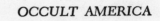

OCCULT AMERICA

BOOKS BY JOHN GODWIN

Occult America
This Baffling World
Alcatraz
Killers Unknown
Killers in Paradise
Requiem for a Rat

Occult America

by JOHN GODWIN

DOUBLEDAY & COMPANY, INC., Garden City, New York
1972

Library of Congress Catalog Card Number 79–168289
Copyright © 1972 by John Godwin
All Rights Reserved
Printed in the United States of America
First Edition

FOR BETH
*My Fellow Writer, Fellow Traveler
and Fellow Sagittarian*

ACKNOWLEDGMENTS

I would like to thank the following people for their kind and generous assistance in my research for this book:
Miss Connie Turner, Mr. Barry Farber of Station WOR, Mrs. Lillian Lindner, Mr. Timothy Green Beckley, Drs. Robert and Sandra Shapiro, "Princess Tahja," Mr. Walter McGraw of the Society for the Investigation of the Unexplained, Mrs. Laura A. Dale and Mrs. Laura F. Knipe of the A.S.P.R., Miss Vickie Hayes of the Parapsychology Symposium, Mr. Allan Angoff of the Parapsychology Foundation, Mrs. Barbara Watters, Mr. Charles Ambler, Dr. Lionel O'Neill, The Rev. Bertha Fischer, Miss Artemis Smith, and sixteen others who prefer their anonymity.

CONTENTS

PROLOGUE

This book is the indirect result of a conversation I overheard in New York's Washington Square Park, about three years ago. Sitting next to me were two young men, busily discussing a method of finding out who had stolen one of their library books.

The method consisted of capturing a lizard, putting it under a magic spell devised by the Hopi Indians, and asking it for the name of the thief. The lizard would then speak—in a very small voice—and reveal the identity of the culprit.

I was both fascinated and bewildered. Not so much by the thief-catching formula as by the boys. They were N.Y.U. students and, judging by their vocabulary, bright ones. Yet they were earnestly contemplating a brand of primitive legendry that Huck Finn might have handed Tom Sawyer in the rural South of a century earlier.

The incident was brought back to my mind over and over during the next couple of months. I went on a nationwide circuit of television and radio shows to publicize what was then my latest book, *This Baffling World*. It dealt with a selection of unsolved true life mysteries and brought me several hundred telephone calls and a round dozen shoeboxes full of suggested solutions.

The astonishing thing was the nature of the solutions that came pouring in. About two-thirds of the puzzlements I had dealt with were of a technical or historical kind. Only three or four concerned ESP, flying saucers or kindred matter.

The overwhelming majority of answers, however, suggested occult explanations for all of them, even though a number of rational causes lay much closer to hand.

At this stage I began to realize that a vast proportion of people in this country were thinking in almost exclusively occult or magical terms—and doing so by preference, regardless of their educational backgrounds. The newspapers, to be sure, had talked about a "wave of American mysticism," but until this experience I'd had no conception of the dimensions of that wave which is rolling over the entire American social horizon.

I became extremely curious about this national phenomenon and set out to find some books that would explain it to me. It took me a while to discover that there weren't any.

Of course, there were books on the occult—rows and shelves of them, from leatherbound tomes to paperbacks. None of them, unfortunately, came even close to telling me what I wanted to know. By and large they fell into two categories—debunkers and boosters—both so preoccupied with effects that they devoted hardly any space at all to what interested me most: the causes.

The debunkers were generally better written and certainly more convincing. But even the best of them somehow seemed to be missing the point of the matter. They could—with wit, erudition and scientific scholarship—prove that astrology is a "pop science," prophecy an art of intelligent guesswork, ESP based on cooked statistics, spiritualism the realm of crooked mediums, witchcraft a rejuvenated fairy tale, Atlantis an invention of Plato—and so on, right down the line. You could almost see the authors dusting off their hands and murmuring, "Well, that's that!"

They appeared sincerely convinced that by pointing out the irrationality of a particular belief they were abolishing it. Which is similar to proving the biological impossibility of the Resurrection and expecting Christianity to evaporate as a result.

The boosters were several degrees more naïve. All of them felt obliged to proclaim that they had begun their work as confirmed skeptics (one of them, so help me, even referred to himself as a "sophisticate"), only to demonstrate within a couple of pages that they didn't know the meaning of the word. The bulk of their output was devoted to a more or less straight recital of miracles and wonderments, sometimes quoted from dubious historical sources, more often from the accounts of "reliable witnesses" (several of whom—when I met them—turned out to be psychopathic liars).

The one thing I was looking for—a dispassionate inquiry into the motivations and workings of America's occultism—seemed not to exist at all. If I wanted one I would have to write it myself. Which, in the course of events, I decided to do.

This appears to be the logical point to present my credentials for the task, such as they are:

I am a rationalist by inclination, meaning that I have no emotional or sentimental leanings toward the miraculous and invariably attempt—by every method at my disposal—to find a rational explanation for what I experience. I have also been around enough to know that this isn't always possible.

I have watched an Australian aborigine die as a result of having a "kudela"—a death bone—pointed at him from a distance of forty yards by a hostile witch doctor. The man had been neither poisoned nor injured. He just died.

I have seen Polynesians, Moroccans and Ceylonese walk barefooted over red-hot fire pits without incurring a blister. I have sweated through a couple of poltergeist hauntings, and I have witnessed a Pakistani fakir suspend his pulse beat by force of will alone. All this, plus a few other events, have given me a lively realization that not all truth comes out of test tubes and that there are more things between heaven and earth . . . etc.

But I am also a newspaperman and what might be termed a trained investigator. And that in turn has made me realize that for every genuine phenomenon there are at least a thousand artificial ones, and that man's faith does not manifest itself by moving mountains, but by seeing mountains move.

The question uppermost in my mind was: what is it that makes him *want* to see mountains move? The answer to that is the key to America's occult upsurge.

There are two standard replies, both embodying a fractional truth. The rationalist explanation can be summarized in the words of New York psychologist M. R. Feinberg: "It represents a throwback to an infantile stage, a flight before the consequences of a totally controlled society." The spiritualist conclusion runs: "The conventional churches have become too worldly and secularized to satisfy man's longing for the supernatural. Therefore the country is seeking a new faith."

Both of these clichés are partly accurate, yet even when taken in conjunction they don't add up to a true picture of the dynamics powering the current quest for mysticism.

In the process of writing this book I conducted around three hundred interviews, coast to coast, with people involved in some fashion with the occult. And there was one question I asked all of them: How did you get into this? The answers pointed to a considerably more subtle set of causes than I had expected.

First of all there emerged a sharp distinguishing line between the young—say under thirties—and their seniors. In the youth group the association with mysticism was almost invariably brought about through some experience with psychedelic drugs. Not necessarily their own experience, but also their friends'. Psychedelics produced a "penchant" for mind expansion, for things beyond the range of normal consciousness, an awareness of—and interest in—a fourth dimension. It also reduced the credibility gap between the rational and the supernatural. There is only a very small step from acid tripping to "soul travel."

Among the older people the psychedelic background was largely replaced by a religious one. Nearly all of them had been devout churchgoers at an earlier stage and felt a definite need for a transcending meaning to life, for a continuity of existence prior to and after their own brief span. Having once believed in miracles there and then, they had no difficulties in accepting miracles here and now. Some had, in fact, developed a positive craving for them and come to resemble occultist hitchhikers, thumbing rides on this, that, and sundry other metaphysical vehicles.

When—for the first time in United States history—the junior and senior groups met in a union of interests, they produced our renaissance of mysticism. They also produced a pattern of characteristics shared by all of them, regardless of age or original motivation.

One is a great desire for rituals, a taste hardly catered to at all in a Western industrialized civilization. At first I was mildly astonished over the accent placed on lengthy—and to me rather pointless—ceremonials in the various cult organizations. Much of the literature germinated by them contains little else but endless ritualistic pageantry that has to be learned by heart and executed correctly down to the minutest detail. I soon learned that for many members these are the most important and satisfying aspects of the creed, that by performing them they achieve a sense of belonging, of worth, that no other function can fully replace.

Another is a common sense of frustration over the ungraspable contradictions of our time. We can get to the moon, but we can't get out of Vietnam. We can quite easily exterminate most of mankind, but not the rats in our urban slums. We are, reputedly, the greatest military power on earth, but appear pathetically vulnerable to the pinpricks inflicted by military midgets. We have conquered jungles and deserts, but seem incapable of rendering a few square miles of city parks safe for pedestrians. The list of paradoxes could be continued almost ad infinitum. In millions of people it has sparked the passionate conviction that there is a basic flaw in our entire thinking process, that we have ignored some universal truth which—if invoked—could bring order into the chaos of our achievements.

The blame for this condition is placed squarely on the skeptics, the pragmatists, the materialists, the whole nebulous class of "them," those who control education and politics and even the orthodox churches and who refuse to see further than their

statistics. In the minds of some occultists—such as the saucerians
—"they" are actually engaged in an international conspiracy to
suppress the truth.

It is therefore perfectly futile for scientific critics to point
out that the most cherished occultist beliefs are based on irration-
alities. They are cherished precisely *because* they are irrational,
supported by faith and emotion rather than concrete evidence.
In this they represent a fingersnap at science, at those icicle-
brained Dr. Frankensteins who seem engaged in computerizing
the souls of mankind.

One of the reasons why so many esoteric cults conjure up
visions of fabulously advanced supercreatures in outer space or
inner earth is because such beings would be able to smite our
human scientists with their own weapons—thus avenging all
the ridicule suffered by the cultists.

The rationalists tend to return these sentiments with interest.
I know ordinarily gentle and kindhearted scientists whose eyes
glaze over with rage whenever the conversation turns to occultism.
For them it means belly-thinking at its worst, a negation of
cerebral progress, a throwback to witch-doctoring. They see occultists as fanatics imbued with what Eileen Garrett—perhaps
the greatest modern medium—termed the "Fascist Impulse": the
conviction that a particular guru has a direct pipeline to God.

In this the rationalists are just as wrong about the occultists
as vice versa. Which might be humorous if it weren't tragic.
And video prophet Marshall McLuhan was equally mistaken when
he delivered his much quoted dictum: "Mysticism is just tomorrow's science dreamed today."

Mysticism, at least the brand now permeating this country,
is nothing of the sort.

It is, on the one hand, a reaction to the peculiar modern
malaise summed up in a passage from Jacques Maritain:

"Having given up God so as to be self-sufficient, man has
lost track of his soul. He looks in vain for himself; he turns the
universe upside down trying to find himself; he finds masks, and
behind the masks, death."

On the other hand it is a revival, in different guise, of an
old American dream: the idea that somewhere on earth there
is room for the kingdom of Heaven. As long as empty spaces

remained, this dream expressed itself in the creation of new settlements, any one of which—the hope was always there— might be the New Jerusalem.

When the land became filled from east to west and lay locked in the armor of its technology, the dream turned inward and became mysticism. But the basic theme is unchanged and unshaken: belief in the perfectibility of the human condition.

JOHN GODWIN

And freely men confesse that this world's spent,
When in the Planets, and the Firmament
They seeke so many new; they see that this
Is crumbled out againe to his Atomies.
'Tis all in pieces, all cohaerence gone;
All just supply, and all Relation:
Prince, Subject, Father, Sonne, are things forgot,
For every man alone thinkes he hath got
To be a Phoenix, and that there can bee
None of that kinde, of which he is, but hee.

JOHN DONNE, "An Anatomie of the World, The First Anniversary."

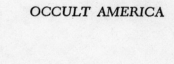

OCCULT AMERICA

I
PEOPLE AND PLANETS

IT HAS BECOME difficult to venture anywhere in contemporary America without being informed that the Age of Aquarius is upon us. There's no escaping the message. It leaps at you from all angles—in the shape of billboards and wall graffiti, in TV commercials and magazine headlines, on highball glasses and bikinis, paper napkins and neckties, from hippie banners and bank windows, on Volkswagens and baby carriages.

The smash hit Broadway musical *Hair* opened with the sung statement that "This is the dawning of the Age of Aquarius" plus the prediction:

> When the moon is in the Seventh House
> And Jupiter aligns with Mars,
> Then peace will guide the planets
> And love will steer the stars.*

* © 1966, 1967, 1968 James Rado, Gerome Ragni, Galt MacDermot, Nat Shapiro and United Artists Music Co., Inc. All rights administered by United Artists Music Co., Inc., New York, New York 10019. Used by permission.

The lyrics, translated into a dozen languages, have since circled the globe, proclaiming the Aquarian Age from Allahabad to Zaragoza.

Yet despite all media saturation a nagging question remains in the minds of the multitude: What, precisely, *is* the Age of Aquarius? With the exception of those who think of it as something vaguely connected with fishtanks, people generally realize that the term signifies an astrological time concept. But when did we get into it—how long will it last—and what does it mean to us?

Nobody at this point has come up with a pat answer. Not even the astrologers.

Aquarius is the Latin word for "water-bearer." It also stands for the eleventh of the twelve signs of the zodiac—the astrological term for the path apparently taken through space by the nine planets within our solar system.

Every two thousand years (give or take an odd century) our earth is said to enter a new astrological age, named for one of the zodiac symbols. The last one was Pisces, a melancholy era filled with chaos and bloodshed. Aquarius—next in line—should bring an advance toward universal brotherhood, enlightenment and greater freedom for all mankind.

So far so good. But when it comes to defining even the approximate start and finish of each age, the situation gets very hazy indeed.

Astrological eras are determined by the relations between the zodiac constellations and the so-called vernal equinox, a point on the heavenly globe where the plane formed by the earth's orbit crosses the celestial equator. The vernal equinox moves westward at the rate of about fifty seconds a year, thus coinciding with a new zodiac constellation every twenty centuries or so.

But astrologers differ radically about the position of the boundary lines between the signs, which varies their estimates as to the advent of Aquarius by nearly a thousand years. According to some the Age of the Water-bearer dawned back in the 1600s, according to others in 1904, while a sizable group maintains that it isn't due until the year 2060 or thereabouts. Still others have us wandering in a transitional period of indeterminate length.

Zolar—perhaps the most popular astrologer in America today —declared in a recent interview: "We're not in the Aquarian Age yet; we've still got one hundred years to go. But we're already feeling it because when you're within five degrees of a sign you begin to get the feeling."

Detractors of the "royal art" point to this lack of unanimity as yet one more proof of astrology's total spuriousness. The same stick, however, could also be used to beat a great many other backs.

Historians, for instance, have divided their subject into chapters which suffer from equally debatable demarcation lines. According to them, Europe's Middle Ages began with the fall of the Roman Empire. But since that empire took an unconscionably long while afalling, the Middle Ages might have commenced at just about any time during the fifth century A.D. In relation to our brief human history this span represents a much wider margin for disagreement than that afflicting the celestial time clock of the astrologers.

Nobody belittles historians because they can't pinpoint the exact date when the curtain ran up on the Renaissance. Why expect an infinitely more difficult feat of astrologers?

But the real significance of the Aquarian Age has nothing whatever to do with its debut. It lies in the fact that the label has become a household cliché in this country. It means that somewhere an invisible wheel has turned full circle and the mystical faith of ancient Babylon is now flowering in the most scientifically sophisticated nation on earth.

Currently the United States boasts some 10,000 professional and 175,000 part-time astrologers. Their incomes range from an occasional $5 to an annual six-figure bracket.

Their clientele consists of an estimated 20 million people, who—during 1969—spent more than $150,000,000 on personal horoscope material. Astrology columns now run in 1,200 of America's 1,750 daily newspapers. Twenty years ago—with twice as many papers on the stands—barely one hundred featured them.

Apart from their sheer weight of numbers, the most remarkable characteristic of the astral devotees is their age—or rather their youth. Most of them are now under twenty-five, whereas only a decade ago the average horoscope follower belonged to

the over-forty group. Which indicates that astrology has ceased
to be a senior citizens' hobby and become the preserve of the
rising generation—with everything that implies.

The only thing that hasn't changed is the lopsided sex ratio
among devotees. Today, as of yore, about three out of every
four are women. A lot of ink has been spilled in trying to
explain why astrology—as distinct from astronomy—casts such a
spell over the fair sex. Some psychologists believe that the atavistic
root cause is that the female menstrual cycle, normally twenty-
eight days, follows the lunar month, creating a kind of kinship
between that planet and femininity.

Strangely enough, this female preponderance among the
followers is not reflected in the astrological hierarchy. All of the
top figures in the field are men. The two best-known women—
Jeane Dixon and Sybil Leek—are regarded by professionals as
Jill-Come-Latelies who jumped on the astrological bandwagon
from different occult vehicles: one from crystal ball clairvoyance,
the other from witchcraft.

The Big Three among stargazers—in terms of fame and
fortune—are such utterly dissimilar personalities that meeting them
makes you forget all about astrological stereotypes. One operates
in New York, two in Los Angeles, and the only feature they
have in common is lots of money.

Bruce King, better known by his pseudonym of Zolar, heads
what may be the world's biggest distributing firm of occult matter.
A massive, gray-mustached man in a rumpled blue suit, he looks
and talks like a rural bank manager with a bad memory for
names and an uncanny one for figures (see Figure 1).

I had heard rumors about his impending retirement—he is
past seventy—but he answered my question by rumbling, "I still
work a longer day than you do!" Glancing around his Manhattan
office, I believed him. It's stripped for action; minimum comforts
and absolutely no frills. The only decorative items were a shiny
globe and a framed certificate for a record tarpon caught off
Fort Lauderdale.

In this headquarters King casts the Zolar horoscopes ranging
from $200 for a personal one to $10 for a simple natal chart.
From there he also runs the production of his thirty astrological
publications—which have sold over 50 million copies—and the

distribution of such occult items as Fast Luck Powder, Jinx Removing Sprays, Seals of Venus, Gambler's Spray and lodestones. Quite apart from Ouija boards, crystal balls, dream interpretations, Tarot cards, incense, self-hypnosis equipment, gold-plated St. Christopher medals, Stars of David, Egyptian scarabs and holy crosses. Not to speak of a line of astrological records, which recently passed the 300,000 mark.

"What accounts for my success?" said King, folding his hands over his stomach in a characteristic gesture. "Everybody can understand me. I explain everything. If you write that Mars squares Jupiter this month in the fifth house and you don't tell people what that means they wonder what that fifth house is. What is a house? So I have every term explained—and in words of two or three syllables. Because when I went into this business the only people we had interested were widows and divorcées and people down on their luck. That was a long time ago."

King got into the business accidentally . . . "Everything in life is accidental." Born in Chicago, he started off as a juvenile actor (in a play he wrote himself), became a clothing model, then a clothing salesman, then a stockbroker. ("Because I'd been to school with a lot of boys who'd gone into the brokerage business, and they were making in a week what I was making per year.")

By 1930 he found himself owning a piece of a radio station in Los Angeles. The station employed an astrologer. "What was his name? Yes—Kobar. That's what he called himself anyway. Oh, he's dead now, but in those days—just after the Crash— he was the only fella who had any cash. Used to get a dollar in the mail for each horoscope. So we made him general manager of the station. I've forgotten the name of the station—but today it would be worth about five or six million dollars."

Later King headed back East, where he bought into another radio station—whose name he had also forgotten—on which Kobar got a regular program. "He'd read a little daily message, maybe about fate or jealousy, and then people wrote in questions together with their birthdates and he'd answer them. We did terrific with that."

One fine day, however, Kobar decided to move back to Hollywood to star in a motion picture. "So," King explained, "I

was left with the horoscope business. So naturally I had to
scramble around to find out what it was all about. I wasn't
even interested in that side of it; I was only interested in the
business part, you know.

"Anyway, I studied and read up about it and then I took
over the astrological part. Well, by sheer accident, the week Kobar
left a man walked in—I forget his name—with a machine where
you put a dime in and turn a handle and a horoscope comes
out. He wanted backing. I backed him and we built these
machines and we put 'em in the RKO and the Paramount
theaters all over the country. Then we went off the air because
we couldn't handle the business any longer; it got too big. I
called it the Astrolograph Company. In those days—this was
1934—business was terrible, you know, but we were selling six
to eight hundred horoscopes a day with the machines; all to
movie audiences.

"The name Zolar?" King smiled under his mustache. "Oh,
that came when I went into chain stores. I was walking past
a Woolworth's one day and the thought occurred to me—why
shouldn't I make horoscopes for the chain stores? Which I did.
I sold them a couple of million horoscopes. In envelopes. And
that's when I took the name of Zolar. Zodiac and Zolar, get it?"

Since then Zolar has sold an estimated 100 million horoscopes
to a larger number of devotees than any other astrologer can
boast. But he doesn't look at his own chart very often. "I did
when I first started. Now only in very important decisions. I've
developed a sixth sense on these things.

"But you know," he added, "by rights I shouldn't be an
astrologer at all. I was born on the cusp of Leo and Cancer—
and that's a very, very good sign for business management and
stuff like that."

If Zolar is the business brain among the Big Three, Carroll
Righter is the showman. He lives—appropriately—in Hollywood,
close to Grauman's Chinese Theater. Six feet tall, impeccably
dressed, and pale-complexioned in a city where everybody sports
year-round suntans, he rarely stirs out into the world from his
pillared house, which he shares with a butler and a cook. The
world, you feel, comes to *him*.

Righter is the greatest living newspaper astrologer, his

syndicated columns appearing in 328 United States and overseas dailies. He was the only member of his profession ever to grace the cover of *Time* magazine. And he almost nonchalantly renamed Cancer people "Moon Children" because he felt that a zodiac sign shouldn't be connected with a disease.

But Righter's special aura does not depend on his astrological journalism, nor his fast-selling books. He plays a quite unique role in southern California; a mixture of father confessor, sage and medicine man to a vast portion of the movie colony and to more local politicians than he cares to mention.

They call him Pappy, and he calls them Libra, Scorpio or Leo or whatever their symbol happens to be—never by their names. Even when you're sitting next to him when the telephone rings (and it rings constantly) you have no idea who he's talking to. It could—rumor has it—even be Governor Reagan himself.

"Oh, Virgo," the soft patrician voice carries all the reassurance of an absolution. "Yes, the aspects are very good for that contract. But I wouldn't sign until—let me see—four o'clock Tuesday morning."

"Aries? I've been expecting your call. You're in Manila, aren't you? I'm happy to tell you that your arm is definitely going to get well. Very soon—within a couple of days."

And so it goes on, virtually around the clock. Righter is one of the few humans who actually enjoys being rung at 3 A.M. by an actor who can't decide whether to take on a lead that might damage his good guy image. He plays doctor, spiritual adviser, business consultant and psychiatrist with equal aplomb. But his real genius lies in conveying the genuine concern he feels for the people he's dealing with. And this is no act. A lifelong bachelor, Righter has made his clients his family. His title Pappy seems almost natural.

His background is as unusual as his methods. Born seventy years ago, of a wealthy and distinguished Philadelphia family, Righter—at fourteen—met Evangeline Adams, the founding mother of American astrology. She told him that his chart was as perfect for planetary interpretation as her own.

He began dabbling in the art then, but first worked as a lawyer, then on several civic projects. During the Depression he not only helped to provide for the physical needs of the unemployed, he also cast free horoscopes for them, telling them when the aspects were favorable for landing jobs.

Righter moved to Los Angeles for health reasons, and in 1939 turned professional.

His fabulous prestige with the motion picture community stems from the occasion when he warned Marlene Dietrich not to go near the studio on a certain date. She disregarded his warning and—sure enough—tripped and broke one slender ankle. His predictions have been treated as gospel by the celluloid crowd ever since.

Today his lavishly furnished rooms are bedecked with lovingly autographed photos of the Hollywood greats; Peter Lawford, Susan Hayward, Ronald Reagan, Tyrone Power, Robert Cummings, Ronald Colman and a score more. The devotion of some of his clients borders on fanaticism. Certain actresses have timed both the conception and the birth of their children according to his charts. Director William Dieterle once ordered the shooting of a movie to commence on a day declared auspicious by Pappy —although the film hadn't even been cast then. The late Clark Gable allegedly set his wedding day to Kay Spreckels on a date recommended by Righter.

But Pappy, who calls himself a "gregarious Aquarius," did not rely on his celestial craft alone. His 162 consecutive parties were launched, according to a local newspaperman, "with enough folderol to start a middling war." Styled to match the zodiac sign of the moment, they featured a live crocodile for Scorpio, an equally live (and extremely obstreperous) lion for Leo, a bull for Taurus, horses for Sagittarius, a goat for Capricorn, and several pairs of human identical twins for the Gemini bash. There was something distinctly Roman about these star-studded shindigs, and the studio set lapped it up.

They also adore Righter's complete involvement with them. He has no standard fees, but charges according to his clients' ability to pay—and he knows precisely who is earning what at any given moment.

Even more, though, they appreciate his genius for "accentuating the positive"—in other words for dispensing bitter pills in sweet coatings. If an actor appears in danger of losing his job, Pappy might break it to him by saying, "You seem to be heading for a period of change in your life. I see some very interesting new beginnings in your chart. You would be wise to prepare for them."

But whether Righter gained his knowledge from his charts or via his batlike attunement to studio gossip is anyone's guess.

For a man of his age he works incredibly hard, keeping his astral charts by his bedside, employing four secretaries and a mathematician, yet never wavering in his unfailing courtesy and tact. There is no doubt about his dedication and none about his belief. "I love people," he once said. "All my life I have wanted to help them. The more people who can be told about—and convinced of—astrology, the better."

At forty-three, Sydney Omarr is the youngster among astrology's Big Three, and cast in an entirely different mold. He is the intellectual of the trio, the "highbrow astrologer" par excellence, skillfully battling to equate his art with modern scientific and psychological trends.

He is also far and away the best writer in the entire field and perhaps the only one of his calling capable of engrossing nonbelieving readers. His popular fame stems from his astrology columns, which appear in 225 newspapers. But he carved a special niche for himself by producing a number of solidly cerebral books that earned him the acclaim of literary critics as well.

Omarr is also a Philadelphian by birth and currently residing in Hollywood. But these are his only similarities with Righter. Whereas Righter luxuriates in the hothouse atmosphere of the movie capital, Omarr gives you the feeling that he might be happier in the academic setting of a college town.

He earned his laurels early in life. Serving with the Air Force in the Pacific during World War II, he went on record by predicting President Roosevelt's death in office. Whereupon the Armed Forces Radio requisitioned him to organize a horoscope-charting show, which made him the only United States serviceman in history ever assigned to full-time astrological duties.

After the war he wrote articles for astrological magazines, read palms in nightclubs (at Madame Bricktop's famous den in Mexico City he demanded—and received—$100 per reading) and crossed swords with some of the most virulent skeptics extant. Most of them began with condescending smiles and finished with outbursts of frustrated fury. Comedian Henry Morgan ended up banging his fist on the table in front of the TV camera, shouting, "Don't you know that I'm the best-informed man in the industry?"

Besting flippant entertainers is one thing, withstanding the onslaught of an infuriated scientist is quite another. Omarr did it—a feat that neither Zolar nor Righter could have accomplished —nor probably would want to.

The occasion was a radio debate arranged by station WPEN in Philadelphia, in June 1951. As Omarr's opponent the network had lovingly chosen Dr. Roy K. Marshall, director of the Fels Planetarium, science editor of the Philadelphia *Evening Bulletin* and sworn enemy of astrology.

As Omarr later put it, "I felt as if I were donning gloves with Joe Louis."

The debate turned into perhaps the most acrimonious and fascinating slugging match ever heard on the Philadelphia airwaves. Halfway through the program's sponsor telephoned the moderator, giving him permission to drop the commercials so that the match could go on uninterrupted . . . greater compliments hath no man.

Dr. Marshall went in for the kill. He would undoubtedly have flattened any astrologer except Sydney Omarr. But it soon became apparent that—while extremely well versed in astronomy —he knew little about astrology. What he knew was largely based on the naïve puff claims made by *some* practitioners of the art; the pulp magazine breed.

This led him into statements of blank disbelief for two hard facts Omarr had up his sleeve.

One was an extract from a speech delivered by Marshall's distinguished colleague and lodge brother, Pulitzer Prize winner and science editor John J. O'Neill. It ran: "While I do not believe all astrology is scientific and worthwhile there is a certain amount of good work being done in that field and it is that which makes me try to do something to help the astrologers."

The other was that RCA—the world's largest communications organization—utilized the principles of astrology to forecast magnetic storms. This was the result of a study report issued by one of their staff researchers, John Henry Nelson, entitled "Short

Wave Radio Propagation Correlation with Planetary Positions."
Its findings were, in fact, based on astrological mores, probably
first mentioned by Ptolemy in the second century.

Neither of these points may sound very earth-shaking to
the average listener, but to an orthodox academician like Dr.
Marshall they were bombshells. They meant that at least some
of his peers had found *something* about astrology that wasn't
"arcane flapdoodle."

Omarr fought with consummate skill. By carefully limiting
his claims, by separating facts from assumptions, by refusing to
be goaded into pat predictions, he stopped his opponent cold.

After three bruising hours the debate ended in stalemate. Dr.
Marshall had not become convinced of astrology's efficacy. But
he had learned that it could be defended on his own intellectual
plane.

The only thing the verbal slugfest really proved was the
barbed-wire gulf that exists between astronomy and astrology.
Which is curious, considering that for the greater part of their
careers the two fields were so closely intertwined that you couldn't
tell them apart.

Astrology appears to be the older of the two, though no
one can say by how much. It was already a highly developed
study five thousand years ago. The Babylonians believed in the
divinity of astral bodies and built skyscraper observatories called
ziggurat (the Old Testament's Tower of Babel) in order to
follow their movements. They weren't just stargazing, but god-
watching. And somewhere along the line came the conclusion
that the motions of these heavenly beings directly influenced
events down on earth.

The observers were priests, their studies were religious activities. The predictions they handed out were limited to matters
of high policy, reserved for the ears of kings. Hence the term
"royal art" for astrology. At the same time, however, the priests
founded universities, thus fusing religion and science into one
occult lump.

It was the democratic Greeks who brought astrology down
from its regal heights. They introduced the popular horoscope,
cast for private citizens to discover auspicious dates for such
mundane matters as marriages and business ventures.

In order to extract higher fees, astrologers tended more and more to match forecasts to their clients' wishes. Astrology began to be tarred with the con man's brush—and the tar is sticking to this day. The racket grew so scandalous that Augustus—the greatest of the Roman emperors—banned the practice entirely; but the edict only lived as long as he.

Astrology and astronomy remained Siamese twins until well into the seventeenth century. Champions of the "royal art" can claim quite truthfully that scientific geniuses like Copernicus, Galileo, Tycho Brahe, and Kepler were all practicing astrologers. But the point is that these men cast horoscopes as a sideline, for a little extra cash, because on astronomers' incomes they could have starved to death. It was expected of them as part of their job.

Nevertheless, it was their discoveries that opened the great breach between the erstwhile twins. They proved the very fundamentals of astrology to be false.

For the ancients had based their theories on the earth occupying a fixed position in space—the centerpoint of the universe. Around it—or rather above it—revolved the moon, the sun, and those five planets they could see with the naked eye. But with the aid of telescopes the pioneering stargazers discovered three more planets up there. Worse—they also discovered that the earth wasn't stationary at all but followed an elliptical route of its own!

The new cosmic knowledge meant the parting of the ways. Astrology and its practitioners were left hopelessly behind. Astronomers took over the university chairs and observatories. Their former colleagues were pushed into dusty corners to read archaic charts for the miserable fees which were all the most ignorant and superstitious section of the populace could afford.

During the nineteenth century astrology hit rock bottom. In most states of the Union the practice was simply bracketed with fortune-telling and outlawed. In fact, the vast majority of astrologers were doing just that, usually with tables that were two thousand years out of date.

But a small, dedicated handful among them were laboring to bring their art into line with the Industrial Age. And—as far as the constellation system is concerned—they succeeded, incorporating every astronomic discovery into their charts. But it still remained to bring astrology out of the back parlor into the modern lecture hall.

This was almost single-handedly accomplished by a remarkable Boston girl named Evangeline Adams. A direct descendant of President John Quincy Adams, equipped with equal quantities of charm, charisma and social graces, she arrived in New York in 1899. She put up at the exclusive Fifth Avenue Hotel, but the moment the proprietor heard that she intended to practice astrology he asked her to leave.

Miss Adams found other quarters, but never forgave the insult. The hotelier must have spent years kicking himself, because her rise on the American scene was meteoric. Within an amazingly short time some very distinguished clients were beating a path to her studio above Carnegie Hall—including Enrico Caruso, King Edward VII, and J. P. Morgan.

Miss Adams's greatest moment came in 1914, when the authorities decided to haul her into court under the law that lumped astrologers together with "men who desert their wives and people who pretend to tell fortunes." Her attorney wanted to have the case dismissed, but Evangeline, grimly clutching an immense briefcase filled with documents, insisted on fighting it out.

Her battle was nothing short of magnificent. She recited intricate mathematical formulas, drew graphs, quoted Ptolemy and Newton. Finally she asked for a chance to demonstrate her art.

Judge Freschi obliged her by giving her the birth details of a man known only as Mr. X. She consulted her ephemerides and Table of Houses, then drew up a horoscope, reading out her findings in a ringing, confident voice. Watching newspapermen could see the judge swallowing hard. He murmured, "This is quite astonishing."

Mr. X, it turned out, was his own son.

After this the verdict was a pretty well foregone conclusion. The judge announced that "the defendant raises astrology to the dignity of an exact science. She has given ample proof that she is a woman of learning and culture, and one who is very well versed in astronomy and other sciences. . . ." He decided that Miss Adams had violated no law.

Evangeline remained an international celebrity until her death in 1932. She had made astrology socially acceptable once more. But although she'd won her own case hands down she only succeeded in rendering the attitude of the law toward astrology more ambiguous. New York still bars "predictive astrology," but distinguishes the art from plain fortune-telling.

This forces practitioners to walk a rather uncomfortable tightrope. Their clients demand predictions—and get them. Most of the time the law turns an obliging blind eye to this. But occasionally an astrologer is arrested, and the antiprediction rule is fairly rigidly enforced on the airwaves. Carroll Righter's radio sponsors are still obliged to insert the disclaimer: "This program is being presented solely for your entertainment. It is not intended to foster a belief in astrology."

In California astrology is still officially forbidden, though the ban is about as effective as Boston's statute against swearing. It is nevertheless the reason why that state's largest astrological organization has to function as a religious body.

Despite the breakthrough achieved by Miss Adams, her art received no governmental recognition of any kind. Some writers in the field have gone to great lengths to point out the opportunities supposedly neglected by this policy. They like to quote Britain as the country that "helped to win World War II with the weapons of astrology."

The facts about this are considerably less dramatic, but the claim contains at least a kernel of truth.

Britain's action was based on the knowledge that certain members of the Nazi high command consulted—or at least listened to—astrologers. Hitler himself was rarely involved in this, but his deputy, Rudolf Hess, and S.S. chief Heinrich Himmler frequently discussed astral charts. Which, incidentally, had not stopped them from harassing astrology and kindred movements in Germany in 1937. (There is a story that Himmler's private safe contained a horoscope of the Führer, prophesying disaster for April 1945, but this may be purely legendary.)

British Naval Intelligence had noted that the names of certain stargazers kept cropping up in connection with Hitler's hierarchy. They were Karl Ernst Krafft, a pro-Nazi Swiss from Basle, Elsbeth Ebertin, a former graphologist who had become her country's leading female astrologer, and Wilhelm Wulff, who seems to have been Himmler's personal Count Cagliostro.

The British—always supreme pragmatists in intelligence matters—decided that it would be wise to keep abreast with whatever advice these people might be whispering to the Nazi entourage. They enlisted a Hungarian-born astrologer named Louis de Wohl and set him up a special Psychological Research Bureau in London. His task was to try and parallel the horoscopic predictions turned out by his enemy colleagues in Berlin. The idea—if nothing else—was original.

De Wohl did a middling job astrologically, but a brilliant one propaganda-wise. When he was right he was startling, when he was wrong he was *very* wrong. Thus he correctly foretold the German invasion of Belgium and Holland in May 1940. But a year later he announced to an American audience in Cleveland that Hitler intended to launch an attack on the United States early in 1942, using Brazil as a springboard.

His *pièce de résistance*, however, was the manner in which he caused the prophecies of Nostradamus to boomerang on Dr. Goebbels. The German Propaganda Minister had utilized the sixteenth century French augur early in the war by altering several of his obscure quatrains (rhymed predictions) to make them forecast the conflict and a complete German victory.

De Wohl went one better. He composed fifty entirely new quatrains—each prognosticating the Reich's impending defeat— and had them smuggled into Germany in the form of astrological leaflets. They were written in German and were such perfect imitations of Nostradamus's oblique originals that they are still being quoted as genuine translations.

De Wohl turned into a successful novelist after the war. His opponents' fate was less happy. Mrs. Ebertin was killed during an American air raid on Freiburg. The Swiss Karl Ernst Krafft came under suspicion of having instigated Rudolf Hess's harebrained flight to England in 1941. Although they hadn't the faintest proof for this, the Gestapo arrested him and had him dispatched to the concentration camp of Buchenwald. He never got there, but was murdered somewhere along the way by the S.S. guards.

American astrologers were never faced with concentration camps, but they have their own crosses to bear. The harshest among them is perhaps their constant struggle for serious recognition—legal, scientific and otherwise. Mere money—and their current earnings are handsome—is no substitute for this.

In the forefront of this struggle are the score of professional organizations which now dot the United States. Most of them are loosely affiliated with the American Federation of Astrologers, headquartered in Washington, D.C., but the connection frequently exists in name only. These bodies function under a vast variety of titles, ranging from the Californian Temple of Astrology (a venerable outfit established in 1908) to the Planetheirs of Toledo, Ohio, and the Wisconsin Starlighters, Inc.

All of these affiliations follow a code of ethics laid down by the AFA, which is considerably more stringent than outsiders may assume. Among other rules members must agree "not to interpolate or to introduce into an astrological deduction, verbally or otherwise, any interpretation which my conclusions appear to warrant, that are irrelevant to the Science of Astrology without first stating definitely that such deductions are neither based upon the life chart nor identified with the science."

Adopting a code, however, is not tantamount to enforcing it, and the AFA and its affiliates do precious little enforcing. They have neither the power nor—it seems—the will.

For a start, only a fraction of the country's practitioners belong to these organizations. The majority are free-lance dabblers, juggling several occult crafts at once and switching from one to the other—or using a mishmash of all—as the occasion demands. As Federation member Ruth Hale Oliver points out, "Plain fortune-tellers put horoscopes in their tents in order to stay out of jail."

But even among serious astrologers there exists an embarrassing tendency to dive off the deep end. After interviewing some fifty of them I noted that at least half also fancied themselves experts on subjects about which they positively radiated ignorance—politics, medicine, even criminology. The spectacle of a homespun little old lady talking star-slanted balderdash about the causes of the 1929 stock-market crash can put you off astrology for life.

So can the off-the-cuff trait assessments, based on your zodiac sign, which some practitioners shovel out by the page. Astrologer Shirley Abbott, for instance, concocted a stellar method according to which you can buy a car that "matches your personality and satisfies your basic needs."

Leos, she recommends, should get Rolls-Royces or some equally deluxe transportation; Libras would be happy with inexpensive economy models; Cancers (sorry, "Moon Children") are in the market for upper-priced, conservative cars and—since they supposedly revere the past—would enjoy an antique car; etc., etc., right around the zodiac. Now I happen to be a Sagittarian, and the vehicle Miss Abbott has in mind for me is a dune buggy, which, I can assure her, would satisfy my basic needs about as much as a pogo stick.

One of the battlers for higher standards of craftsmanship is Al Morrison, former president of the Astrologers' Guild of America. Morrison, who currently edits the Guild's authorative publications, is far from happy about the present upsurge of his art.

"There's too much greed, too much cheap commercialism, too much charlatanism," he growled. "And too many facets that have nothing to do with astrology. Astrology is *not* an occult religion or anything of the kind, damit. It's an exact science—like chemistry or physics. Remember that when you write about it!"

A tall, loose-jointed man with piercing light eyes beneath bushy brows, Morrison took his B.A. at the University of Tennessee, later worked as a federal Food and Drug inspector. His astrology is entirely self-taught, he never attended classes. He received his first fee for a reading ($5) in 1953, turned professional nine years later, now gets up to $100 per consultation.

He lives in a studio six flights up in an extremely ramshackle building in New York's Greenwich Village, his habitat so crammed with tomes, charts and files that the wallpaper seems to bulge. Above his desk hangs a portrait of psychiatrist and author Karen Horney.

Although Morrison is a highly distinguished lecturer, he never developed what you might call a rostrum manner. His speech is abrupt, dogmatic, and totally devoid of mock modesty. And he has a disconcerting habit of lacing technical dissertations with frequent "groovies," "uptights," and "you know, mans," which somehow don't fit into his purist style.

This may be the result of his unique association with a music-recording outfit, located a couple of flights down from his office. Known as Apostolic Studios, it is probably the only disk company in America run on astrological lines. Morrison is its guiding spirit and he carefully charts the aspects of each working week. If he pronounces a particular day inauspicious, no production takes place.

The studio specializes in what Morrison calls "a predictive brand of music"—rhythms that allegedly foreshadow the sounds of the future. To my layman's ears it sounded just like good, slick commercial rock fare. But Morrison's astrological charts on the wall are treated with a delicate reverence rare in rock circles.

Through Apostolic Studios, Morrison hovers on the fringe of the mystic mélange that passes for astrology in a large segment of America's youth. Its most glamorous exponent is Wanda Lawris Moore—though I doubt whether Morrison would approve of her methods.

At twenty-five, Wanda Moore considers herself a "New Ager" in the ultimate sense of the word. "I don't care about all those quibbles on the start of the Age of Aquarius," she says. "I'm an Aquarian Child because I *feel* I am. Way deep down. That's all that matters."

If Wanda is a sample of the Aquarian Age, then by all means let's have it. She is hauntingly beautiful, with shoulder-length blond hair, a sullen, bee-stung mouth, and a figure so reminiscent of a *Playboy* centerspread that you want to look for the staples in her midriff (see Figure 2).

Unlike most astrologers, who tend to cluster in big cities, Wanda lives in rural New Jersey. She occupies a studio room on the top floor of her parents' house, which she keeps in permanent semidarkness, sweet with burning incense, and bedecked with psychedelic lights, show-biz souvenirs, posters, stellar charts, and pictures of Indian gurus, handsome actors and Jesus Christ.

Wanda is astrological and spiritual adviser to a throng of under-thirty entertainers and musicians, among them teenage idol Tim Buckley. But her brand of astrology differs radically from Morrison's "exact science."

"Of course I believe in reincarnation," she said, sitting gracefully on the floor. "How can I help it—I've lived many, many times before. I've been both a man and a woman, married and single. The first time I became aware of my previous lives I was just three years old. My father had taken me to a lonely mountain spot, and I suddenly pointed to a hillside and said, 'Daddy, I've played here before.'"

"*Déjà vu?*" I asked.

"More than that. It was absolute certainty. I can't explain it so that you'd understand—but I *knew*."

Wanda is supremely contemptuous of what she terms the "astrological elite,"—the professionals who, according to her, "commercialize on the appeal of all things shrouded in mystery."

She calls herself a New Age Astrologer, a title which apparently covers a whole slew of beliefs. She always uses the so-called Karmic house in her horoscopes as a means of discovering her clients' former lives. With this she combines Indian mysticism, based on the teachings of Baba Ram Dass, a smattering of Rudolf Steiner's anthroposophy, plus an American brand of spiritualism handed down by a New Jersey psychic.

Her strongest creed, however, is that of the Atlantean Incarnates, the "Brothers of Light" who claim to have lived on the Lost Continent of Atlantis thousands of years ago and who—in various reincarnated shapes—frequently run into each other on earth. "I constantly keep meeting fathers, husbands, brothers and sisters from my past lives," she said dreamily. "We recognize each other in a flash. You catch the other's eye—and in the same instant we both know who we were."

Wanda predicts that in the year 2000 the earth's axis will revert to its original position (as it was in Atlantean times). The caps of the poles will melt, water will flood the continents and most of humanity will "lose their vehicles"—her euphemism for

dying. She will be just fifty-five then, but the prospect doesn't
worry her. "I'm rather longing for that day," she added. "After
all—this is only one life. . . ."

Wanda also practices out-of-body travel—her spirit covering
long distances while her physical shape stays at home. How?
"I blank out my mind," she explained, "slow down my breathing
and pulse rate and concentrate on a patch of light somewhere
in the back of my brain. It takes me from three to fifteen
minutes—then I'm off. Sometimes I take lone journeys, sometimes I visit friends that way. No, they can't actually *see* me,
but they always sense my presence. You wouldn't understand . . .
it's a feeling."

Currently she leads a sternly ascetic life; doesn't smoke,
drink, eat meat or indulge in other fleshly pleasures. But this is
a relatively new routine.

Until 1967, Wanda raced with the subjet setters. For a
time she was mascot and member of a Californian motorcycle
gang similar to the Hell's Angels. She rode her own machine,
clad from neck to foot in black leather, her golden mane streaming in the wind. Later she came back East and founded the
Nirvana Club in Greenwich Village; a psychedelically oriented
rendezvous dive, featuring hard rock and open twenty-four hours
a day. "Which meant that I got hardly any sleep at all."

But after six months of clublife, Wanda suddenly packed
up and retired to a lone house on top of a mountain in Wayne,
New Jersey. There she meditated, practiced Yoga, went from
two packs of cigarettes a day to none, and read immense
quantities of occult lore.

The metamorphosis took almost a year. What came down
from the mountaintop was the New Age Wanda, lecturing to
select groups of Aquarian disciples and casting Karmic horoscopes
in a room permanently filled with incense.

It is by no means certain, however, whether the New Age
will require human astrologers at all. Because at the moment
the "royal art" is being computerized, like almost everything else.
Professional stargazers are as fond of the computers as nineteenth-
century handweavers were of power looms, but the general public
has taken to them in a big way.

First on the scene was a New York outfit called Time

Pattern Research Institute, Inc., which began operations in May 1967. The company uses an IBM 360-30 computer, plus an internationally famous astrologer named Katina Theodossiou. Stored in the machine is a memory bank containing some twenty-five million pieces of information. Miss Theodossiou feeds in the clients' year, month, date, time and place of birth and within two minutes receives a detailed report that might have taken her up to a week to prepare personally.

The horoscopes are meaty affairs, running to ten thousand words and include a character analysis and the client's future aspects. At the time of writing they are the most expensive of their type, at twenty dollars each. But within three years the company sold over 300,000 of them and now has outlets in some two hundred American department stores.

Its closest competitor came from France. Conceived by—of all people—the head of a national supermarket chain, it set up its first computer in the Pan-Am building on Paris's Champs Elysées and did traffic-stopping business. The IBM 360-25 machine was programmed by France's top astrologer, André Barbault. Known as Astroflash, it contains almost a year's work on part of M. Barbault—planetary interpretations that are said to allow nearly two *billion* possible combinations.

Astroflash II, its sister apparatus, debuted in New York's Grand Central Station in June 1969, amidst a tremendous flourish of starlets, mini-skirted hostesses and sundry celebrities. Its horoscopes come in English, French or Spanish—at choice—cover fourteen pages and cost a mere five dollars (see Figure 3). The United States firm running the operation here is planning to install other centers in Chicago, Dallas, and San Francisco.

The salient point, of course, is: how do these Frankenstein readings compare with the flesh and blood type? In order to decide this my wife Beth (a fellow Sagittarian) and I took out a computer horoscope each and at the same time had readings done by two live astrologers. Then we compared notes. The result was rather like the proverbial curate's egg—good in parts.

The planetary positions on the computer charts were as accurate as those on the hand-drafted samples. The only deviations in the computers were the trifling results of rounding off everything to even degrees without minutes. The prediction

of aspects—as it turned out—were an equally mixed bag on all—
about half right or 50 percent wrong, take your pick.

The psychoastrological profiles were a different matter. There
the human astrologers won by miles. They had, after all, met us
face to face. Unlike the machines, they could think, listen, use
their intuition, get our vibrations. Their assessments were at least
partially accurate. The computers floundered in a sea of nebulous
generalizations, as much applicable to us as to virtually any pair
of adult, heterosexual, passably rational Homo sapiens.

But astrological conclusions should, by rights, be completely
divorced from personal contact or intuition. Ideally a horoscope
should be based on pure spherical trigonometry, demonstrating
the correspondence between man and celestial movements.

A horoscope is a map of the heavens for a given moment,
with an inner ring depicting the earth and an outer circle showing
the various planets and solar bodies. The simplest horoscope, the
natal chart, pictures the solar system at the precise moment of the
person's birth.

The inner circle is divided by "cusps" into twelve "houses,"
each representing a sign of the zodiac. Each of them is said
to have a ruling planet, but since there are only nine planets,
several of them rule more than one sign. The planets have
various characteristics, which affect each other when they are in
"conjunction"—that is only 10 degrees apart. The effect can
be good, hampering or disastrous, depending on the nature of
the planets and whether they are "trine"—120 degrees apart—
"sextile," "square" or in "opposition"—at opposite sides of the
circle.

These are only a few of the factors involved in reading a
horoscope. Equally important are the positions of the two "lights"
—sun and moon—the conversion of True Local Time, that is
earth time, into Sidereal Time (star time), and the ascendant,
or rising sign, meaning the degree of the zodiac on the eastern
horizon at the moment of birth. And in the majority of natal
charts these intricate calculations are rendered haphazard by the
fact that most clients don't know the precise moment of their
birth.

Forecasting the future by horoscope involves a brain-spinning
maneuver called "taking transits and progressions." This means

drawing up a new celestial chart as it will be at some distant date, comparing it with the original natal horoscope and trying to interpret the interactions and combinations between the two. Results depend entirely on the skill of the interpreter.

Predictive astrology, therefore, is by no means the exact science its exponents claim it to be. Not even within the modest limitations staked out by those who claim that "astrology can forecast rain, but it can't tell whether you, personally, will get wet."

Can it tell anything at all? There seems to be no hard and fast answer to this. You could visualize astrology as an immensely intricate, finely constructed piece of machinery resting on an invisible foundation. And the foundation is the question whether or not celestial actions influence earthly events.

To quote Sydney Omarr: "We do not claim that the planets have the power to *cause* events to occur nor to cause people to react the way they do. What we do claim is that there is a correspondence, a coincidence, between planetary patterns and mundane actions, reactions, events."

No astrologer has put it better, but it still leaves the vital theory of causation as vague as ever. Proofs of any connection are, to say it gently, tenuous. We know that the full moon has an influence on the behavior of certain types of lunatics as well as animals. We know the relationship of the moon to ocean tides and the effect of the planets on electromagnetically controlled forces on earth. A Japanese biologist recently discovered that the composition of human blood alters in relation to sunspot cycles.

But all of this is still a mighty long way from the assertion that—for example—because Mars occupies a certain position in the sky war will break out on earth.

On a more personalized level the proofs are somewhat stronger. During the 1930s psychologist Carl Gustav Jung— Freud's favorite pupil and prize opponent—began to have horoscopes cast for his patients. He believed that they clarified traits in patient personalities which he might have missed. He never claimed to know why this should be so, but developed a theory of "synchronicity" in partial explanation. This, roughly speaking, is what men like Omarr expound today—the existence of a mysterious but consistent parallel between movements above and below.

Jung, in due course, became sufficiently convinced to tell one of his lecture classes, "The fact that it is possible, in an adequate fashion, to construct a person's character from the data of his nativity, shows the relative validity of astrology."

It took thirty years before the first American psychologists followed in his footsteps. Today a number—mostly in California—use horoscopes to aid in their probings of man's unconscious. One has even suggested that astrology might be admitted as an adjunct to his own field.

But the ultimate distinction so far came from NASA, America's Space Agency. In November 1969, this august scientific body invited ten hand-picked astrologers to witness the Apollo 12 moon launch at Cape Kennedy.

Nothing of the kind has happened since the rulers of antiquity consulted the Delphic oracle before marching into battle.

II

THE VOICES
OF PROPHECY

DURING APRIL 1969, travel agencies and airline offices throughout the United States experienced a noticeable slump in California-bound bookings. The reason for this was a widespread conviction that the Golden State was about to vanish from the map. If not entirely then at least partially.

The disappearance was to be caused by a series of devastating earthquakes, which would make those portions of the state west of the San Andreas fault slide into the Pacific Ocean.

The San Andreas fault runs six hundred miles through California, starting north of San Francisco and extending southward to Los Angeles. It has been held responsible for the catastrophic quake and fire that destroyed much of San Francisco on April 18, 1906. But there was not the slightest indication that it would repeat the act sixty-three years later.

The warning voices had not been raised by seismologists but by oracles. A whole chorus of them, varying slightly about the exact date but harmonious on the theme that the end of the state was at hand.

Nobody knew who or what started it. Some local chroniclers tend to blame a large-scale misinterpretation of the writings of the late Edgar Cayce. The "Sleeping Prophet" had indeed predicted the eventual obliteration of Los Angeles and San Francisco. But he had given himself a fairly wide margin of fulfillment—the entire second half of the century.

There was the psychic Dutch-born housewife, Elisabeth Steen, who saw recurring visions of San Francisco swallowed by earthquakes and tidal waves. These visions had come to her for four years and in due course persuaded her husband to move his family to Washington. Mrs. Steen foresaw April as the disaster month—but she never claimed to know *which* April.

Scientists of the California Institute of Technology forecast a "creep" along the San Andreas fault early in April. Except that the earth movement known by that term is so slight that you couldn't feel it even if you were standing right beside the fault.

Yet in some mysterious fashion a goodly section of America's soothsayers fastened on April 1969 as the fatal span. True, the stars of the profession kept aloof, most of them refusing to comment one way or another. Some of the lesser fry, on the other hand, went overboard. They pinpointed not just the month, but the day, hour and minute of the impending holocaust; several painting downright orgiastic pictures of the destruction in store.

In Los Angeles, San Diego and Bakersfield the heads of six spiritualistic churches ordered their congregations to leave California and head for the hills of Georgia and Tennessee. Several hundred actually packed up and went. As far as we know they haven't returned yet.

In Santa Barbara an augur named Andrew Widrovsky envisioned "two titanic earth convulsions, followed by five tidal waves and a deluge of radio-active ash that will cover the entire south-western part of the state," and advised his disciples to either take flight or wear "antiradiation belts" (sold by him) as protection.

The favorite date at first was April 4 at 3:15 P.M. Chief reason for this was the fact that Governor Ronald Reagan (who allegedly had "inside information") would be in Arizona then. When that day passed prognosticators switched to April 18—the anniversary of the great 1906 quake—and excitement mounted.

Thousands of citizens kept ringing police stations, civil defense offices and newspapers, demanding to know when the earthquake would commence. When no precise information was forthcoming, some charged that the authorities were "suppressing the truth in order to avoid a panic." Stores and bars displayed posters promising "These premises will remain open during the Scare." Retailers offered "Earthquake Helmets" and "Quake Cushions," and one fashion show ran with the title "How to Be Best Dressed for the Earthquake."

At 5:13 on the morning of April 18, Mayor Joseph Alioto of San Francisco threw a giant "Earthquake Party" in the city's Civic Center Plaza. Despite the ungodly hour, several thousand people turned up to sing, dance, drink and watch the destruction of their town on the screen—by means of a rerun of the classic disaster scenes from MGM's movie *San Francisco*.

The hippies of San Francisco's Haight-Ashbury, however, didn't join in. Their particular choice was April 19 at 8:19 A.M., as indicated by half a hundred storefront mystics. Some of the beard-and-bead set decamped for the day, most of them stayed put and awaited the end with an equal mixture of stoicism, apprehension and glee.

So it went on, right through April. California, as it happened, did not slide into oblivion. But if the great nonevent proved anything, it was the amazing grip of prophecy on the minds of millions of Americans.

Divination in one form or another is probably as old as human society; it certainly predates written history. The ancients used it as a matter of routine. It was part of every known religion; including the monotheistic faith of the Hebrews.

With the coming of the Christian era in the West, however, the practice fell into disrepute. The Church fathers regarded it with the deepest suspicion as a hangover from paganism, even when they didn't ban it outright. But from that time dates the striking parallel between unrest and augurism. The more turbulent the present, the more uncertain the future, the greater became the demand—and hope—for preview glimpses into it.

With acute social tensions and turmoil currently sweeping America, it isn't surprising that the United States now harbors a greater number of seers than any country has ever possessed before. The astonishing thing is the uniformity of their methods. For despite an encyclopedic mass of divination practices, our soothsayers confine themselves to a tiny handful.

Other civilizations made use of an immense variety, ranging from the humorous to the gruesome. You could, for instance, foretell the future by the sound of a person's laughter. You could also do it from the state of his—or her—exposed entrails.

Then there was Alectromancy, based on the grain pecking of sacred cocks. Pyromancy, the observation of fires on sacrificial altars. Ornithomancy, interpreting the flights of birds. Sycomancy, which depended on the withering process of fig leaves. Ichthyomancy, looking for omens in the innards of fish. Tyromancy, studying the mildew forming on cheeses. Psychomancy, by conjuring up ghosts; etc., etc., and almost ad infinitum.

Out of this multitude of methods, United States practitioners utilize only a small fraction. One is a form generically known as Crystalomancy. This includes tea-leaf and coffee-ground reading and crystal ball gazing. The others are dream interpretations (Oneiromancy), card reading, palmistry, and a fairly recent innovation called Pyramidology, which isn't real augurism at all but a kind of architectural analysis.

In any case, most of our topflight forecasters admit that they regard these aids merely as means to achieve concentration. They are—or claim to be—clairvoyant. The word comes from the French and means "clear seeing." It denotes a sixth sense, an undefinable, often erratic ability to look forward and backward in time, to read thoughts, to observe things that are not material, and it does not depend on any sort of operative tool.

Jeane Dixon, our most publicized prophetess, is frequently photographed with a crystal ball. In actual fact she uses it rarely. Her general predictions are mostly based on revelations and visions in true biblical style. On a personal level she often depends on touch—"tip fingers," as she calls it—using the ring finger of her left hand to channel in on her subject. In recent years she has also taken up astrology.

There is little of the solemn ritualism of past ages in contemporary American seers. Their equipment is stored almost entirely inside their heads. Their studios and workrooms appear about as mystical as insurance offices. But what they may lack in magic paraphernalia they make up for in the communications branch.

America's prophets author best sellers, pack lecture halls, star in TV shows, run radio programs, write newspaper columns and publish periodicals. No group of augurs in history has ever reached anything approaching their audience.

And in no Western industrial society were they ever listened to with greater reverence. Entire bookstore shelves are filled with their biographies, most of them as inaccurate as they are worshipful. Magazines turn out "human interest" pieces on their private lives in assembly-line fashion. Every New Year pages of newsprint and hours of air time are devoted to their prognostications on every conceivable topic, from international politics to skirt lengths. At the turn of the decades of 1960 and '70 the volume of their voices reached crescendo levels.

In theory they suffer from the same legal ambiguity as their astrological colleagues—though "suffer" is hardly the right word for it. Most United States communities possess some form of legislation against fortune-telling, but the wording varies not only from state to state but from county to county and city to city.

Los Angeles, surprisingly, boasts the most comprehensive ordinance in the entire nation. The city outlaws the advertising not only of fortune-telling but of astrology, clairvoyance, mediumship, palmistry, necromancy, psychometry, prophecy and numerology —all arts through which an estimated nine thousand of its inhabitants earn their living. A rider, however, specifically exempts "ministers who fully conform to the rites and practices prescribed by their church or religious organization."

This exemption prompted the lower ranks of the soothsaying profession to equip themselves with Reverend and Doctor of Divinity titles. Both are easily available. The Church of Universal Brotherhood in Hollywood sells them at $10 each, complete with Ordination Certificate. The recipient D.D. is then entitled

to found a new church and expound as many prophecies as
he—or she—can dream up. Which accounts, at least to some
extent, for the breathtaking proliferation of religious cults in Los
Angeles.

The upper stratas of augurism are in any case immune from
legal molestation. The process works according to a curious in-
verse ratio: the more publicity, the higher the fees, the less
chance of being arrested for "fortune-telling." As one Chicago
cop put it succinctly, "A fortune-teller—that's anyone who
charges less than eight bucks a sitting!"

Since the leaders in the clairvoyant field collect between
$20 and $150 per private consultation, they are well beyond the
borderline.

The remarkable exception to this rule is Jeane Dixon, the
sibyl of Washington, D.C., for Mrs. Dixon gives her profession
as "real estate broker" and charges no actual fees for her psychic
services. Which puts her in a class strictly by herself. And in
more ways than one.

Jeane Dixon regards her talent merely as a means to an
end. "I use my gift to catch people's interest," she explained,
"so they'll listen to my real message, and it works."

Mrs. Dixon's particular message is so tightly entwined with
her prophecies that you frequently can't tell where one stops
and the other begins.

It is an odd fusion of Catholic mysticism with the most
virulently right-wing brand of Republicanism. The resultant mixture often makes her augurisms read like Goldwater campaign
pamphlets.

Her annual predictions for 1969, published by *Newsday*,
were partially devoted to a seven-step plan hatched by "three
decision makers" of the Soviet Union. The amount of prophecy
involved was no higher than that routinely dispensed by political
journalists, except that Mrs. Dixon revealed the initials of those
decision makers to be "S," "P" and "A."

The rest of the list consisted of forecasts so broadly generalized that it would have taken a total and miraculous reversal of
world trends to prove her wrong. After all, even nonpsychic
mortals might have guessed that money would lose some of its
buying power, that there would be marches and demonstrations

in America and a flare-up in the Middle East, that the police would again be charged with brutality and that Governor Reagan of California would "continue to have trouble with riotous activities." One of her very few specifics proved completely false: she predicted "a great change in the leadership of Red China this year."

But, as Mrs. Dixon pointed out, her purpose does not lie in her premonitions but in the message behind them. The gist of it, roughly, is that drug distribution, pornography, rampant crime, racial conflicts and student riots are all part of the planned destruction of this country's moral fiber, blueprinted by "the organizational geniuses of the USSR." The "wonderful and trusting people here in America" are their unwitting tools. Mrs. Dixon knows this because she picks up "thought patterns and plans from the leaders of the opposing forces by telepathy."

She also knows, though evidently from a different source, that "God never said that all people were equal. He said that all people were equally His children." Which may not be quite in line with the Declaration of Independence, but apparently is the Gospel according to Mrs. Jeane Dixon, née Pinckert.

Despite her telepathic pickup, Washington's own Pythia doesn't have a particularly lucky hand with world affairs. Contrary to her pronouncements, the United States did not go to war with Red China in 1958, Walter Reuther did not make a bid for the White House in 1964, nor did the Berlin Wall come down that year. Presidents Johnson and de Gaulle did not meet in 1966, and that year also failed to come up with the negotiated peace in Vietnam she had promised.

When asked about her misses, she usually explains that she had seen the correct signs but had misinterpreted them. Occasionally, however, stronger corrections are required. Thus her syndicate hastily withdrew Mrs. Dixon's newspaper column scheduled for October 20, 1968. She had gone on record with the statement: "I still stand by my New Year's prediction and see no marriage for Jackie Kennedy in the near future."

October 20 happened to be the day Jackie became Mrs. Onassis.

In print Mrs. Dixon rarely rises above the average level of press prognosticators—handing out solid shots of Capitol grapevine laced with random prophecies, which sometimes score, frequently miss and mostly remain unverifiable. For her revealed Second Coming of Christ, for instance, we will have to wait until the year 2000.

The private Mrs. Dixon is quite a different matter. To start with she has considerable charm, which doesn't come through in her writing. She is pretty in a matronly way, disarmingly modest and rather fey—except when she gets into politics. Her blue eyes have a strong, steady, curiously distant gaze; you remember it longer than any of her other features. She speaks very simply and directly, accentuating the words with expressive gestures of her white-gloved hands.

She does a tremendous amount for charity—something few psychics seem to bother with. And she unfailingly returns every personal fee that arrives with the three thousand or so letters in her weekly mailbag.

Nearly all of her famous predictions were made privately and only revealed after they—allegedly—came to pass. And here lies the rub. Most of the celebrities to whom they were uttered —from Winston Churchill to Carole Lombard—are dead and cannot be interviewed. Other widely quoted prophecies were heard only by her intimate friends, who are not what you might call impartial witnesses.

Documented evidence—that is precise, unequivocal forecasts of certain events given at a verifiable date—are scarce. Which makes it somewhat difficult to assess Mrs. Dixon's rating as an oracle. But there is no doubt about her caliber as a public figure. She has become an institution, her name synonymous with psychic powers, her entire image a living symbol of clairvoyance. And that to millions of people who take a decidedly dim view of the "message" that goes with it.

No one in this country quite matches Jeane Dixon's status in her field. Her closest rival doesn't really count, because he is an Englishman who only spends part of his time in America.

Maurice Woodruff divides his life between a five-hundred-year-old country mansion in Kent and an exceedingly plush penthouse beside New York's East River. An amiably garrulous man in his mid-fifties, with a shock of gray-mottled hair, he looks like Hollywood's idea of a benign country doctor. He is, in fact, one of the world's leading clairvoyants. His United States television shows broke several audience records, he receives up to five thousand advice-seeking letters a week, and his syndicated newspaper column achieves a worldwide circulation approaching 50 million.

Woodruff calls himself a clairvoyant-astrologer and uses both methods to about equal degrees. His readings are conducted in a unique manner—he hardly lets his clients speak at all. Woodruff does all the talking; he rarely asks any questions. Then, at the end of forty minutes or so of solid monologue, he sits back and waits for queries. Usually there aren't any.

As far as Woodruff's public predictions are concerned, you can judge for yourself. Here is a sampling of his prophecies for 1970. By the time you read this they *should* have materialized:

• The great sensation of 1970 will be the discovery of a cure for cancer. It will happen by fall, possibly in September.
• Jackie Kennedy Onassis will have a son.
• The war in Vietnam will peter out late in the year. As the war dwindles in Vietnam, another will flare up in Korea.
• Ronald Reagan will lose California's next fall's election.

Both Dixon and Woodruff—like the majority of seers—use their powers almost solely for predictive purposes. But this doesn't apply to another of the big leaguers, who resembles an occult one-man band.

The Reverend Clifford Matthew Royse, Jr., known in his native Chicago as Mr. Psychic, is a singular combination of deep trance medium, religious mystic, telepathist, parapsychologist, card reader, psychometrist and prophet. Not to mention his secondary talents, such as blindfolded reading, facial transfiguration and astral projection. With this goes a knack for lecturing and broadcasting, a flair for publicity and considerable business acumen.

A heavy, balding man, looking older than his thirty-eight years, Royse is the son of five generations of mediums, the husband of a fellow psychic and the father of a prospective one. Probably no other family in the United States is so steeped in the occult. He met his wife, an attractive brunette named Eursula, while both were attending the Light of Truth Church of Divine Healing, in which he became an ordained minister in 1956. They now have two sons, of whom the older already exhibits psychic talents.

The Royses operate an institution called Chicago Psychic Center, in suburban West Lake Street; an extensive complex with lecture rooms capable of seating two hundred people. It also houses a restaurant which not only features prime steaks, strolling minstrels and organ music, but also ESP readings at your dinner table, sometimes performed by Mr. Psychic in person.

Apart from running a daily radio program, Royse holds classes, lectures to civic groups and gives private readings at $25 each. Mrs. Royse offers hers for only $15.

But the most remarkable thing about Chicago's Mr. Psychic is his annual list of printed predictions. Not only are they widely circulated and unusually specific, but Royse frequently reprints lists from previous years—something that requires a quite uncommon amount of courage. For the penalty for being specific is being wrong . . . and that on a pretty massive scale.

While he correctly prophesied President Johnson's last health setback, the hospitalization of the late Senator Dirksen, the remarriage of Mrs. Lee Harvey Oswald, the explosion of China's second A-bomb, the Chicago taxi strike of 1965 and the lawsuits dogging the Krebiozen cancer drug, he was way out on at least twice as many counts.

Among other startlers he had foreseen the assassination of Fidel Castro and the natural death of Charles de Gaulle for 1966, Egypt's first atomic bomb test for 1967, and the death of President Nasser, the breakup of the Huntley-Brinkley news team, a Conservative government for Britain and a new Pope for 1969.

However, it's only fair to add that Royse could have avoided most of the above boo-boos had he chosen to be a little more obscure in his language.

He could, for instance, have followed the example of the California-based augur Criswell (of "Criswell Predicts" fame) and dealt in pronouncements like the following typical one for 1970: "I predict that one of our movie stars will be found to have feet of clay when the divorce hits the courts."

Has there ever been a year over the past four decades when *some* movie star did *not* display feet of clay in a divorce court?

The general haziness that afflicts the prophetic profession often makes it hard to determine just who said what and when and where about whom. Virtually all soothsayers in this country —and scores abroad—now claim credit for having forecast the murder of President Kennedy. More than that—they also remember having written frantic letters and/or telephoned the White House in their anxiety. If you were to believe only half of them, the late President's staff must have been inundated with warning missives, each citing the nature, date and locality of the impending peril. All of which were not only ignored but also mysteriously lost somewhere down the line.

But the obscurancy is not necessarily deliberate. Augurs— regardless of their sincerity—have to cope with the most intangible of all media. They lack the mathematical system that forms the basis of astrology. They have no technical jargon at their disposal, no real means of communicating how they arrived at their predictions. Most of the time they don't know themselves. Whereas astrologers can declare that such-and-such will happen because Jupiter is in conjunction with Saturn, prophets can rarely go beyond saying, "I feel . . ."

Those among them who read cards or claim religious guidance have at least a frame of reference. Their visions were spelled out by the Tarot or came from God. The rest can only speak of "images" and "vibrations"—the very vaguest of terminologies.

The more intellectually curious are currently making serious efforts to come to grips with their own phenomena. To trace back, pinpoint and possibly explain exactly how the process worked that made them utter a particular forecast.

The reason this hadn't happened earlier may be the generally low educational level of most psychics, their tendency to distrust research from fear that analysis might weaken their gift. One of the exceptions is thirty-three-year-old Alan Vaughan, a Classics graduate of the University of Akron, Ohio, who happens to be precognitive.

Vaughan stumbled on his own ability while actually investigating the phenomena in others. He went to Europe on a grant from the American Parapsychology Foundation and studied at research centers in Germany, Holland and England (see Figure 4).

"I was studying mediumistic prophecy," he remembered. "On
a purely experimental basis I started recording my own dreams.
This was in the spring of 1968, while working with Professor
Bender in Freiburg. Well, I had a couple of dreams which—
somehow—linked up with several newspaper headlines I read to
form a definite prediction. Professor Bender called this 'synchronicity'—which means a meaningful coincidence.

"Later I found this pattern operating again and again. I
became fairly proficient at recording my dreams the moment I
woke up. I also learned to meditate with a certain purpose in
mind. Both these methods sometimes coalesced with newspaper
captions, assembling into prophecies; distinct mental pictures of
future events. But there's also a disturbing element called 'displacement'—that is certain aspects you associate with one event
actually pertain to another. And this can really throw you off."

He pulled at his pipe. "I'll give you an example. On November 12, 1969, I meditated on the Apollo 12 moonshot. I had
the clear impression that there was something wrong with either
the fuel or the electrical system that would cause an explosion.

"Now these details were pretty accurate," he said, "only they
didn't apply to Apollo 12 but to the next lunar launch, Apollo 13.
If you'll recall, a fuel cell exploded, knocking out most of the
electrical equipment, nearly killing the astronauts. And that is
what we mean by 'displacement.'"

"How do you go about this meditating with a purpose?"
I asked.

"I sit in a chair, straight up, not too comfortable, because
I don't want to fall asleep. I relax completely, but I don't
have to close my eyes. I distill my mind and wait . . . wait to
see if anything comes. Sometimes nothing does. At other times
images come, which I have learned to interpret. If I described
the images to you you'd probably say, 'Oh, that's nothing.'
But it's a matter of practice, you see, of analyzing past impressions, of keeping records and noting sequences. Then reflecting
back on how things have happened previously. And the more I
analyze, the more I can get out of the material that comes to
me."

Vaughan is not so much interested in the veracity of his
talent as in the mechanics behind it. He carefully dates each

of his predictions, records the time and circumstances in which it was made and files it away for future reference. By comparing prophecies made at various periods and under different conditions he eventually hopes to construct something resembling a basic framework for precognition.

His extensive scientific training gives him very exacting standards. He spoke apologetically about a premonition he recorded in London, concerning a Japanese train that he foresaw being derailed by an earthquake. His forecast, as it turned out, named November instead of January as the time of the disaster.

Vaughan, whose languid manner and long fair hair seem at odds with his Kirk Douglas chin, belongs to an entirely new breed of sensitives. He uses his gift solely for research purposes. His consultations and lectures are given free of charge. So are his services in numerous laboratory experiments. He earns his living as science editor of a magazine and with the books he writes. He and his wife, plus a gregarious German shepherd dog named Meka, inhabit an apartment in the distinctly unfashionable Williamsburg section of Brooklyn, New York.

Yet he appears to have been the *only* seer in the world who actually wrote out—and registered—a clear prediction of Robert Kennedy's death by shooting. He kept a copy and mailed the original from Germany to the Maimonides Dream Laboratory in Brooklyn (of which more later). It arrived there on June 3, 1968—just forty-eight hours before the murder took place in Los Angeles! The letter—with the date stamp—is on file in the laboratory's record section.

The fulfillment of Vaughan's tragic vision sparked a project which may in due course provide a blueprint for the entire subject of precognition. The idea originated in England, but Vaughan's letter persuaded one of the laboratory's volunteer workers to extend it to America.

Robert Nelson is the thirty-three-year-old manager of the New York *Times*'s College and School Service Department. An Ohio psychology major, he first became fascinated by the paranormal when his identical twin brother William developed a gift for telekinesis—that is the mysterious power to move physical objects by mental effort alone.

The same month that Vaughan's Kennedy prediction arrived,

Nelson established the Central Premonitions Registry, of which he is director as well as 50 percent of the staff (see Figure 5).

"The CPR has a triple purpose," he explained in his sharp, slightly twangy Midwestern voice. "First of all, we were trying to set up a clearinghouse to either prove or disprove the existence of precognition. We're asking anyone who has any premonitory claims to send us their dreams, premonitions, hunches or whatever for our special filing system which will show how many of these prophecies actually come true.

"The second goal is to locate people who demonstrate a genuine psychic gift. We hope to encourage them to participate in ESP experiments in order to discover—for instance—what brain-wave activity accompanies their precognitive dreams.

"Thirdly," he added, "we hope to set up a 'Precognition Alert.' Meaning some kind of Early Warning System which may actually prevent disasters."

"What are the results so far?" I asked.

He grinned and opened the drawers of a row of steel filing cabinets. "This—" he said.

"This" was the first systematized and indexed prophecy bank in the United States. It housed the 950 predictions from over 500 persons the CPR had received by February 1970.

All were date-stamped and filed into one of thirteen different categories. The bulkiest was "Prominent Personalities —Injury or Death," which contained a special subfile just for the Kennedy family.

Other categories run from "Natural Disasters" and "Civil Unrest" to "War and International Relations," "Aircraft and Ship Disasters," "The Space Race" and a slender one marked "Economics."

Most of the filing and much of the clipping, letter writing and news monitoring is done by the slim, dark-haired and comely Mrs. Nelson, a former Peace Corps worker in Africa. Neither she nor her director-husband receive any pay for their CPR work and no grant has been forthcoming so far. But one large-circulation weekly is giving them financial assistance in return for first grabs on any prophecy story with a sensational flavor.

If Nelson had merely wished to prove the existence of precognition he has already done so. His files contain a whole batch of letters which—by fairly stringent standards—can pass as prophecies. A few came from professional psychics, most from ordinary men and women.

There was Mrs. Mildred Barton, a forty-two-year-old housewife in Cincinnati, Ohio. On January 14, 1970, the bureau registered her dream prediction, which concerned the killings of United Mine Workers official Joseph Yablonski and his family. At that time the police had released no clues whatever on the slayings.

Mrs. Barton wrote: "There were three men present . . . two killers and the director of it. A young blond-headed girl is involved . . ."

Seven days later three men were arrested and charged with the murders. Later a federal grand jury also indicted a blond woman named Annette Lucy Gilly.

On June 10, 1969, a New England book salesman named Rex Coile filed a prediction that the New York Mets would win the World Series. The odds against them doing so were then given at 100 to 1. They did.

Malcolm Bessent, a professional sensitive, wrote: "A Greek oil tanker, black in color, will be involved in a disaster having international significance within 4–6 months. (Onassis connected—perhaps the imagery is symbolic, but I feel that the ship may represent him personally.)"

Bessent's letter was registered on December 9, 1969. On February 7, the black-painted Greek tanker *Arrow* broke in half off Nova Scotia, spilling its oil cargo into the sea. Both Canada and the United States feared contaminated beaches, thus causing international concern. The *Arrow* belonged to the Sunstone Marine Co., Ltd.—which is owned by Aristotle Onassis!

It is too early to judge whether Nelson will succeed in cataloging augurism into some form of calculable and practically useful pattern. But his project is already off to a far sounder start than a previous attempt.

The inspiration for this likewise came from England. It dates back to 1859 and an eccentric London publisher named John Taylor. That year Mr. Taylor brought out a book entitled *The Great Pyramid*. He had never actually *seen* the pyramid, but by studying its various measurements decided that it embodied a prophetic message for all mankind.

A whole row of disciples on both sides of the Atlantic improved on Taylor's original idea. In what grew into a veritable
library of books they demonstrated that the mammoth structure
was a stone oracle. The ancient Egyptian architects had actually
predicted future history in its outline, interior and contents. It
was just a question of discovering the key formula; you could then
proceed to read the future like a mathematical textbook!

The Great Pyramid of Gizeh is a titanic edifice, covering
13 acres, rising to 481 feet and weighing 6½ million tons. It is
constructed entirely of stone blocks—some of them weighing over
50 tons—and with such dazzling precision that the joints where
the blocks were fitted are hardly discernible.

The trouble is that we don't know when it was built, we don't
know how it was built, and we aren't even sure why it was built.
Archeologists put the date of construction at somewhere between
5000 and 4000 B.C. But the engineering puzzle of just how those
monster blocks were hoisted into place with the primitive tools
then available has never been satifactorily solved. Neither has the
original purpose of the structure. It is generally believed to have
been the tomb of King Cheops, but no royal mummy was ever
found inside.

Discovering the key, the yardstick cipher, to this man-made
mountain was quite a task. Taylor thought it was the "sacred
cubit" of the Bible, about twenty-five inches. But later a Scottish
astronomer named Charles P. Smyth adopted what he called
the "pyramid inch," which he thought was the smallest measuring
unit employed by the pyramid builders.

Armed with these measuring units thousands of Pyramidologists proceeded to measure history—past and future—from the
base, the flanks, the chambers, the walls and the maze of
internal passages and corridors of the stone giant. They counted
one inch as equaling one year and came up with some astounding
results.

The pyramid, according to them, not only marked the date of
the creation of the world (4004 B.C.), the Flood, the Resurrection
of Christ and the Barbarian invasion of Rome, but also the First
and Second World War, the 1929 Stock Market Crash, the Depression and the Atom Bomb. Plus what other great events still lay
ahead.

The measuring was done in a rather freewheeling style: now one passage, then another, now the circumference of the base, then the height of a gallery. If the same enthusiasm and laissez-faire had been applied to, say, the vital statistics of the Empire State Building, they might have yielded a couple of prophecies too.

The pyramidic prophecies filled several hundred books and tens of thousands of pamphlets and brochures. However, as Bertrand Russell remarked, "It is a singular fact that the Great Pyramid always predicts history accurately up to the date of publication of the book in question, but after that it becomes less reliable."

In due course the Pyramidologists quite literally measured themselves to a standstill. For the application of the pyramid inch to the inner passages could only go as far as the date calculated as August 20, 1953. There it ends at a blank wall—clearly the end of the world!

When the expected grand finale didn't take place just then, the more dedicated disciples maintained that the world, in fact, *did* end at that date. Judgment has already been passed upon us and we are now merely awaiting its execution in a kind of interim period that will last no longer than about thirty or so years.

But not all pyramidic lore is based on measurements. In his book, *The Symbolic Prophecy of the Great Pyramid*, H. Spencer Lewis—founder of the Rosicrucian Order in America—mentioned the birthdate of Jesus engraved on an inside wall in symbols denoting October 4, 4 B.C.

Now this is a well-nigh miraculous discovery, in view of the fact that the Great Pyramid has NO ornamentation, inscriptions, carvings or hieroglyphs of any kind, either inside or out. With the exception, that is, of the graffiti left by two generations of British Commonwealth troops. Which—take my word for it—bear no relation whatever to the birth of Jesus.

Episodes like this have left many earnest clairvoyants with a distaste for any kind of mechanistic approach. They prefer to rely solely on their own sensibility.

This also applies to one of the most successful of our younger psychics. Daniel Logan uses no implements except his mind. "No, I don't see any 'images,'" he told me. "Nothing visual at all. With me it's entirely a matter of thought processes and words. But the two are almost instantaneous. As a matter of fact, very often I find myself saying things to people that I can't remember having *thought* of at all. It's as if the words had been on the tip of my tongue all the time."

His autobiographical book *The Reluctant Prophet* is aptly titled. Logan—who changed his name from the somewhat unpronounceable Olaschinez—wanted first to be an actor, then an author. Prophecy was almost foisted upon him. But at thirty-five he has caught the spotlight both as an exceptionally intelligent writer and lecturer and as a TV augur of startling accuracy.

Network audiences heard him predict five years ago that the Vietnam war would drag into the 1970s. They heard him name the Academy Award winners for 1966, '67 and '68 several weeks in advance. They heard his forecasts of the 1967 race riots as well as that year's unusually heavy snowfalls and record rains.

They also heard him tell actress Betsy von Furstenberg that she was negotiating about property in Switzerland—which she promptly denied. After the show, however, she confided to producer David Susskind that there was indeed "something about a house and land in Switzerland" which—for legal reasons—she couldn't discuss.

Logan is a small, highly strung man with very prominent brown eyes, his Scythian chin beard forming a strange contrast to his juvenile voice. He dresses meticulously mod—unlike most psychics, who tend to be rather sloppy about their appearance. He seems to live on his nerves and is prone to stage fright, in the wider sense of the word.

"I'll never forget my first professional consultation," he said with a wan smile. "The first one I ever got paid for. I had no idea what to charge. And I was absolutely petrified. In the cab to the lady's place I kept thinking: 'Oh, my God, what if I go dry—what if nothing happens? What if she has terrible secrets and that's the only thing I receive?' Well, as it turned out she was very nice, gave me a cup of tea, and we had a very good reading. But I'll never forget that taxi ride."

Yet all traces of tension disappear the moment he faces a client. A calm, cheerful certainty takes over and somewhere in him a supersensitive antenna starts picking up signals, linking him with the other person in a delicate two-way rapport.

Hardly anyone notices the grueling strain this involves. "In the beginning," said Logan, "I didn't know how to limit myself in these sessions. Sometimes they went on for an hour and a half, leaving me depleted and ill afterwards. Now I restrict them to forty minutes. Twice a week—and I only see about three people on each of these days.

"I charge a maximum of twenty-five dollars a reading. I don't make my money from being a practicing psychic, most of it comes from writing and lecturing. But occasionally I'll put in overtime."

One of these occasions was when he rescued a client from the clutches of a unique pair of confidence crooks. The lady, whom he describes as a "wealthy, well-educated New York society matron," seems to have suffered from an overdose of spiritualist gullibility. She came under the spell of her masseuse, who also happened to be an effective medium.

With the aid of a Ouija board—allegedly operated by the matron's late father—the medium-masseuse persuaded her to set up a $100,000 trust fund for an invalid nephew. The cash, however, was then turned over to the masseuse's attorney—likewise suggested by the Ouija board. The fund, somehow, was never set up; at least not for the nephew. The lawyer found better and more personal uses for the money.

It took Logan only one session to see through the fraud, but months to persuade his client to do something about it. Eventually the attorney went to jail and the psychic masseuse up for trial. But whether the lady will ever see her money again even Logan can't predict.

Logan was born in New York, but recently found that he couldn't take the city any longer. He now lives in the country, "way upstate," in a little house with a few acres. He doesn't live exactly alone. With him are a pet robin, a pet sparrow, a parrot, a chihuahua and a cat. And he hopes to add a couple of horses.

Clairvoyants may share the same power, but their efforts in utilizing it vary immensely. What is an exhausting struggle to Daniel Logan comes as easy "as turning on a tap and letting the water flow" to Irene Hughes. She knows neither uncertainty nor psychic tensions. Her smile remains serene and a little frosty no matter what questions you put to her (see Figure 6).

Mrs. Hughes is both a consultant psychic and head of an educational nonprofit organization called The Golden Path. She also writes a predictive column that appears weekly in twenty-eight newspapers.

Her office and headquarters is in downtown Chicago—a suite of rooms lavishly decorated with crucifixes, holy pictures and zodiac signs, mixed with photos of herself in company with various celebrities. Even the plastic light switches bear a praying-hands motif. A small nursery school type blackboard in the lecture room has "God is All" chalked on it in stiff letters.

When I called on her she was wearing a silvery sparkle dress that matched her silvery sparkle hair. But she sat behind a very businesslike desk and her poise was as crisply impersonal as an account executive's.

"I was born in Tennessee, very near the Mississippi border, and I had my first psychic experience at the age of four," she started. "It was what my mother called a revelation of things that were going to happen in my own life. And they did. That very week."

She smiled frigidly at the middle distance. "From then on it seemed like I was in contact with everything that was happening. So by the time I was nine I said to my mother, 'I'm going to marry a man from Michigan and I'm going to live in Chicago.' And my mother said, 'Chicago—that's the other side of the world! How do you ever expect to get there?' But it happened."

Her self-assurance is absolute. "I don't allow my clients to tell me anything about themselves. Not during the early part of the session, anyway. I'll tell them! No, I don't talk about their characters. I may deal with some situation that happened in the past. Sometimes I get the indication—well, here's your husband who died in a plane crash on August 12, 1959. It comes to me perfectly clearly—a plane falling, maybe in flames, seeing the plane crash, the man dying . . . everything. All in pictures—extremely clear pictures."

Unlike most of her colleagues, Irene Hughes doesn't pull punches. "I give everything that comes," she declared firmly. "I feel that it's their reading and I'm only the channel through which it flows. Within me I feel in a state of prayer—the soul part of me—and so if a really tragic situation arises then I'm told how to go about it, and I follow that, very calmly and quietly. And I find that—usually—people are not upset."

In print Mrs. Hughes comes through as rather less than crystalline. In her columns she frequently fights losing battles with both syntax and logic. She uses a curious staccato style that sometimes reads like those subtly bewildering cables you get from business companies whose native language is not English.

Her New Year's prognostications for 1970 included enigmas like: "Total reevaluation and new economic structure for our nation which began in 1969 with the downward trend of the market on the exact dates as predicted."

Or: "I predict that the Middle East situation will be far worse in 1973, and that Russia and China will be involved in that war plus fighting against each other and that we will be drawn into a violent and atomic war late in 1973."

Personally I've never heard of a *non*violent war, atomic or otherwise.

Points of grammar notwithstanding, Irene Hughes's regular stock market forecasts have a large and faithful following among Chicago's business community. This despite her avowal that "I don't know one stock from another."

She is one of the very few sensitives who can make her talent work on her own behalf. "I always dress according to my own weather predictions," she assured me. "And I'm the best weather prophet there is."

Could she make a fortune in the stock market or on the race track?

She must have been asked that one many, many times before. Her answer was categorical: "I will tell you this: I do not believe that just because a person wishes to gamble that they will lose their gift. I do not use it in that way—I've never had the desire to. But if I ever felt that I wanted to use it in that way, I think I'd go ahead and do it. But I've no desire to have a lot of money lying around that I can't use. All I want, you know, is just enough money to buy food and clothing and to pay the rent."

A few blocks away lies the studio of the third of Chicago's star prophets. Joseph DeLouise is a late arrival in the psychic Hall of Fame and decidedly the odd man out. He did not leap into prominence until four years ago and he remains a part-timer. He spends about four hours of his working day at his hairdressing salon, the rest in his consulting office.

DeLouise is that rarity—a blue-eyed Sicilian; a feature set off by his mass of black hair and dark goatee (see Figure 7). He was born in 1927, in the small Sicilian town of Jubelena ("Sorry, I can't spell it for you") and came to America aged five. Both his father and grandfather were "healers" in the old country. But it was the son's first brush with the occult that enabled the family to emigrate.

"It was because I found some money on that little farm patch we had," he explained. "Gold coins. I was shown where to dig by—well," he seemed slightly embarrassed "—well—I would call it a spirit, maybe. My mother said it was my dead uncle. Anyway, when we dug it up it turned out to be his life's savings. And with this money we went to the United States."

The DeLouises were bitterly poor. Young Joseph grew up in what he terms a "ghetto part of town." He has since acquired an extensive vocabulary, but south Chicago still lingers in his "dose," "dese" and "dems."

He originally wanted to become a priest, but after mastering a bout of TB he went to a hairdressing school on the GI Bill. He opened his own salon in 1955.

In between shampoos, haircuts and sets, DeLouise worked hard to develop his paranormal abilities. He gained a local reputation, though he did not become nationally famous until the end of 1967.

On December 15 of that year the Silver Bridge across the Ohio River at Point Pleasant, West Virginia, collapsed during rush hour traffic, hurling forty-six people to their deaths. And then several hundred thousand listeners remembered the words "that hairdresser guy" had spoken over Radio WWCA on November 25: "Before the end of 1967, a major bridge—not as large as the Golden Gate or Brooklyn bridges, but sizable—will collapse, causing many deaths and headlines!"

It was a prophecy precise and time-narrowed enough to be sensational. Almost overnight Chicago's "psychic hairdresser" found himself a national celebrity. But it was only a start.

For the beginning of 1969, DeLouise predicted "a terrible train wreck on the IC line south of Chicago on a foggy night and involving two trains." Early on the morning of January 17, an Illinois Central passenger train, in dense fog, plowed into a freight train at Manteno, forty-five miles south of Chicago, killing three and injuring forty-nine people.

On February 25, 1969, DeLouise told a radio interviewer that he "saw" an airliner crashing southwest of Chicago. Seventy-nine passengers would die. "And I see the number 330—yes, 330. Only I'm not sure if that is the time or the flight number . . . I think it is the time." On September 9 an Allegheny Airlines jet collided with a Piper sportsplane over Shelbyville, Indiana, about 135 miles south of Chicago. All of the eighty-three persons aboard both aircraft died. And the time was 3:31 P.M.!

DeLouise's greatest "hit" came to him while a press photographer was taking pictures in his studio. The cameraman wanted the psychic gazing into his crystal ball. DeLouise posed. And then—something in the crystal triggered . . . something.

"I saw this blurred newspaper headline. It said TED KENNEDY—blank, blank—DROWNS. The second thing I saw was a woman's face. There were bubbles coming out of her mouth. I knew it was a woman because her hair—like it was streaming in the water. I didn't know if it was his wife or who—but it was a woman.

"I had my Predictions of the Year all written out already. But after some thought I inserted this. And we sent it to the newspaper."

The Chicago Sun-Times toned it down to a very terse, "I see tragedy involving water around the Kennedys." Which was how it appeared in the magazine section of December 29, 1967. On June 25, 1969, Senator Edward M. Kennedy's car plunged off a Massachusetts bridge, drowning the passenger, one Mary Jo Kopechne.

On Joseph DeLouise's studio desk are two telephones and they ring constantly, endlessly. The voices at the other end sound strained and anxious. He nods, makes appointments, jots them down on a sheet in front of him. The page is full, and still the phones keep ringing.

"It's time spent away from my hairdressing business, so I have to charge a fee," he said apologetically. "So I charge ten dollars for a consultation, up to an hour."

"That's very little," I commented.

"Yeah, well, there's a selfish reason for that—I don't want to feel guilty. For ten dollars I can give them *my* impressions without having to doctor them up, y'understand?"

He shrugged. "Because—I dunno—sometimes I think I see nothing but tragedies."

"And how do you handle—tragedies?"

"I get vibrations about who can take it and who can't. Not always, though. I had this girl in here once and she kinda—forced it out of me. Said she could take it . . . only she couldn't." He shook his head. "I told her that by the time she was thirty-one she'd be a complete alcoholic and that she'd have lost both her children to her husband. And about her automobile accident, with her face scarred. Well—it didn't do her any good, I'm sure of that."

He suddenly seemed very small and melancholy. "I look into my crystal balls—I use two of them, you know—and I keep seeing these headlines and it's always disasters and tragedies and more disasters. Sometimes it scares me.

"And what I've got—it doesn't work for myself. I lost about two thousand dollars on the market when I tried. I don't know if it works for my wife or our six kids, either. But I know it works for others."

I left him then. A kindly little man with an outsized gift, staring at his telephones with a worried expression. They were both ringing at once. . . .

These are the voices of America's prophets, and they are very loud in the land. Amplified by a million megaphones, disseminated in acres of newsprint, funneled through video tubes, boomed from radio receivers.

The voices are not clear. Frequently they are wrong, sometimes contradictory, often irrelevant. Their message—if they have one—is so muffled that it mostly does nothing but add to the general din.

But the fault does not lie with the prophets alone. Many of them possess a genuine if erratic form of mental vision, which science has never properly explored or even classified. It could be compared to the beam of a flashlight which—at odd moments— shines into a pitch-black vault. Only to be flicked off again before the details of the interior have become clear, leaving the beholder with a blurred and fading picture of something half-seen.

Then come money and fame and the thrill of having a huge audience hanging breathlessly on every utterance. And with it the demand for more glimpses—more details—specific details—minute details. . . . Like the goose that has laid one golden egg, the augur has to keep on laying to hold the attention of that admiring multitude.

It can't be done, because the gift—whatever it is—doesn't work that way. So the prophet learns to embroider visions, to magnify and finally to invent them altogether. And the more he— or she—fabricates, the more oblique and generalized he has to become in order to give them at least an average chance of fulfillment. From being a seer he deteriorates into a mere calculator of odds, laboring frantically to keep up with the clamor.

This is the reason why the lesser lights in the field frequently score better than the stars, and the rank amateurs often best of all. There is no public pressure on them, they can bide their time until a real vision comes. They are also less ego-involved, less tempted to color their glimpses with their own ideas and prejudices.

The villain of the piece is the unholy dread of the future that grips nations when their traditional signposts and guidelines are obliterated. In such times anyone who appears to know what lies ahead—who demonstrates some degree of certainty—is seized upon as a rallying beacon against the darkness on the horizon.

Frightened people don't realize that our society could no more coexist with infallible day-to-day prophets than with invisible men. We would either have to destroy them or become their slaves.

III
THERE BE WITCHES . . .

IN THE YEAR of our Lord 1957, the Massachusetts legislature solemnly exonerated six women who had been hanged as witches almost three centuries earlier. The bill, however, carried a prudent amendment barring any payment of damages to their descendants.

With this act the state senate drew a final line under North America's one and only literal witch hunt. Ironically, it did so just at the start of the first witchcraft boom this country has ever known. Within ten years covens were gathering from Back Bay Boston to the Hollywood Hills, practitioners were buying their craft equipment in special boutiques and metropolitan New York alone boasted an estimated five thousand working witches.

By comparison the town of Salem, Massachusetts, has little to show for the outburst of witch hysteria that once made it a household whisper. The Essex County Superior Courthouse displays a few yellowed sheets of handwritten trial records, six rusty pins and one lone death warrant. There are some more documents

1. Bruce King, better known as "Zolar," heads what may be the world's largest distributing firm of occultist material, including thirty astrological periodicals.

2. Wanda Lawris Moore, one of the new generation of astrologers. Celestial adviser to a throng of under-thirty showfolks, she considers herself a reincarnated Atlantean.

3. Comedian Flip Wilson and hostesses at the gala debut of the astrological computer Astroflash II in New York's Grand Central Station (PHOTO: SAM SIEGEL).

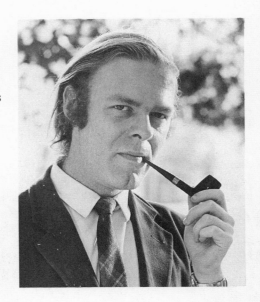

4. Alan Vaughan, a psychic with a scientific turn of mind, one of the few men in his field to analyze his prophetic images (PHOTO: JOHN LARSEN).

5. Robert and Nancy Nelson, who operate New York's Central Premonition Agency, designed to register and check prophecies from every part of the nation.

6. Irene Hughes, Chicago clairvoyant, newspaper columnist and adviser to large numbers of Midwestern business executives.

7. Joseph DeLouise, who divides his time between prophecy and hair-dressing, pointing at the press clippings featuring some of his predictions.

8. An old and somewhat demure print showing one of the "bewitched" children of Salem Village during America's only literal witch drive in 1692.

9. Louise Huebner broadcasting. Mrs. Huebner is the official County Witch of Los Angeles—the only such post in the Western world.

10. English-born Sybil Leek, now a resident of Texas, and the most popular witch in America (PHOTO: JOHN LARSEN).

11. Witch Hazel and Dr. Leo Martello. Two of New York's leading witchcraft practitioners shown here in full regalia.

12. Prince VanDercar, a Miami sculptor who heads the Royal Order of Warlocks & Witches, a secret organization allegedly functioning in units of ten.

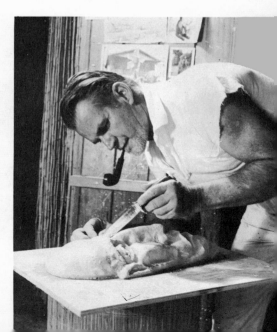

in the Essex Institute and a restored "Witch House" in North Street—the erstwhile home of magistrate Jonathan Corwin, who conducted the preliminary grilling of the accused.

That is all. No dungeons, no ducking stools and torture instruments, no burning sites—not even a preserved gallows to clear up the running dispute on whether the Salem witches were strung from trees or crossbeams.

But then the Salem witch craze was a diminutive affair, as these things went. Measured against the scale and ferocity of its Old World models it seems—in retrospect—like a mild gust at the tail end of a hurricane.

The American colonies caught merely the dying ripple of a tidal wave of dementia that had swept Europe with shattering force for over two hundred years. It caused an accumulation of mass horror that remained unmatched until the extermination camps of our own era.

The popular concept of "medieval witch burnings" does an injustice to the Middle Ages. Hardly any witches were burned during the so-called Dark Ages in Europe. Witchcraft rated as a misdemeanor, akin to watering milk, but several notches below sheep stealing in criminality. The village "wise woman" (the word witch derives from the Anglo-Saxon *wicca,* meaning "wise one,") was esteemed both as medico and midwife and lived in fairly amiable coexistence with the local priest.

Occasionally the civil authorities might whip a hag whose spells they considered antisocial. Sometimes her neighbors accused her of hexing livestock and promptly stoned her to death. But these were rare events and always confined to a few unpopular individuals. Popes as well as kings made pronouncements against anyone "paying heed to vain and idle fancies about people alleged to be witches."

It must rank as one of history's grimmest paradoxes that witch-hunting proper began only with the dawning of the more enlightened age we call the Renaissance. Early in the fifteenth century the Church began to equate witchcraft with heresy and to excommunicate those involved in the practice. From a minor felony, the craft became the most dreaded and hated form of crime extant.

The reason for this altered attitude lay in the avalanche of new ideas, discoveries and inventions that was rolling over Europe, battering the entire social and political framework of the Continent. The ruling nobles, the dominant Catholic Church and the common people were all equally bewildered and frightened by the winds of change buffeting them from every direction.

Clearly Satan was stalking the land, sowing doubt and confusion in the minds of man. Clearly he had helpers in their midst—and who was better suited as the devil's Fifth Column than those "magick weavers" with their weird spells and incantations? Here were the natural scapegoats for every menace abroad, from fiery meteors in the sky to the rise of the heretical Hussites in Bohemia!

The Catholic Church officially proclaimed witchcraft to be a form of Satanism and ordered its investigative arm—the Holy Inquisition—to root out this newly elevated brand of heresy. The results would have been ghastly in any case. They became nightmarish when Pope Innocent VIII decided to codify this charge into a legal doctrine.

In 1485 he ordered two of his inquisitors to work out a court manual aimed at the detection of witchcraft in all existing forms. The men he chose were Germans, Heinrich Kramer and Jacob Sprenger, both learned theologians at the University of Cologne. They were the Himmler-Eichmann combination of their time; parchment-dry bureaucrats with not a spark of wit or compassion between them, but painstakingly thorough and steeped in every judicial angle of their task.

Their brainchild, entitled *Malleus Maleficarum*—"Witches' Hammer"—became the handbook for witch-hunters everywhere. And even in its stilted original Latin, the book sends cold shivers down your spine.

It formulated a trial procedure that gave the accused virtually no chance of proving innocence. She was entitled to neither defender nor legal counsel since, as the scholarly authors put it, "whosoever pleads on behalf of a witch becomes himself tinged with the sin of heresy."

The prosecution could summon any number of witnesses— the accused none. False witnesses could be punished by the court, but their testimony might nevertheless be retained and cited with full effect. Nor need those witnesses ever confront the accused "lest the wrath of the witch or her Satanic master do them injury."

The most important evidence was the general character and reputation of the accused, as described by neighbors, clergymen and town officials. But there again she stood to lose either way. If her behavior could be interpreted as immoral or eccentric, the fact weighed heavily against her. If, on the other hand, she had been charitable, friendly and a regular churchgoer, this was likewise regarded as highly suspicious since "Satan in his cunning will often command his followers to don the mask of piety so as to better deceive the righteous."

Apart from testimony, there were numerous other clues that could be regarded as proofs of witchcraft. Among them Messrs. Kramer and Sprenger listed "devil's marks,"—imprints which Satan allegedly bestowed on his disciples. These could be birthmarks, moles, warts or blackheads which somehow failed to bleed when pricked by a sharp point. At the start of the examination, therefore, the accused was stripped naked and jabbed in every part of her body with special needles, including her breasts, nipples and sex organs. This was considered the preliminary or "light" portion of the questioning.

The *Malleus* laid down that from the moment of her arrest the inquisitors were to "entreat the accused with great earnestness to confess her guilt." But the authors held out little hope that she would do so voluntarily. "Experience has shown," they submitted, "that most witches will remain stubborn in diabolic taciturnity until subjected at least once to the painful question."

The "painful question," of course, was torture. Kramer and Sprenger left the technical details to the local judges, but they stipulated a few basic ground rules. One of them was that the devices used for the purpose should be inscribed *Soli Deo Gloria* ("Glory be only to God") and that they be sprayed with holy water beforehand. They also ruled that torture should only be applied once during any particular examination, but that the procedure could be "continued" indefinitely until either a confession had been obtained or the presiding judge was satisfied that the accused had nothing to confess. "Great care must be taken," they admonished "that the accused should not die while thus questioned. Nor should she be permitted, through negligence, to inflict death upon herself while safely confined."

The consequences of the "continuance" ruling were hair-raising. According to contemporary records a German woman named Maria Holf was tortured fifty-six times in the course of one week, until she finally expired on the rack. Other suspects underwent the "painful question" eight or ten times in a single day, the inquisitor always punctiliously closing one examination and starting another an hour later.

The means used ranged from the simply brutal to the most elaborately sadistic, with every shading and gradation in between.

The first stage was usually a plain lashing administered with a horse whip. It was intended as little more than a foretaste.

Then followed more ingenious methods. The victim's finger- and toenails would be torn out with pincers. Red-hot irons might be inserted into her vagina and rectum. She could be spread-eagled on the rack—a long table fitted with ropes and windlasses —and her arms and legs dislocated in gradual twists. The strappado meant that her wrists were bound behind her back and she was hoisted to the ceiling by a rope attached to them. Heavy weights were fastened to her feet and she was lowered in sudden jerks until the strain pulled her arms from their sockets.

There was the spider—a sharp iron fork to mangle her breasts—and the Spanish boot, a metal clamp that could be tightened over her legs until it crushed the ankles. There were thumbscrews and toescrews, burning feathers dipped in sulfur and applied to her armpits and groin, and pots of boiling oil to cook the flesh off her fingers one by one. In the intervals the torturers might pour brandy over her shaven skull and pubic hair and set it alight.

An element of macabre clownishness hung over these proceedings, rendering them even more repulsive. As protection against the alleged witch's powers, judge and assessors wore blessed herbs and consecrated wax around their necks, the timid ones adding up to a dozen amulets on their hats and collars. The torturers were constantly crossing themselves, drinking infusions prepared from blessed objects and fingering talismans made espe-

cially for their safety. When their victim's howls of agony grew
unbearable they pushed a pear-shaped wooden gag in her mouth
which—for some reason—was painted in gay candy stripes.

The only escape from the "painful question" lay in confession and repentance. But this was by no means a simple matter.

The accused, by then half-insane with pain and despair, had
to "remember" practices completely beyond her ken. This she
usually did by elaborating on hints fed to her by the inquisitors. . . . "And how many times did you kiss the devil's arse
on Candlemas Eve? Four times—five? Five, you say! Write this
down, clerk of the court."

In this manner most of the fables that cling to witchcraft
rituals to this day were fabricated.

After confession the witch's fate was usually—though not
always—sealed. For the *Malleus* permitted inquisitors to promise
the accused her life providing she confessed and repented. The
promise need not be kept too literally. *Another* judge, for instance, could have her executed afterwards. Or she could be released and in due course rearrested and tried again.

But occasionally, when there were strongly mitigating circumstances involved, the judge might sentence her to life imprison-
ment; *murus largus*—in a cell—or *murus strictus*, chained in a
dungeon.

This, however, was quite exceptional. The usual sentence
ended in the phrase: "We pronounce that you have truly fallen
into the sin of heresy; and as one so fallen we cast you forth
from this our ecclesiastical Court, and leave you to be delivered to
the secular arm."

Although death was not mentioned, the sentence meant
exactly that. For the "secular arm," on pain of excommunication,
was forced to burn her at the stake. If her repentance had moved
the judge, he could recommend that "special mercy be extended."
Which meant that she was strangled beforehand.

So far I have referred to witches in the female tense only,
which is not strictly accurate. They could, in fact, be of either
sex and bore the same label. In the early stages of the drive,
those charged were nearly always women. But as the hunt gathered pace and momentum, tens of thousands of men were also

roped in and dealt with in the same fashion. From start to finish, though, women continued to outnumber men by about ten to one.

Perhaps the most sinister aspect of the process arose from the judicial ruling that a witch's confession was acceptable only if it named other witches. The more persons implicated the more valid the confession.

It takes no great imagination to realize the inflating horror generated by this rule. In order to escape torture prisoners blurted forth any names that came into their convulsed minds. Strangers, neighbors, friends—their own brothers, sisters and parents . . . anything to get out of that reeking, blood-smeared torture chamber!

And so the manic machine ground on. Those named were arrested, put to the "painful question," and made to divulge yet more names. They in turn produced still more—and so on and so forth until the witch-hunting snowball became an avalanche that threatened to bury Europe.

For with every new wave of trials and convictions the panic fear of the population rose. There were witches everywhere: next door—in your church—in your own home—plotting with Satan against your property, your health, your immortal soul! People denounced each other by the millions, and frequently the informers themselves landed on the accused bench at the next assizes. Priests, aldermen, mayors—occasionally even the inquisitors—were caught in the cogs, mauled into "confessions," and burned in the marketplace.

It would be quite unfair to saddle the Catholic Church with the sole blame for this continental pogrom. The Roman Church burned the most witches simply because it happened to be dominant in the largest portions of the Christian world.

But in those countries where Protestant factions rose to power—northern Germany, Scandinavia, the British Isles, Switzerland, the Netherlands—the drive went on with, if anything, even greater fervor. If there was one matter in which the followers of Luther, Knox and Calvin agreed with the popes it was their dread and loathing of witchcraft.

Statistics on the subject read like battle reports. The bishop of the south German town of Bamberg boasted that he alone had sent "a goodly 600 witches" to the stake. His colleague in nearby Würtzburg claimed 1,900 over five years. Toulouse in France burned 400 in a single day, Como in Italy 100, Calvinist Geneva in Switzerland 500 within three months (including a seven-year-old girl), while Trier in the Rhineland seems to have broken all records with 7,000 burnings. So it went in town after town, right across the map of Europe.

The frenzy was worst in Germany, where an estimated 200,000 went to the stake, with France and Scotland as her nearest rivals. In England a "mere" 1,000 were put to death, mostly by hanging instead of the customary fire. The total number of victims is difficult to assess; historians guess at somewhere between 300,000 and one million. But to this must be added at least another million women and men who were jailed, driven into exile, whipped, branded or mutilated as suspected witches.

The madness subsided very gradually toward the close of the seventeenth century, though it kept flickering right into the eighteenth. England stopped executing witches in 1682, France in 1745, Germany in 1775. The last official witch-burning took place in Poland in 1793.

But by the time the fever reached the North American colonies across the Atlantic, Europe was already satiated with the stench of burning flesh. For New England, witch-hunting was still something of a novelty. It says a great deal for the horse sense of its inhabitants that they recovered so quickly and so thoroughly.

The whole outburst remained more or less confined to the obscure little village of Salem in the Puritan Massachusetts Bay Colony. Until 1692 the community's only claim to fame had been the insufferable backbiting it meted out to its resident clergy, rendering their lives a misery. But in that year the Reverend Samuel Parris got his own back with interest.

Parris, who had come to Salem from the West Indies, owned a black woman slave named Tituba; a big, wildly talkative female, deeply immersed in the voodoo lore of her home island of Barbados. This lore she dispensed, night after night, to the Parris's nine-year-old daughter, Elizabeth, and several of her neighborhood girl friends.

One winter night—for reasons never fully explained—the

girls went into hysterical fits, screeching like epileptic monkeys and biting at the hands that tried to restrain them.

The Reverend Parris quickly diagnosed their condition. Only a week earlier he had written to a friend: "There be witches here in Massachusetts as wicked as any thou finds in the Indies . . ."

Now he leaned close to his gibbering daughter. "Elizabeth," he demanded, "art thou and thy friends bewitched?"

The girls must have been waiting for just that cue. In unison they screamed, "Osburn, Good, and Tituba!"

Sarah Osburn was a bedridden invalid, Sarah Good an ancient and hideous beggar woman. On Parris's request, magistrate Jonathan Corwin issued warrants for the arrest of both Sarahs and Tituba.

These were the first in a wave of arrests that shook the colony for the next ten months. Suspects were hauled to Salem courthouse in batches, where they were confronted by the "afflicted children." At the sight of some of them the terrible little moppets fell into convulsions, yelling that they were being pinched, strangled, stabbed and kicked by invisible imps. Occasionally they would "see" spirits or animal shapes hovering around the accused, and naturally some of the spectators began seeing them also. . . . "Look, a yellow bird is perching on her shoulder . . . Nay, 'tis a yellow face peering!"

This practice was called "the crying out" and the girls quickly became pastmasters at it. The Reverend Parris encouraged them heartily, for with every confrontation his power in the community grew (see Figure 8).

In a way the accused were lucky. The Puritan officials were ignorant of the finer points of witch-grilling, as expounded by the *Malleus*. Those who confessed and appeared penitent were merely jailed—Tituba among them. When the craze had evaporated they were hurriedly set free.

Nor were they tortured, at least not in the customary meaning of the term. They were, of course, pricked for witchmarks, but —"to preserve due modesty"—by a jury of women. On Bridget Bishop, a very lively tavern keeper, they actually discovered a "witch's tet" between "ye pupendum and anus."

The worst fate befell those who were either too honest to "confess" and repent or incapable of doing so. The former consisted of nineteen women and men who were hanged, and the invalid Sarah Osburn, who died in jail. The latter of one black mongrel dog, put to death in nearby Andover for "grivously bewitching four Christian persons," and failing to regret it.

But by the fall of 1693, revulsion set in. The girls had "cried out" a few too many folks, including Lady Phips—wife of the colony's Royal Governor—who made short shrift of the accusation.

Pending charges were dropped, the remaining suspects released. Now it was the turn of jurors and informers to repent, which they did with almost as much gusto as they had shown at the trials. Judge Sewall, who had thundered condemnation over the accused, read out his own confession of sin and error to the congregation of his Boston church, asking that they pray for him. The notable exception were the juveniles who had started it all—most of them stayed firmly unpenitent.

Several years later the children of thirteen of the condemned witches succeeded in getting their sentences quashed—posthumously. The court then ordered a total of £597 12s. to be distributed among the heirs of the executed. Not, perhaps, a regal sum, but that much more than all the surviving relatives of Europe's witch-hunt victims ever received.

Six of the condemned, who had no children, were left unexonerated until the Massachusetts senate took up their case again some 287 years later.

Scores of historians and sociologists have in the meantime tried to fathom the causes of New England's witching hour.

Some saw it as an attempt by the colony's ruling theocracy to put the fear of the devil into their secular opponents. Others explained it as a reaction against crushing guilt complexes fostered by the Puritan sin-and-damnation creed. Still others regarded it as half-conscious juvenile revenge against oppressive elders.

The truth may be a combination of all the above reasons. Unfortunately none of them offers even the slightest clue for the present resurgence of the "craft."

For witches have emerged as something like the glamor elite of America's occult scene—socially not only tolerated but prized. They pose for magazine spreads, add tang to cocktail parties, tout their autobiographies, give interviews on television and offer advice to newspaper readers. Los Angeles—always an oblique step or two ahead in such matters—even appointed an official County Witch in 1968.

The post—the only one of its kind in the Western world— went to small, raven-haired and exquisite Louise Huebner. If Mayor Yorty had intended to dispel, once and for all, the notion that witches are necessarily hook-nosed scarecrows, he couldn't have made a better choice (see Figure 9).

Mrs. Huebner, who won a beauty contest at age three, has starred in several films and run her own TV series. Her first official appearance took place at the Hollywood Bowl, when she cast a spell designed to give her capacity audience of youngsters "increased sexual vitality." Holding a candle aloft, her brown eyes flashing, she made the crowd chant after her, "Light the flame—bright the fire—red is the color of desire."

Louise lives in a Spanish-style hilltop villa near Hollywood, together with her husband, three children, assorted turtles, cats, dogs and beetles, and an uncommonly charming rat named Melissa.

"No, they're not familiars," she told me, "they're pets. But I do have a great—well, attraction—for my beetles. I don't believe witches need familiars or most of that other junk."

The "other junk" were the potions, salves, herbs and suchlike considered indispensable by many practitioners. "My grandmother is all nutty on those things, but I don't go for them. Oh, sure, I believe they work, but that's not because of the ingredients but because of the people that make them."

Louise's own spells are woven quite unpharmaceutically in the privacy of her bathroom. Why the bathroom? "Well, it's small and intimate. I light candles, watch their reflected glow in the mirror and chant."

"Chant what?"

"Whatever it is I want. I mention names—things . . ." She trailed off deliberately. "Well, yes, I do act out my spells. You know—dramatize them. Sometimes I recite poetry that appeals to me. It's all just to get myself turned on, really. I've found out that if you tense up your body—become very much aware of it— then the whole thing works better." She gave a short giggle, like a college freshman describing a rather ribald sorority rite. "But I'm fully dressed. You don't have to be naked to be effective."

Her approach to the entire business is as down-to-earth as that of a French housewife toward onion soup. She merely chortled when I suggested that witchcraft might be a form of religion.

"I have no religion. Some people are religious about astrology and some are very religious about eating wheat germ. But witchcraft is just me—it's how I operate. To me it's as natural as making love."

She aimed a slender index finger at me. "Look, my family's been mixed up with the occult from way back. It was coming out of my eyeballs. My grandmother is a real, honest-to-God old-fashioned fortune-teller. And I was psychic when I was a baby. People noticed it all the time. Only I thought then it was a gimmick—a trick I'd learned. I thought I was fooling people, being very clever. Then, gradually, I realized that there was something very odd about myself. No, don't call it a gift—that's a word that bugs me—makes it sound—oh, supernatural. When it's really so human; just an extension of my personality. It may have to do with hormones. It certainly has to do with my emotions."

"But it was something you consciously developed," I ventured.

"It developed as part of my growing-up process." She sounded a little impatient. Like someone trying to explain differential calculus to a mathematics junior. "I grew up in my marriage. And if you're married to a painter—a very involved painter—like I am, you have to do something of your own, otherwise you'd die. So"—she smiled brightly—"I became very busy with my own . . . art."

Busy is the right term. Apart from her municipal duties as Special Events Coordinator and Cultural Movement Chairman, her numerous radio and television spots, her newspaper column and civic club appearances, Mrs. Huebner also made a highly successful record entitled "Seduction Through Witchcraft" and wrote two books, the latest called *Never Strike a Happy Medium* (pun intended).

All this on top of running a decidedly lively household

which, besides husband, children and animals, includes ghosts.
"What kind of ghosts?"
"Oh, just strange things." She shrugged. "You know—foot-
steps shuffling down the hall when there's nobody there—that sort
of business. I think my big boy, Mentor, is the cause of it. He has
the type of energy that disturbs his environment."
"But it doesn't seem to disturb you."
"Uh-uh. I've lived with it too long."
Louise may be nonchalant about her ghosts, but she is very
serious about her poetry. More so, perhaps, than about her spells.
Her poems deal with a multitude of subjects, but they all share a
detached, ironic quality that seems odd coming from such a
pronounced ego. Here, as a sample, is the last part of one on the
theme of her own eventual demise:

> . . . If nothing gives to my resistance
> And no one echoes back my shout
> With the force of sheer emotion
> I will tumble into space
> And for all my damned commotion
> Leave no trace.

Despite her unique official position, Mrs. Huebner is not an
ideal subject to interview about witchcraft. Hers is an entirely
personal affair, uninvolved with the mainstream, an expression of
her own psyche rather than part of a worldwide fraternity.
Others in the craft take a much more universal view. The
most celebrated among them is a plump and erudite English lady
in her forties, who resides—of all places—in Houston, Texas.
Sybil Leek was born of Russian-Irish parentage in Stafford-
shire, and came to the United States in 1964. With her aquiline
nose, full lips and bushy eyebrows she has a distinct gypsy appearance, but her speaking voice is pure English drawing room.
She rose to fame after her chattily informative *Diary of a Witch*
became a national best seller. Since then she has talked and
written more on the subject than anyone in this country and is
probably the only extant witch with a popular image (see Figure
10).
She takes a teacup-cozy approach to her craft, mingling it
with astrology, augurism, occasional ghost-hunting, levitation sé-

ances, sundry psychic phenomena and doses of homespun philosophy. She now edits an astrological monthly, casts horoscopes and
gives extended lecture tours. She seems to have abandoned spells,
but until recently her household included a perky little raven
named Hotfoot Jackson and two boa constrictors.

To Sybil Leek witchcraft is very much a religion, but one
predating Christianity—or any other faith—by thousands of years.

"It is not anti-Christian and not heathen," she told an interviewer. "It's the Old Religion because it seems to go back
to the time when man was first on earth, when he had those
religious, spiritual feelings. I think it's a great mistake to think
that man did not have religion until Christ and Buddha appeared.

"Basically, it is absolutely designed to be in tune with the
components of the universe—male, female; positive, negative; action, reaction.

"Our rituals are linked with the seasons—spring, summer,
autumn, and winter—and we keep very much to the universe.
What we're really doing is giving a general hymn of praise to the
universe and all the things in it."

This is one view of witchcraft, and certainly the most benevolent. Picturing disciples of the craft as nature worshipers is excellent public relations, and even true as far as it goes. But it
does not—by a long stretch—cover the entire movement.

In the course of researching this chapter I met close to forty
self-proclaimed witches in seven states of the Union. By and
large I found them distinctly simpatico. They were bright,
amiable, had a sense of humor, and were quite devoid of the
priggish pomposity you find in so many occultists.

But I also discovered that not one group ever agreed with
another as to what, exactly, constitutes witchcraft. They couldn't
even agree to disagree, but invariably insisted that *their* particular
brand of practice was the only valid one. In that respect they
bore a striking resemblance to the eternally bickering Christian
denominations. Which means that virtually every generalization
about them is apt to be simultaneously accurate and false; applicable to one bunch but not to another.

Even terms like movement, cult or fraternity convey a wrong
impression. For while most American witches are loosely or-

ganized in small units, there are also thousands of adherents like
Elizabeth F., a pretty Baltimore photographer who, quite solo,
practices weekly conjurations in her streamlined bachelor apartment.

This makes it quite impossible to establish the number of
witches in this country. Practitioners range from dedicated full-
timers, like Leo Martello of Manhattan, to housewives and teenagers all over suburbia, who go through what they deem to be
witchcraft rituals for occasional kicks.

There are, however, some fundamental facts on the subject.
If nothing else, they will at least help to crack a few widespread
misconceptions concerning the craft.

To start with, witchcraft definitely derived from various forms
of primeval nature and animal cults; hence the tag "Old Religion." The legend of witches riding on broomsticks, for instance,
is directly traceable to pagan priestesses sticking a pole between
their legs (symbolizing a penis) and galloping around the village
fields to insure their fertility.

With the coming of new, better organized and highly militant
creeds like Christianity and Mohammedanism, the old cults were
forced to withdraw to isolated regions and finally to dive completely underground. They were never totally eradicated, but
became obsessively secretive and stealthy; mainly for security
reasons. They retained some of their acquired know-how about
herbs, drugs, weather changes and animal behavior, which gave
their adherents certain advantages over their neighbors—who frequently resented it. But during those centuries of underground
existence they also became perverted into something darker,
power-oriented, sometimes covertly vicious. The fairy-tale witch
was the lineal descendant of the pagan village priestess forced
to shun daylight and deprived of the social status she thought
rightfully hers by virtue of her special knowledge.

At no time or place were witches devil-worshipers. This is a
grotesquely tragic misunderstanding, initiated by the Christian
Church and lingering to this day, aided and abetted by works like
Rosemary's Baby, wherein author Ira Levin portrayed a nest of
New York Satanists and dubbed them "witches."

The fact is that witches believe in neither devil nor hell. They
have two chief divinities: the fecund Moon Goddess and the

phallic Horned God—both easily recognizable as male and female fertility symbols.

But the Church authorities saw only the god's horns and decided forthwith that he had to be Satan. Hundreds of thousands of people—the vast majority quite unconnected with witchcraft—paid with their lives for this identification error.

The imagination of certain theological scholars added the trimmings. The Witches' Sabbat (from the French s'esbattre—"to frolic") became a demoniacal orgy with a climax designed to send chills through every Christian soul. After feasting, dancing, and boasting of the evil they had wrought, the entire company would line up behind the person of Satan (who was invariably present) and bestow the osculum infame—the Kiss of Shame—on his buttocks.

Then it was the turn of the new female initiates to seal their entry into the order by sexual intercourse with the devil. The experience was vividly described by thousands of them—after a spell in the torture chamber had refreshed their memories. Some of the physiological details varied from case to case, but all agreed that it was an exceedingly painful business. Satan's sex organ, it appeared, was colossal and the sperm he ejected cold as ice. The inquisitors took good care not to make the ritual seem attractive.

Like all effective propaganda tales, this one also had certain ingredients of truth. Witches did meet in secluded spots to celebrate festivals and maintain contact. And there is no doubt that their rituals had strongly erotic overtones—as have all nature and fertility cults.

Some may even have believed that they actually flew to these Sabbats. Craft adherents used to smear their naked bodies with ointments and salves containing substances like aconite, belladonna and hemlock, plus aromatic grease. Both aconite and belladonna produce wild excitement and delirious hallucinations and may very well have given their users the sensation of flying through the air.

But the distinctly anti-Christian and blasphemous parts of the ceremony—the disfigured crucifix, the obscenely garbled creed, the urine used as holy water, the left-handed blessing, the abuse of the cross and trampling of the Host, the chants reviling Jesus and extolling Satan—were in reality lifted from the Black Mass of the Satanists and had nothing whatever to do with witchcraft. Whether erroneous or deliberate, it amounted to the most fatal mixup in history.

As the followers of the Old Religion became more hard pressed, the size of their gatherings shrank. This produced the traditional coven; still the basic unit of craft adherents. Theoretically, a coven should consist of six women and six men, plus a high priestess, thirteen people in all. In the United States, at least, very few covens come in the standard numbers. Some are larger, most are smaller, and the ratio is usually heavy on the female side. In one Chicago coven I counted nine women and one solitary male.

The number of functioning covens in America is a moot point. Sybil Leek, for instance, recognizes only a handful as authentic and refers to the rest as "sordid little clubs." But one of my inside contacts assured me that there were at least twenty thousand organized members in this country. So the matter seems to be anyone's guess.

The preponderance of women is certainly due to the fact that witchcraft is a matriarchal creed. Leadership always rests with the high priestess, even though her husband may belong to the same coven. This is the reason why witches are known by the feminine label, whatever their sex. The term "warlock," which supposedly denotes a male witch, actually means a wizard or sorcerer—a different breed altogether.

There are, however, no "white" and "black"' witches. The popular notion about this is pure *Wizard of Oz* stuff. Witches are no more inherently good or wicked than, say, Presbyterians. Some of them certainly try to use their powers for malevolent purposes, though they'll rarely admit it. But to persuade an entire coven to aid them is pretty difficult. Like most private organizations, witching groups exist mainly for their own benefit and can rarely be argued into working for someone else's misfortune rather than their own good fortune.

Thus nearly all the spells woven by these groups are beneficial —to members of the group, that is. The reason for this is not benevolence but sound, healthy egotism. Most witches consider any other kind of effort simply a waste of energy.

Although there seem to be about as many brands of witches

as there are covens, all of them fall—roughly—into two main categories: garbed and "sky-clad."

The garbed variety wear long flowing robes or cloaks during their ceremonies. Sky-clad witches perform in their bare skins; the traditional costume for rituals.

There is also a large, amorphous subsection called Gardnerians. These are followers of the late Dr. Gerald Brosseau Gardner, the British occultist-writer who founded the world's first witchcraft museum on the Isle of Man in 1950. More orthodox craft members use the term derisively. But the only difference I noticed about Gardnerians was that they were eminently approachable and publicity conscious and therefore tended to monopolize the limelight.

Regardless of philosophy, every coven has—or should have—a "Book of Shadows." This is the witches' bible, the only written scripture of the craft, and contains all of the charms, chants, spells and incantations in use. One of the tasks of the high priestess is to copy it in in her own hand, then destroy the original. Eventually she passes her copy on to her successor, who repeats the process.

The matriarchal structure of the craft does not mean that the only prominent members are women. The New York City scene, for instance, is virtually dominated by Dr. Leo Louis Martello (the doctorate stems from a spiritualist ministry he no longer practices).

Martello is a short, black-bearded man of immense vitality, with shoulder-length hair and a slight lisp. He looks rather like a dry-cleaned version of Rasputin with beads ("I wore them long before they were *in*."). He is somewhere in his thirties, but won't reveal his exact age ("Believe me, I'm *thousands* of years old.") (see Figure 11).

His small, chaotic apartment lies in a rough patch of mid-Manhattan, but the aura of violence around him doesn't faze him in the slightest. He strides about, frequently in full craft regalia—beads and cloak flapping—tossing the witches' salutation, "Blessed Be," to all and sundry. Most people grin back—perhaps because he manages to make it sound like an indecent proposal.

Martello represents witchdom's antithesis of Mrs. Leek. He has no time for the established moral code and even less for anything that smacks of established religion—particularly his own. "I was baptized into the Catholic faith as a helpless infant," he comments, "and the six worst years of my life were spent in a Catholic boarding school."

Among his works is the so-called "Witch Manifesto," a document demanding (a) the moral condemnation of the Catholic Church for the torture and murder of witches, and (b) a suit for $500 million in damages and reparations, to be paid by the Vatican to their descendants.

As an expert hypnotist and graphologist, he earns part of his income by analyzing the handwriting of job applicants for business firms. He also writes and speaks on a wide variety of occult subjects, cultivating a waspish turn of wit that often lands him in hot water. During one live radio show a lady panelist asked him why he thought God had created man. Martello snapped, "Maybe He was disappointed in the monkey!"

He has large numbers of private clients who come to him, singly or in groups, for something he terms "Psychic Psychology." It amounts to advisory sessions on intimate problems, couched sometimes in occult phrases, more frequently in an earthier form.

One client, who happened to be a high-class call girl, wanted to know whether to go ahead and take a cheaper apartment. She was afraid that the move might induce her clients to demand lower rates. Martello's answer was prompt and to the point: "If they come to you for the sake of the decor, tell them to f—— the wallpaper!"

His advice isn't always that pithy. Psychic Psychology, in fact, is a quite elaborate blend of occultism and psychoanalysis, peppered with a dash of pure Martello.

To alleviate hostility, for instance, he teaches clients a mental ritual:

"Visualize the person you hate in your mind—See him clearly—Take a dagger and stab him in the heart—Take his body and place it in a coffin—Close the lid—Dig a big hole in the ground—Push the coffin into the hole—Cover the coffin with dirt—After the coffin is fully covered say this, 'Peace be unto you—Peace be unto me—I am free.'"

He claims that this little ceremony works—even if the victim concerned is already dead.

Martello never teaches his classes actual witchcraft techniques. On this portion of his activities he is amazingly tight-mouthed. But he snorts contemptuously at the idea that there is anything supernatural about them.

"That's a lot of eyewash," he insists. "Witchcraft is as natural as electricity. It's merely natural physical forces accentuated and utilized. All our rituals are simply devices to focus concentration—no connection with 'magic' at all."

He belongs to a standard-sized coven in New York—"But I'm the only exhibitionist among them. The others keep under cover."

There is no doubt that Martello finds being a witch tremendous fun. His puckish gleefulness is contagious. Whether he appears on television or before live audiences he hams his role to the hilt; twirling his black beard, knitting evil brows, but ready at any moment to burst out giggling.

"Oh, I've been steeped in this thing all my damned life," he grinned. "I remember back at the boarding school when I was five I invented a witching game for the kids. And guess who was the witch?" He nudged me slyly. "Yours truly, of course. And in a charming fringed shawl.

"A few years later I started practicing hypnotism on my comrades. Absolutely *horrified* the dear Fathers when they caught me at it—I had one fellow stretched between two chairs in a rigid trance. You should have heard the uproar.

"Oh, and I also studied palmistry. That was in Worcester, Massachusetts, where I grew up. I had two neighborhood gypsies as tutors when I was—let me see—just six. At sixteen I was on radio, giving handwriting analyses. And from 1964 to '65 I lived in Tangier, Morocco, studying Oriental witchcraft. So you might say I'm full-fledged in the craft."

"How do you practice it?" I asked.

"In various ways—it's a complex subject." Martello smiled quietly to himself and began telling me about his newsletter. It is in these evasions more than in anything else that you can feel the serious core beneath all his surface Halloweening.

His *Wicca Newsletter*—perhaps the oddest publication in the country—is a labor of love. A deplorably produced but amusing little sheet, it jumbles the latest coven news with two-line reviews, snatches of gossip and other scraps liable to interest witchdom.

Martello's assistant editor in this enterprise calls herself Witch
Hazel on the masthead. In the flesh she is as lusciously rounded
as a brunette peach, but determined not to reveal her surname.
"Hazel is my real first name," she said, waving charcoal eye-
lashes, "and I *am* a witch. So the name fits, doesn't it?"
It does. Almost as perfectly as her sweater.

Hazel is in her early twenties and on occasions wears a scarlet
cloak and gold chain over a miniskirt and black kneeboots. The
effect is likely to win any number of male converts for the craft.
She has a fresh, homey sophomore voice that makes witchcraft
sound like a spiritualist branch of the PTA.

"I'm in my sixth or seventh reincarnation now and I've been
a witch in several of my earlier lives," she confided brightly.
"I see witchcraft basically as a means of self-improvement. It
brings out—well, latent powers that most people allow to lie
fallow. No, I never cast 'hexes.' You see I believe—most of us
believe—that evil wished upon another person bounces back
threefold on the wisher."

"But couldn't you wish a million dollars for yourself?" I
wanted to know. "Or a movie career?"

She shook her long black tresses. "It wouldn't work like
that. Fulfillment might be linked with unforeseeable consequences.
Like the death of my father, for instance. Or some horrible
disfigurement for me."

"Well, what do you wish for then?"

"Lots of things." She thought for a moment. "I can control
the weather, for instance. Make it bright when I want it. Once
I wished for a familiar—a cat. And it arrived on my doorstep the
next day."

Despite its deceptively naïve ring, this wishing process is the
root formula of modern witchcraft. Witches actually wish in
unison, focusing and tuning their individual wills through incantations and chants until the whole coven becomes a psychic
one. No longer a group of people, but a single-willed, cohesive
mass.

The aim of the ritual is to harness invisible forces and give
them a certain direction and purpose—rather like a hydroelectric
plant harnesses, transforms and directs waterpower.

The procedure is democratic. Individual members voice their

wishes, but the entire coven has to agree on their worth before it goes into action. Contrary to Hazel's opinion the goal is often purely materialistic.

In the Chicago coven I mentioned earlier, one of the lady members had bought some shares (I'll call them ABC) on the stock market. They weren't doing too well, and she wanted the coven to exert its power for their betterment. Her request was discussed and granted.

She had brought her share certificate, which passed from hand to hand and was finally laid on the altar—"to help us focus the psychic power," the high priestess told me afterwards.

Then the high priestess pronounced, "ABC shares *must* rise— *must* rise—" and the entire group took up the chorus: "ABC shares *must* rise, ABC shares *must* rise . . ." The chanting went on and on, the black candles on the walls flickering, the long cloaks of the chanters rustling accompaniment.

I made a point of checking the financial pages a week later. The shares had gone up—slightly.

These gatherings are called Esbats (as distinct from the purely festive Sabbats) and can be held for considerably weightier purposes. Dr. Gardner repeatedly assured his British audiences that they had witches' powers to thank for foiling the projected invasions of their island by the Spanish Armada and Hitler's Wehrmacht. He left out Napoleon. Nor did he explain why the spells hadn't worked on Julius Caesar and William the Conqueror.

The late doctor's disciples are not disturbed by such inconsistencies, nor by the constant pinpricks they suffer from more tradition-bound practitioners.

"We feel that mistakes might have crept into the rituals over the centuries and we try to sort them out. This makes us far more flexible than traditionalist groups, who want everything to remain exactly as handed down."

The speaker was Dr. Raymond Brian Buckland (his degree is a genuine Ph.D. in anthropology from King's College, London). The Bucklands, husband and wife, were initiated into the craft by Gardner's own high priestess before coming to the United States in 1962. Today they have a Gardnerian coven in suburban Brentwood, Long Island.

Anyone less witchlike would be hard to conceive. Mr. Buckland—whose witch name is Robat—looks almost fragile, with finely drawn features, a little pointed beard and sharp blue eyes. He is aloofly polite, with a touch of formality and academic precision in his speech. He works as an editor of manuals for an overseas airline. His wife—Lady Rowen to the witchworld—is a private secretary in Long Island.

"At the moment our coven is oversubscribed," he said, sounding apologetic. "Sixteen members instead of the correct thirteen. But we have equal numbers because we work in pairs— male and female—as nature intended."

"Clothed or naked?"

He looked slightly pained. "We prefer to call it 'sky-clad,'" he corrected me. "Yes, we do shed our clothing. Not for erotic reasons—that's nonsense—but because we believe that clothes hamper occult emanations. There's power in the human body, you know."

The Bucklands have long ceased trying to hide their creed from their neighbors. They now operate a Museum of Witchcraft and Magick—the only one of its kind in America—as an adjunct to their home. Their coven meets about once a month in a special basement room, with Lady Rowen—a cool, slender woman in her thirties—presiding as high priestess.

"This secrecy business among witches is largely a tradition," Buckland explained. "Doesn't make much sense these days. Matter of fact, our neighbors often come to see my wife with their eye and sinus troubles. She has a herb garden and she works wonders with teas and potions and that kind of stuff."

They have two sons of whom the older was initiated as a witch at six. The young one has shown no interest in the occult so far. "He's more for outdoor games," his father added regretfully.

To Buckland the main attraction of witchcraft lies in its relative freedom. "There is a 'personalness' about the craft. Witches work in small, close covens—no big organized hierarchy handing down dogmas and prescribing rituals. Each coven governs itself."

Witchcraft, then, is a uniquely democratic institution. This applies even to the imperiously titled Royal Order of Warlocks and Witches, headquartered in Florida. Its spokesman is a rugged, pipe-smoking Miami sculptor who calls himself Prince VanDercar and once—during a severe draught—put a cryptic ad in the Miami *Herald:* "I am making Kahuna Rain God." The next day it rained (see Figure 12).

According to VanDercar, the Royal Order is organized in units of ten, each unit electing its own representative to act on its behalf at the next highest level—the Shaman coven, a meeting of ten representatives from ten base units. Each representative must answer to the nine members who elected him (or her) and can be demoted at any time.

"In this system," explains the Prince, "no one can gain control or power. All orders come from the bottom upward."

However, since the Order is a secret organization we have no means of telling just how many—or how few—covens belong to it. It may, for all I know, consist exclusively of Mr. VanDercar and the handful of Miamians (mostly young and mostly female) who attend his gatherings.

The laissez-faire attitude of the creed has resulted in a totally bewildering variety of coven practices; some as sedate as Methodist prayer meetings, others outright orgy clubs. There are covens dabbling in voodoo and covens trying to swing elections via psychic emanations. And all in the name of the "Old Religion."

At the time of writing several dozen solo witches also flourish in Reynosa, a small Mexican town just across the United States border. They advertise in general terms on radio, television and handbills, but actually specialize in draft evasion. For a flat fee of four hundred dollars—or its equivalent in merchandise—they promise to use their powers to keep young Texans out of the services and Vietnam.

Sometimes the powers of these "brujas" seem to work. Sometimes they don't—"Because the spirits were against me"—and the boy gets drafted. Either way his parents have paid in advance. Even at one customer per week it would be an excellent business, and some of them average ten.

Because of the hothouse proliferation of witching procedures it is quite impossible to describe any one coven as typical. The three or four ceremonies I witnessed personally all differed from each other, except in certain very basic steps.

The most elaborate took place in the Disneyland-Gothic

living room of an advertising executive in Los Angeles. The hostess didn't object to my presence, but asked me not to look anyone in the eye. "It spoils our concentration, you understand."

The coven members—five women and four men—first undressed, then purified themselves in salt water. Most of them were young and beach proportioned. The high priestess was the oldest; a remarkably well-preserved matron, wearing only green garters and an enigmatic smile. None of them spoke to me.

A circle, nine feet in diameter, had been drawn on the well-polished floorboards. In the center stood the altar—a small table draped in black velvet—and around the edge of the circle burned four black candles.

On the altar lay the Book of Shadows—a loose-leaf manual— a black-handled dagger called an athame and a long sword. The high priestess raised the sword to begin the ceremony (she is the only member allowed to touch it) and recited in standard sermon tones:

"Listen to the words of the Great Mother, who was of old called amongst men Artemis, Diana, Aphrodite and many other names. Whenever you have need of anything, once in a month, and better it be when the moon is full, then shall ye assemble in some secret place . . ."

The formalized drone went on for several minutes, ending with a fervent shout—taken up by the others: "Blessed be the great goddess. Without beginning, without end . . . everlasting to eternity . . . Blessed Be."

The coven members joined hands and the high priestess gave a brief reading from the Book of Shadows—occult formulas in colloquial English on how to keep your house safe from fire and how to make a thief return stolen goods.

Incense was lit in silver burners. From somewhere an invisible tape recorder began breathing mood music—quite appropriately Grieg's "Dance of the Trolls."

The coven started to dance around the perimeter of the magic circle. Slowly at first, then faster and faster as the music gathered pace. Their gyrations became wilder, more abandoned, sweat glistened on their suntans, clouds of blue incense mingled with the smoke of the candles like a soft sponge blurring the edges of reality.

The high priestess went around with a silver whip, flicking the dancers—not too lightly—on their bare haunches. At this the leaping and weaving grew frenzied—the panting of the dancers could be heard over the music.

The heavy perfumes of the women's bodies blended with the sweat, the aroma of incense and melting candle wax in a pungent exciting whole. The men, at least, were showing unmistakable signs of stimulation.

The dance ended on the last convulsive blast of the music. The coven, tense and breathless, went into the wishing part of the ritual.

I have solemnly promised not to reveal details of the requests. They were, in any case, quite mundane; concerned with eminently practical matters such as success in a business partnership and the salving of someone's marital relations. But as each request was transformed into a unified chant—a strident appeal—no, command —to mighty powers, the coven's conviction seemed absolute.

"What can we do?" my hostess replied to me afterwards. "We can do anything!"

She had voiced what is probably the basis of modern witch-craft—the urge for power. Not necessarily power over others, but power to control one's own life. Whether the spells cast by practitioners actually influence events is more or less immaterial. The adherents believe they do, and things go their way sufficiently often to reinforce that belief into conviction. Such conviction alone can be enough to give them a steady, forceful self-assurance that sets them ahead of the great mass—and frequently exerts very real influence on their surroundings.

For in an age where everyone except computer cards gets duly stapled, folded and mutilated, one of the greatest attainable boons is the feeling of being a manipulator instead of the eternally manipulated.

IV
THE HOSTS OF
L. RON HUBBARD

EVERY DAY of the week some tens of thousands brightly colored, badly printed leaflets wander through mail slots, under windshield wipers and into the hands of pedestrians, inviting all recipients to CROSS THE BRIDGE TO TOTAL FREEDOM AND TOTAL POWER!

Those who follow up the address find themselves in a curious hybrid establishment, resembling a cross between a political ward headquarters and an army recruiting station. Actually it is neither, but one of the 362 nationwide branch Missions of America's— and perhaps the world's—fastest growing religion: scientology.

"Religion" does not really describe this phenomenal mass movement. Scientology, in fact, only became a church as an afterthought.

Its founder, Lafayette Ronald Hubbard, explains it as "a religious philosophy possessing a technology for spiritual recovery and the increase of individual ability." But this is no clearer a definition than its title—from the Latin *scio* ("knowledge") and the Greek *logos* ("study"); making it the "study of knowledge."

What, then, *is* scientology? The most expressive answer to this question was supplied to me by a nineteen-year-old adherent in Chicago: "It's like—Wow!" he said, dreamily shifting his gum. "Like you never existed before and suddenly you're alive, man. It's . . . it's a state of *being!*"

Scientology has several claims to uniqueness. It represents the first attempt ever made to incorporate elements of psychoanalysis into a mass organization. It is also the first to use electric machinery for the purpose.

It is the only creed involved in this country's occult upsurge that actually originated here. Whereas all the others derived their inspirations either from Europe or the Orient, scientology is as home-baked American as Rotary or the Ku Klux Klan. Yet paradoxically, its world headquarters is located in England, much of its literature is printed in Scandinavia, and its founding father rarely sets foot on his native soil.

But the Church's outstanding peculiarity is its running conflict with the authorities. Ever since its inauguration, eighteen years ago, scientology has been in and out of one judicial hassle after another; not merely in the United States, but on three continents.

At first glance the causes of these constant legal scrapes seem utterly mystifying. Scientology advocates nothing that could be considered contrary to established social mores. It espouses neither political upheaval nor sexual license. It is opposed to narcotics, uses no "fine print" contract forms and its economic doctrines are —if anything—starchily conservative.

Nevertheless, both the United States and British governments have at some stage taken measures against the movement. The Australian state of Victoria even set up a special Royal Commission to investigate it.

In 1965 the Commission issued a report declaring that "scientology is evil; its techniques evil; its practice a serious threat to the community . . ." The government thereupon banned scientology in the state.

Being banned in Victoria does not exactly constitute ultimate

proof of wickedness. In Australia the state enjoys a comically
Bostonian reputation for banning and proscribing with more zeal
than judgment. Victorian customs officials once impounded a
children's book filled with games, puzzles and coloring pictures,
designed to keep sick youngsters occupied. Sole reason for its
seizure was the title—*Fun in Bed*.

But in America too, the AMA branded scientology "a serious
threat to health." The British Home Office barred Mr. Hubbard
from teaching in the country. In July 1968 police stopped a
planeload of seventy American scientologists at London airport
and made them return to the United States. They had been
bound for a conference at their international headquarters in East
Grinstead.

The movement's British spokesman, David Gaiman, claimed
that "we are in the middle of the biggest witch hunt since the
reign of James II." In order to draw public attention to the
Church's plight, he began a hunger strike outside Number 10
Downing Street, the residence of Britain's prime ministers.

On that occasion Bernard Levin, a columnist of the London
Daily Mail and ardent civil libertarian, wrote:

"David Gaiman has written to the Home Secretary announcing his intention to starve himself to death. He has sent a copy of
his letter to me.

"I hope I will not seem unduly vindictive when I say that if
I believed Mr. Gaiman meant his threat I would regard it as the
best news I have heard for some considerable time. What makes
his news all the more welcome is that he has not only promised
to starve to death himself but declared that others of his curious
persuasion are no less determined to do so."

What is it about this "curious persuasion" that aroused such
hostility in the usually gentle Mr. Levin? And what is it that
engendered repressive actions from such totally diverse bodies as
the U. S. Food and Drug Administration, England's Socialist
Home Office, and the ultrastodgy state government of Victoria?

Church spokesmen hint at some form of international cabal
against their movement, fostered by unnamed "negative powers."
In London the Church distributed replicas of Wild West posters
announcing:

WANTED—1,000 pounds Reward to anyone furnishing the name and documentary proof of any member of any CONSPIRACY to deny advanced technology to England and/or attempting to discredit new healing developments that would increase the health and ability of the British People. Forward any such data to The Guardian, Dianetics and Scientology Organizations.

Ron Hubbard put it less obliquely in a letter he wrote to *Life* magazine: "Those attacking Scientology run mental institutions. They make millions out of it. They advocate brutal, murderous actions against the insane. They are terrified of losing the avalanches of money gouged out of governments. They see Scientology taking it all away with kind, effective measures. There is no question in their minds but that Scientology works. That's why they are attacking it . . ."

Whatever the forces arrayed against scientology, they have—to date—been decidedly ineffective. The movement's rate of growth can only be described as fantastic. According to sober estimates, the Church has probably quadrupled its membership over the past five years. It now has somewhere between three and five million disciples in the United States, plus several hundred thousand more abroad. And this despite an almost unanimously bad press, sundry scandals, and several splinter factions within its ranks.

The riddle of scientology is not easily solved. It has to be explored, layer by layer, before the pattern falls into shape and you get an idea what it is that inspires so much fanatical devotion on the one hand and such bitter animosity on the other.

My first encounter with the workings of the Church took place at its East Coast headquarters in New York's sedately respectable Hotel Martinique. And my first impression was one of vibrant, garish dynamism.

The walls of the premises were plastered with graphs, charts, lists and announcements, life-sized portraits of L. Ron Hubbard, and cartoon posters of little men flying, stumbling, cheering, exploding or hitting each other with clubs.

Wherever you looked there was *action*. Telephones ringing,

typewriters rattling, books and pamphlets being delivered, displayed, sold, swarms of people rushing in and out of offices, rustling files, marking papers, yelling "Hi, there" across partitions and laughing uproariously about unheard jokes. The place was alive with the kind of excited purposeful movement you find backstage in a theater just before the curtain goes up.

The second impression was of youth and good looks. The premises seemed populated by attractive girls and boys in their early twenties, the lasses wearing tiny miniskirts, the lads mostly in semimod garb. They displayed a good deal of affection for each other, frequently exchanging hugs or pecks on the cheek. There was nothing in the least sly or self-conscious about them, they exuded simply warmth and a great gladness that made watching them a pleasure.

Listening to them was a different matter. Their talk was so richly studded with incomprehensibles like "preclear," "engrams," "OT Three Expanded," "Standard Tech," "Space Org," and "power processing," that they might have been personnel of the Martian air force.

In any case, I wasn't left to listen for long. A girl came over and sat down beside me. She seemed to consist entirely of auburn hair, long nylon legs and a peekaboo blouse with lots to peek at. "Hi, my name is Daphne," she breathed. "What's yours?"

I told her. Daphne smiled radiantly. "This your first time here?" I admitted it was. "Well, look around. You'll like it." She gathered up a sheaf of papers and swayed away. After a few steps she turned around and waved at me, her teeth gleaming. "Bye— see ya soon."

I had imagined that Daphne might be some sort of hostess. But she was merely one of the office staff who had taken a moment off to make contact. Suddenly I was no longer a stranger.

A whole crowd of us then gathered in the adjoining auditorium for "Group Processing." The processor was a lady named Yvonne Gilham; a striking, curvacious brunette with a cheerful nursery school manner.

She made her class go through a series of simple maneuvers, such as circulating and meeting twenty new people, looking around and finding somebody we liked, thinking of something we really wanted to achieve, and thinking that everybody around us wanted us to achieve it.

Each routine—about a dozen of them—was rewarded by one of Miss Gilham's standard comments: "Good," and "Very good." She invited suggestions from the audience and one—put forward by a young man with an excruciating stammer—received a "Beautiful!"

The next stage was "Money Processing."

All of us were told to take out a dollar bill. "Now look at your dollar bill—from both sides—and upside down," (Miss Gilham showed us how). "Wave your dollar around—smell your dollar—rub it against your cheek—feel the weight of it . . . very good." Her voice rose. "Now screw up your dollar," she shouted. "*Throw* it away! Think of something pleasant—forget about your dollar, you couldn't care less about it. Now—find a dollar! Pass your dollar around—give it away—take one you've been given . . . that's right. Very good."

I glanced around the audience. They were playing along with tremendous enthusiasm, hurling, finding and exchanging their notes, shouting and jostling as they tossed them high into the air, scrambling under chairs to recover them amidst roars of laughter punctuated by colliding heads. The stammering youth climbed on his chair and caught a bill in mid-flight.

In conclusion the audience applauded the processor. Miss Gilham applauded back. "And that's for you all . . . very, very good."

Filing out we passed a special table with a Success Book. It contained page after typed page of testimonials. Glowing tributes to the powers of dianetics and scientology from people who had found relief from aching wisdom teeth, sinusitis, allergies, backaches and myopia.

Others had undergone even more remarkable improvements.

One disciple had written: "Right after Clear I hit a keyed out OT state and could change my body size about 1¼ to 1½ inches in height by actual measurement. Some people swore it was 2 to 3 inches, which it might have been, but it was 1¼ inch different the time I measured. The ability was under control and I would do it at will."

Another statement read:

Duplication of data often brings interesting abilities into view. I'm OT I. While studying with intention in the privacy of my bedroom, I heard a noise in the adjoining den. I looked around to "see" what it was, and behold, I looked right through the wall into the next room as though no wall was there. When your intention is very strong, you can do what you intend to do! Wow! Do you intend to go CLEAR? And O.T.?

Clear ⚡ 2313.

At that point I didn't know the meaning of the terms "Clear" and "O.T." Neither did most of the other visitors, although they beckoned from every wall. Just above the table hung a poster showing a leaping man letting go a jagged scream: "I WANNA GO CLEAR!"

Elsewhere people were lining up to take a "Free Personality Test." When my turn came I was handed sheets containing forty questions, each with three alternative answers which had to be ticked off. The questions dealt with an extensive range of problem fields: self-confidence or lack of it, relations with others, ambitions, fears, doubts, prejudices, and so on.

My form was worked over by a grave-faced girl. She made a graph pattern from my replies, using various shadings to illustrate positive and negative trends. I had answered the questions as honestly as possible. As a result her penciled graph showed vast areas of negative shading.

She looked at me compassionately. "Here," she said, indicating the dark patches, "is where scientology can help you."

"How do you suggest I start?"

She handed me another form. "This is for the Communication Course. Fifteen hours, any day of the week, one hour a day. It costs fifteen dollars."

I thanked her and promised to think it over.

From that moment on I was at the receiving end of a steady torrent of reminders, mingled with an infinite variety of booklets, periodicals, handbills, tickets and proclamations.

The letters ranged from the well typed to the almost illegibly hand-scrawled, the headings from a pally "Hi, John," to a formal

"Dear Sir." Their style was not so much high-pressure as elbow-nudging, the theme always identically urging, prodding, encouraging to "Hit the Road to Freedom."

Hovering over everything was the enigmatic but benign figure of L. Ron Hubbard; a kind of ubiquitous Big Brother with the menace removed. Virtually every article in every brochure and magazine carried his byline, every quotation was credited to him, every testimonial offered him thanks. He was, it appeared, the linchpin of a private universe, the fount of all wisdom, the living hope for all humanity.

Hubbard, in fact, is the object of a personality cult unparalleled since the followers of the late Aga Khan drank their leader's bottled bathwater to be cured of stomach ache.

Yet not one scientologist in ten thousand has ever seen him in the flesh. They are surrounded by his busts and pictures, they listen to his resonant, disembodied voice on tapes and records, they watch his image on films, but the man himself remains as remote and luminous as an aurora borealis.

As I delved deeper into the organization I was astonished at how little most scientologists knew about their idol. Their only source is a brief, uninformative biographical sketch, which appears over and over in various Church publications. Yet some knowledge of Hubbard's career and character is absolutely essential if you want to comprehend the nature of scientology.

Lafayette Ronald Hubbard ("Ron" or "Elron" to his flock) is a large, burly man with reddish-gray hair and exceptionally smooth skin. He dresses impeccably in clothes of a casually nautical type, radiates patriarchal self-assurance and looks somewhat like a vintage Wallace Beery (see Figure 13). His present wife is a pretty Texan named Mary Sue.

Hubbard was born in Tilden, Nebraska, in 1911, and received civil engineering training at George Washington University. His tendency to apply engineering terms to the human psyche probably stems from his education.

He had a colorful early career, including movie script writing, wartime service in the navy and a stint as singer and banjo player on a radio program. Everyone who knew him was struck by his surging energy, his rare capacity for equally large chunks of talk and action.

His special forte, however, lay in magazine fiction. He allegedly churned out 15 million published words, pounding at breakneck speed on a special electric typewriter with extra keys for common terms like "and" and "the." His opponents frequently refer to him as a "pulp fiction hack," but this indicates that they probably haven't read his work.

Hubbard did write for the pulps, but an amazing proportion of his output was excellent. He specialized in science fiction fantasies and although he never quite reached the classical levels of, say, Isaac Asimov or Ray Bradbury, some of his stories were hauntingly memorable.

Perhaps his greatest—and certainly his most significant—piece was a nightmare entitled "Typewriter in the Sky." In it the hero, Mike de Wolfe, finds himself forced to participate in a historic melodrama written by a mysterious—and omnipotent—novelist named Horace Hackett.

Whether he wants to or not, Mike has to play out the role in which the author has cast him. He has to fight for his life, has to kill others in order to survive—never knowing how the plot that holds him captive is going to end.

It ends happily. Mike gets back to his home and to his own century. But he is seething with fury against Hackett, whose strange power made him undergo the adventure.

And then a thought—almost a revelation—strikes him. Could Horace Hackett be—up there—God, in a dirty bathrobe? . . .

That's the story, and you don't forget it in a hurry. And you remember it again when you see legions of scientologists acting out the roles that somebody—with a typewriter—has assigned to them.

Hubbard achieved national fame in 1950. In that year an article by him appeared in *Astounding Science Fiction* describing a new approach to mental health called dianetics (from the Greek word for "thought.")

Shortly afterwards a thick volume appeared under the title *Dianetics—The Modern Science of Mental Health*, which Hubbard claims to have written in three weeks. This is believable, insofar as the book is certainly the worst thing he ever wrote . . . as well as the most successful.

The opening sentence reads: "The creation of dianetics is a

milestone for Man comparable to his discovery of fire and superior to his inventions of the wheel and the arch."

Reviewers had very mixed feelings about it, but the general public thought differently. The book became a fabulous runaway bestseller, retailing more than 1½ million copies and triggering a nationwide cult of massive proportions. For a while dianetics replaced psychoanalysis as the favorite fad of the Hollywood movie colony. College kids banned together in Dianetic Clubs, housewives tried out the new therapy on each other at afternoon parties.

A Hubbard Dianetic Foundation was established in Wichita, Kansas, where patients received thirty-six hours of therapy for five hundred dollars. Hubbard flew back and forth across the country, addressing vast audiences (sometimes accompanied by a drummer who kept time to his word rhythm) and gathering in more disciples.

His book's basic theme had zeroed in on something which millions of Americans thought not only valid but highly relevant. This was the theory of the "engram."

An engram is a traumatic shock of varying intensity which humans suffer while still in the womb or in early childhood. There can be scores of them, sometimes caused by physical jolts ("Mama sneezes, baby gets knocked unconscious") sometimes by emotional upheavals. But whether they are inflicted prenatally or in infancy, engrams are the cause of *all* psychosomatic ailments and mental aberrations later in life.

The way to eliminate them is through a process called "auditing." By asking the right kind of questions a trained dianetic auditor can pinpoint a particular engram and—by making the patient remember every detail connected with it—gradually erase it.

The procedure is long and involved, especially since the auditor has to try to send the patient back along his "time track" to his very earliest engram, the "basic-basic" or BB. Once this has been dissolved the rest go a little easier.

After about twenty hours of auditing the patient becomes a "release"—that is free from *major* ills. The next stage is the "preclear" and later—much later—he may go "clear." A "clear," according to Hubbard, is a superior being. He—or she—does not get colds, his wounds and injuries heal faster, he is free from any kind of neuroses, gains a noticeably higher I.Q. and improved eyesight.

But dianetics did not last long enough to produce many clears. It fizzled almost as fast as it had ignited. Public interest waned, several of Hubbard's lectures turned into fiascos, with parts of the audience walking out. And in February 1952, the Dianetic Foundation in Wichita collapsed.

To most observers it seemed that Hubbard's time in the limelight was over and that dianetics had gone the way of the dinosaurs. Which merely goes to show how mistaken observers can be.

For in the spring of 1952, Hubbard was already assembling the pieces of a new creed, fused with dianetics, but infinitely more evolved . . . scientology. Whereas dianetics was subject to limitations, scientology knows no bounds. While dianetics dealt only with this life, scientology deals with past lives and the hereafter. While dianetics simply sought to heal individuals, scientology's aim is to raise all mankind to semidivine levels. While dianetics focused on this earth, scientology reaches out for the universe.

Hubbard, temporarily headquartered in Phoenix, Arizona, gave scientology its official launching late in 1952. The press was, to put it politely, cool.

Reporters listened poker-faced while Hubbard expounded on his discovery of "life energy in such a form as to revive the dead and dying." He also explained that everybody was 74 trillion years old and had been reincarnated innumerable times in what he called "spirals." *Time* magazine commented that "his latest ology is compounded in equal parts of science fiction, dianetics . . . and plain jabberwocky."

But once again the media showed itself out of step with a very large segment of the population. For what chiefly aroused journalistic derision struck multitudes as a scientific device of supreme importance.

This was the instrument Hubbard introduced as an essential aid to auditing: the electropsychometer or E-Meter. As he put it: "An auditor auditing without this machine reminds one of a hunter hunting ducks at pitch black midnight, firing his gun off in all directions."

The E-Meter consists of a small box connected to two wires which are clipped onto jam cans. The box contains a battery which sends a very light electric charge through the body of any-one holding the cans. With the subject clutching the cans, the auditor asks questions, watching a dial on which a needle indicates emotional fluctuations in the subject while answering. The needle also responds to sweaty palms and squeezing of the cans. The movements of the needle supposedly help the auditor decide whether or not his subject is answering truthfully.

The E-Meter, then, is a very primitive type of lie detector. What appalled me personally was the blind confidence most scientologists place in its accuracy.

As a former crime reporter I have had fairly extensive experience with the most advanced form of lie detector, the Keeler polygraph. Despite its technical sophistication, no court in the world admits the results of polygraph tests as evidence. Any police officer will tell you why: the polygraph won't work on psychopaths, morons, or habitual liars who tend to believe their own lies. It also gets stymied by certain psychological hang-ups. I know the case of a convict whose wife had divorced him while he was in prison. At his polygraph test the man answered the question whether he was married with a truthful "No." The machine, however, registered this as a lie. The reason was simple —as a devout Catholic, the convict did not believe in divorce. Subconsciously he was still a married man.

The results of the Keeler polygraph depend almost entirely on the interpretation of complex graph patterns by highly skilled operators. To try and read similar deductions from the momentary jerks of a needle would be futile even if the E-Meter registered as many reflexes as the polygraph. As it is, it can't give the auditor any clue on whether the subject is fantasizing or not.

As a technical instrument the E-Meter may be useless. But as a magic symbol of the auditor's powers it turned out to be invaluable. Its very presence—the responsive sway of the needle combined with the sage prodding of the operator—made lying difficult for the impressionable.

The E-Meter contributed immensely to the upsurge of sci-entology. But it also got Hubbard into legal difficulties.

The machines were sold to scientology auditors for prices

ranging up to $144. Some of these operators implied—possibly
without Hubbard's knowledge—that the meters could be used to
detect "engrammic diseases" such as asthma, tuberculosis, heart
ailments, stomach ulcers and even some forms of cancer. Others
went further and claimed that they could also eliminate radiation
burns from atomic explosions.

The Food and Drug Administration eventually filed charges,
claiming that certain statements connected with the E-Meter were
"false and misleading." Some of the machines were confiscated
and the case dragged on through various courts over a period of
nine years. In the end, however, Hubbard triumphed.

His victory was entirely due to a step he took when he shifted
his operation base to Washington, D.C., in 1955. There he established the Founding Church of Scientology as an unincorpo-
rated independent church, able to ordain ministers, perform
marriage ceremonies and bury its dead.

This, no matter how hotly the U.S. Government Attorney
said otherwise, altered the legal status of the E-Meter as well as its
operators. In a decision handed down in 1969, the U.S. Court of
Appeals stated that "from the viewpoint of Scientology auditing or
processing is a central practice of their religion, akin to confession
in the Catholic Church."

Even before this decision, Hubbard had safeguarded himself
by ordering all machines to bear the notice that "the E-Meter is
not intended or effective for the diagnosis, treatment or pre-
vention of any disease."

The purpose of the E-Meter, in fact, lies far beyond that. It
is the instrument that guides scientologists toward the ultimate
aim of "clear." and both the process and the goal have altered
dramatically since the earlier, simpler days of dianetics.

Hubbard now emphasized the existence of Thetans, tiny
beings a quarter to two inches long, which are indestructible
and eternal. Thetans arrive in the human body around birth, and
they have been wandering from body to body, from planet to
planet, since time began.

Quite apart from the human's own engrams, he is also saddled
with the engrams the Thetan has brought along from billions of
years of previous lives. These, too, must be found and eradicated

before the state of "clear" can be reached. Thus it is just as important to "process past lives" as it is to work on the present.

When the human dies, his Thetan flies off to an Implant Station to await assignment to another body. Before being given one, however, it is implanted with a number of goals, one of them the goal "to forget."

Implant stations are scattered throughout the universe; most of them on Mars, some on Venus, a few on earth. They also exist in (on?) Heaven, which place Hubbard claims to have visited twice. The time of his first arrival he dated at 43,891,611,177 years, 344 days, 10 hours, 20 minutes and 40 seconds from 10:02½ P.M. Daylight Greenwich Time, May 9, 1963.

He wrote a detailed description of Heaven: "The gates of the series are well done, well built. An avenue of saints leads up to them. The gate pillars are surmounted by marble angels. The entering grounds are very well kept, laid out like Bush Gardens in Pasadena, so often seen in the movies. A sign on the left says, 'This is Heaven.' The right has the sign, 'Hell.'"

But getting back to earth . . .

A human's state of "clear" is achieved when he or she has shed all the engrams of his present and his Thetan's previous lives. This is indicated by the needle of the E-Meter swinging slowly and smoothly from side to side. He then becomes what is known as an "Operating Thetan" or OT and joins the ranks of scientology's elite.

The road upward, however, is long, hard—and expensive. It involves many, many sessions with the E-Meter, some of them— during "power processing"—lasting several hours. The auditor's questions probe into the most intimate spheres of the subject's life, bringing out past misdeeds (including rather tenuous ones, like a murder committed twenty-nine lives earlier on the planet Jupiter) revealing sexual aberrations and erotic desires and fantasies which the subject may have confessed to no one before.

Priests and psychiatrists, of course, get such revelations every week. The ominous difference is that the auditor is bound by neither a confessional seal nor a medical code. He is at liberty to pass on anything he learns to his scientology superiors, who can file it away for future use. The mere possession of such information gives the Church a hold on its members that is nothing short of frightening.

Auditing, though, is merely one part of scientology. The gargantuan rest consists of a constantly changing, shifting and fluctuating series of more or less interlocking study courses and training programs designed to teach the philosophy, disciplines and ethics of the Church. Since the order, importance and price of these courses is being perpetually rearranged they are extremely difficult to keep track of.

"That's because the orgs (organizations) are evolving, improving and expanding all the time," a Los Angeles scientologist explained to me. "If you just drop out for six weeks you find the pieces reshuffled on your return. Keeps you on your toes."

This permanent flux is generated by a stream of bulletins which Hubbard issues over a worldwide Telex network maintained by a nerve center called HCO (Hubbard Communications Office). They take the form of policy letters and commands, introducing new practices, abolishing or modifying others, establishing or scrapping courses, giving extremely shrewd and practical advice on salesmanship, finances and administration.

Many of these shifts seem to serve no other purpose than to produce action—movement—for its own sake. Peacetime armies operate on the same principle—about 70 percent of their activities are designed simply to keep soldiers busy. But some of the changes are clearly the result of outside pressures on the Church. In recent years Hubbard peremptorily discarded certain practices that handed scientology's opponents too much ammunition to fire at the Church.

What remains permanent is the skillful dovetailing of the programs, by which students of one course are induced to go on to the next, higher, costlier one. Scientology employs some unique methods in accomplishing this.

I know a young and very shy New York girl who signed on for the lowest rung of the ladder; the aforementioned Communication Course at fifteen dollars. While still in the midst of it, her instructor told her that she would need massive auditing sessions, costing a thousand dollars.

She was frankly aghast at the sum—more than she had owned in her life. But her instructor arranged for her to take gratis

"Money Processing," which caused her not only to lose her awe of large figures but also of banks. She promptly went to her bank manager and obtained a student loan of a thousand dollars —which paid for her auditing.

I should note here that the girl is still in scientology, and convinced that she'd had her money's worth—and more.

The above is a fair sample of the Church's price bracket. The structuring and fees of the courses, however, alter so often that anything quoted here may be outdated by the time you read it.

At the moment, anyway, "Grades of Release" run from I to IV and cost a total of $750. The Special Briefing Course comes to $775. OT Sections go from I to VIII and vary in price from $75 to $875. The Class VIII Auditor Course—which members who have achieved Class VI and OT III are encouraged to take—costs $1,775 (with a 5 percent discount for payment in advance).

There are numerous other discounts and ways of cutting costs by taking courses in prepaid batches, with new bargains being offered several times per season. You can, for instance, save a substantial sum of the three-thousand-dollar total on the eight OT Sections if you sign up for all of them in one Total Power Package instead of taking them singly.

Salesmanship for all courses is constant and very persuasive, with ads and slogans placed in every scientology publication. My personal favorite was: "Three Billion Preclears Need More Class VIII Auditors"—the three billion referring to the population of the world.

Even the state of "clear" has been considerably modified. Once it was the ultimate apex, but now Hubbard identifies no fewer than eight OT levels of Total Freedom above it. Reaching them is costly, as will be seen by the prices given, but the results seem to border the miraculous.

Changing body heights and peering through solid walls, as described in the Success Book, is only part of it. Scientologists in the lower echelons have assured me that Operating Thetans can read other people's minds, shift heavy objects without touching them and actually materialize things by simply imagining them.

If this is the case, then the world is richer by thousands of superpowered citizens, for the toal number of OTs has reached the five-figure mark.

I only met three of them myself, two men and one woman. All three were handsome, poised and pleasantly outgoing people, but the only special feature I noted was that the lady was suffering from a bad attack of laryngitis. I don't know whether any of them read my mind.

For the past four years the OTs have had competition from another elite group of scientology. This is the Sea Org, the Church's private navy, now comprising seven small ocean craft divided into Pacific, Atlantic and Mediterranean flotillas.

The task facing Sea Org is greater than any fleet has ever tackled: to help "Ron" in his purpose line "of clearing this Universe for the next billion years." Which is the reason why Sea Organization contracts run (according to Clause 6 of the form) for 1 Billion Years.

Recruiting is done with an unusual accent on selectivity. One pamphlet states: "If almost any person in the Sea Organization were to appear in a Scientology group or Organization he would be lionized, red-carpeted and Very-Important-Personed beyond belief. For the Sea Organization is composed of the 'aristocracy' of Scientology."

This is no idle promise. Sea Org members wear stylized naval uniforms with gold lanyards and certainly cause ripples at Church gatherings. At the Los Angeles center I watched three girls hurl themselves upon one of these aristocrats and bear him off to the nearest armchair, where they kept him surrounded, busy and immobilized for the rest of the evening.

Originally only Class VI Clears were eligible to join the Sea Org. But—like most scientology rules—this has been altered. Now any graduate of Standard Dianetics can enlist—providing he doesn't mind committing himself for the next billion years.

The prestige of the Sea Org derives largely from the fact that they work "directly under Ron." For currently the Church's founding father has no permanent land abode but sails the seas (mostly the warm Mediterranean) on board a converted four-thousand-ton passenger ferry that acts as scientology's flagship.

This was the result of another of those amazing shifts that have punctuated the career of L. Ron Hubbard.

In 1959 Mr. and Mrs. Hubbard left Washington and moved to England. There Hubbard bought a superb country mansion,

Saint Hill Manor, at East Grinstead in the green hills of Sussex, thirty miles from London.

Saint Hill became the Church's international headquarters, the advanced training college for scientologists as well as the stately home of the Hubbards. Flocks of students—mainly from America—streamed to the eighteenth-century mansion, some of their activity spilling over into the little town of East Grinstead.

It was this, apparently, that got the Church into trouble with the British government. As one of the locals related to me over a glass of lukewarm English beer:

"Well, you see, they started buying up property right and left. Bought a hotel and a couple of shops and about twenty houses. Well, that's all right as far as it goes, only they started throwing their weight about after that.

"How? Well, some of the people around here didn't go for this here scientology lark, and they didn't mind saying so. Next thing we know that crowd puts up an order declaring a whole list of shops 'off limits'—including this pub we're in now. *Off limits*, I tell you, just like they was some kind of bloomin' army and we were an occupied town! Bloody cheek, I calls it. . . ."

As a response to bitter complaints from East Grinstead the local Member of Parliament demanded a full-scale investigation of the Church in the House of Commons.

The government hesitated for several years, but in 1968 the Ministry of Health took fairly drastic action. The College of Scientology and all other scientology establishments were deprived of their status as educational bodies. Foreign nationals would no longer be able to come to—or remain in—England for the purpose of studying or teaching scientology.

The ministerial dictum (brought down on very little concrete evidence) affected Hubbard's own residence in Britain. He and his wife became seafaring rovers in the Mediterranean, touching United States ports only at rare intervals.

British scientologists were not hit by the ban, and Saint Hill continues to flourish as worldwide headquarters of the Church.

But it is doubtful whether the aggrieved East Grinsteaders had much to do with the government's action. The real cause probably lay in scientology's almost paranoid attacks upon its enemies.

Both the AMA and its British counterpart, the BMA, have indeed been highly critical of the Church, and a number of psychiatrists did warn their patients against contact with scientology. Hubbard's responses, however, were delivered in tones not heard since the days of Dr. Goebbels.

The Church's newspaper, *Freedom-Scientology* (Edition No. 3), ran an article in which he declared, in his own inimitable style:

"So psychiatric activities consist of Political Treatment. That is very certain now. This was the deadly secret we in Scientology might have found out and which made them terrified of us, ridicule us, fight us and spend over $2 million to try unsuccessfully to get rid of us.

"Over the world they were running Death Camps.

"A few times they missed and certain political actions came to light—Ezra Pound the poet, Governor Long of Louisiana, General Walker of Little Rock, managed to become known about before they were de-personalized.

"So be mystified no longer. We weren't up against any mental treatment—only violent brutality known as political treatment.

"So that's what we ought to brand it.

"These dumb birds were trying to form a total police state, but the police hate them and the army deserts at every chance. How do you form a police state with the police and army on the side of the population?

"That's not their only mistake. Their biggest one was attacking us.

"The Commies would have won in the end. Revolution is not far off if political treatment is allowed to continue. Some of the 'very best people' are involved.

"If we can expose and eradicate this bestial tendency in Western government before it is too late, the society will not fall into the chaos desired for a Communist take-over. It's our one chance. Expose them fully and fast."

Various issues of the same publication ran cartoons showing British Members of Parliament groveling on their knees before whip-swinging devils dressed in doctors' smocks; a shrouded skeleton figure with a scythe labeled "Psychiatry" mounted on a rhinoceros trampling "Human Rights" under its hooves; and the same figure, standing before a pile of bleeding corpses tagged "Germany," "Russia," "Poland," and "Austria," beckoning to three waiting men marked as "The Western World." The caption beneath read: "Next."

The English are somewhat more sensitive to abuse than Americans, and reacted accordingly. In the United States nobody batted an eyelid when Hubbard wrote:

"Every time we have investigated the background of a critic of Scientology, we have found crimes for which that person or group could be imprisoned under existing law.

"We do not find critics of Scientology who do not have criminal pasts."

Together with such virulence, however, goes a mimosa-like sensitivity on the part of the Church. Every criticism—no matter how restrained—is answered by concerted screams of "religious persecution" and a broadside of libel writs, accompanied by a barrage of invective and character assassination that would do credit to *Pravda*. Scientology's idea of religious freedom, apparently, is that it entitles the Church to belabor opponents with a sledge hammer while itself remaining shielded against any retaliation.

Coupled with this outlook on top is a positive mania for security within the Church. Until quite recently scientologists were subjected to controls reminiscent of Orwell's 1984. They were applied by a special "Ethics" department, which played the role of the Thought Police.

At every stage members had to undergo routine security checks—given with the E-Meter—which, they were told, could detect guilt. The object was to weed out doubters as well as infiltrating reporters. But this was merely a secondary function for Ethics.

Their main task consisted of tracking down and punishing infringements of Church policy. There were a great many of those, classified by Hubbard into Misdemeanors, Crimes, and High Crimes. In the minor brackets penalties ranged from suspension of pay or the enforced wearing of a black mark to day and night confinement on Org premises.

But for High Crimes (Hubbard called them "Suppressive Acts") punishment was grim. The offender was labeled *enemy* and proclaimed "fair game." Which meant that he "may be deprived of property or injured by any means by any Scientologist without any discipline of the Scientologist. May be tricked, sued, or lied to, or destroyed."

Considering the confidential data the organization has on all its members through auditing, this could have catastrophic consequences for the offender.

Not only members, but outsiders as well—husbands, wives or families—could be branded "suppressives" if their influence was considered contrary to Church interests.

The member involved was then ordered to "disconnect" from them—totally and immediately—or face a "suppressive" label himself. The results of this were not only torn friendships and business associations but frequently broken homes. Unless, of course, the outsiders concerned changed their views and joined the Church.

Most of the above, however, belongs to the past. Late in 1968 some of the harsher Ethics measures were canceled by policy order. This included confessional security checks, "fair game" proclamations and "disconnections." The milder penalties are still in force.

Still in force, too, are the rumors. Malevolent rumors of ex-members suddenly dying after breaking with the Church, going insane, or being crippled in accidents. Rumors of beatings and kidnapings perpetrated by "persons unknown," of "suppressives" kept imprisoned in secret hideouts.

I have not been able to substantiate a single one of these tales —and neither has anybody else. But they circulate so persistently that I rather suspect they were set in motion by the scientologists themselves, *pour encourager les autres.*

Whatever their origin, there is no doubt about their effectiveness. Of the half-dozen scientology dropouts ("squirrels" in Church parlance) I interviewed, every one implored me not to mention his or her name. No concrete reasons, just vague qualms . . . "You never know what might happen."

It is this peculiar brand of discipline that has earned the Church the sobriquet Fascist—usually from critics who are blissfully unaware of the nature of Fascism.

In truth, scientology displays none of the salient Fascist characteristics: racism, nationalism and militarism. Negroes, Jews and Latinos are well represented in the membership, and I never heard of a single instance of discrimination against any of them.

The Church *is* authoritarian; insofar as all power flows from above, while the rank and file have no influence on policy. But the same applies to the majority of business firms, not to mention most of the nation's newspapers.

The autocratic nature of the organization remained intact even though Hubbard officially resigned from it in 1967. To all practical purposes his withdrawal made no difference whatever. He is still the founding father, still wields unchallenged authority, and the steady stream of his orders and proclamations over HCO flows on as before.

At the movement's Los Angeles Celebrity Centre stands an ornately elegant settee more or less permanently unused. It bears a card, "Reserved For L. Ron And Mary Sue Hubbard." As far as anyone could tell me, no lesser derrière has ever touched it.

Most members, however, take such details in their stride. For scientology gives them what the outer world does not offer, and which they crave. A secretive, nestlike warmth, complete with a private code language; instant and demonstrative approval; and a distinct and attainable purpose in life.

At the moment of joining their lone "I" is transformed into a mighty "WE," their anxieties and handicaps reduced to soluble problems of soul engineering, their social limitations overcome by general acceptance, offered simply because they *are* members. Scientology has no wallflowers.

Nor does it have sex discrimination. Women rise as fast as men in the movement and wield equal authority. Promotion and rewards come rapidly; at twenty-five a member can be among the top executives of an org. It is an essential tenet of Hubbard's creed that the "Up Statistics person" (his term for an achiever) should be encouraged by every financial and psychological means.

This accounts for the Church's pronounced egalitarianism, which ignores status acquired outside the fold. The high school dropout may rank higher than the college major if he sells more literature or enrolls more students.

And to all disciples Hubbard extends a message that acts like balm on bruised psyches: you are *not* a fleeting speck in the cosmos, you are immortal and perfectable, you *count!* No matter how flawed your present being may be, you can—through your efforts—attain heights undreamed of by most humans. You are mankind's spearhead thrusting into the realm of the gods!

Scientology's inherent tensions lie well below the surface. They are quite undetectable in the blandly serene youngsters who answer every question with stereotypes and invariably reward your inquiry with uniform "Very goods" and "Thank yous."

But occasionally some grit gets into the machine.

I had made an appointment at the Church's Los Angeles headquarters, also called Saint Hill, after the English original. The dispenser of information there, I was told, was one Michael Brisnehan.

Mr. Brisnehan turned out to be a friendly and relaxed young man, with a drooping Mexican-style mustache that made him look like Zapata's kid brother.

He talked readily, but since he had only been in scientology for nine months his knowledge of past developments was sketchy.

In the midst of our conversation I felt a tap on my shoulder. Behind me stood a little round lady, wearing glasses and a curiously fixed expression. "There has been a mistake," she said. "Please follow me to the office."

I did. The lady glanced at a slip of paper. "The person you must see is Mr. Gordon Mustain. He will see you at two o'clock."

"Well, I have to get my car checked this afternoon. I'd rather—"

"Thank you. Mr. Mustain will see you at two o'clock."

"But, look, I promised the man at the garage—"

"Very good. Mr. Mustain will see you at two o'clock. Thank you."

Mr. Mustain saw me at two o'clock.

Gordon B. Mustain, Deputy Guardian for Public Relations, had a quick smile and an apology for the mixup. He was an impressive personality, sharp-featured, handsome and completely at ease, yet with an athletic spring in his movements. His eyes were alert and cordial and never left mine.

He didn't address me by my first name, as most scientologists are apt to do, and always referred to "Mr. Hubbard" instead of the customary "Ron." His whole attitude implied that here was one knowledgeable adult speaking to another.

Hubbard's claims of having visited Venus and Heaven? "Well, they needn't be taken—er, literally," he explained gently. "You could look at them as—shall we say allegories."

And those Ethics measures of fair game and security checks and disconnections?

Mustain smiled disarmingly. "Much of this has been misunderstood by outsiders. These measures were necessary while we were under attack. We had to defend ourselves, you'll understand that. Anyway, as you know, they've been discontinued. Things have changed."

"Well, maybe," I ventured. "But some scientologists I've talked to—"

"Excuse me," he interrupted. "Did you interview other people before me? Where?"

"Here. On the East Coast. In Chicago. All over the place."

"How many?" His smile had disappeared without trace.

"Oh, ten—fifteen. Quite a lot."

"Could you give me their names?" he asked tensely.

"Not offhand," I said. "There were too many. I'd have to look up my notes."

"Then please make out a list for me. All the people you talked to and where." He sounded urgent. "Also when these interviews took place." He added, "This is very important."

I left then. And I knew that I wasn't going to give Mr. Mustain any names.

Downstairs young people were thronging around the information counter, leafing through books and pamphlets, raptly gazing at posters urging them to CROSS THE BRIDGE TO TOTAL FREEDOM . . .

V

THE HERITAGE
OF EDGAR CAYCE

OF ALL the strange personalities who ever bestrode the metaphysical scene, the most bewilderingly implausible was Edgar
Cayce. Even after a dozen books and millions of words of
magazine copy about him, the man still defies explanation as well
as classification.

He was a healer who performed the vast majority of his cures
on patients he had never met. He was a psychic so deeply disturbed
by his gift that he often prayed to be rid of it. And he was a
prophet who found himself forced to rely on other people to tell
him what it was he had predicted (see Figure 15).

Perhaps the most astonishing item about Cayce is that he
reached his current near-legendary fame only after his death.
Among artists and composers this may be fairly customary. But

in America's occult world—geared, as it is, to personal charisma —this constitutes a singular achievement.

Ask any given group of people today what they know of Evangeline Adams or Cheiro—both giants in their time—and chances are they won't be sure whether you are talking about movie stars or cocktail mixtures. Mention Edgar Cayce and at least half of them will show instant recognition, "Oh, yes—the 'Sleeping Prophet.'"

A quarter-century after his passing, Cayce's heritage virtually dominates supernaturalism in this country. Yet his heirs are so averse to picturing him as the traditional prophet figure that one of them admitted recently, "We have made a cult out of *not* being a cult."

The movement that has formed around this legacy could be compared to the concentric growth rings of a tree. The inner core is the Edgar Cayce Foundation. Then comes the closely connected Association for Research and Enlightenment (ARE), with a current membership of thirteen thousand. Around this have developed some eight hundred very loosely affiliated study units known—ineptly—as "Search for God" groups. They number between three and thirty people each and are scattered throughout the United States, Britain, Canada and Australia.

But all this doesn't begin to describe the extent to which Cayce permeates America's metaphysics. His name crops up everywhere and constantly; often in connection with projects that would have made him shudder. His teachings—or what passes for them—are utilized in enterprises ranging from attempts at rediscovering Atlantis to retailing copper bracelets to arthritis victims.

It would be illogical to attribute this to the fact that his biography, *The Sleeping Prophet*, made the best-seller list of 1967. Books on van Gogh and Ernest Hemingway have sold equally well without resulting in a comparable surge of public interest.

Cayce, it seems, struck a chord in America's mind that no other mystic has sounded. Or rather he spanned an entire octave, harmonizing purely physical relief from suffering with the farthest reaches of occult cerebration.

Edgar Cayce (pronounced Kay-see) was born in 1877 near

Hopkinsville, Kentucky, as the son of barely literate farming parents. He dropped out of school at the ninth grade and throughout his career his letters remained uniformly ungrammatical and mispunctuated.

He was a thin, stoop-shouldered man with mild blue-gray eyes behind rimless spectacles, and a receding chin. No psychic in history ever had a less dramatic exterior.

But at twenty-four, Cayce discovered that he possessed—or was possessed by—a totally inexplicable gift. He could, while asleep, diagnose the ailments of people and prescribe remedies for them. People he had never laid eyes on.

The procedure he adopted soon became a standard ritual. He would stretch out on his study couch in his shirt sleeves and very quickly fall into self-induced slumber. His wife then gave him the name and address of a particular "patient," most of whom had communicated only by mail.

Cayce opened each sleep diagnosis with the words: "Yes, we see the body." Then followed a detailed rundown of the person's state of health and an equally detailed cure for the ailment involved.

Few of the suggested remedies were within the realm of orthodox medicine; but then neither was Cayce. He prescribed exercises of the Yoga type, special diets, electrical treatments, massages, poultices, herbs, tonics and endless varieties of medicinal mixtures nobody had heard of before. He prescribed inhalations of old brandy for tuberculosis, "peach-tree poultices" for convulsions, castor oil packs for epileptic fits, "oil of smoke" for leg sores and "bedbug juice" for dropsy. Very frequently he ordered spinal manipulations to be given by an osteopath. Very rarely he recommended surgery.

After the first few years there was always someone in the room to take a stenographic recording of Cayce's words. These sessions became known as "readings"—and Cayce could take readings on himself as well as others.

But on awakening he always professed utter ignorance of whatever he had said. His own statements had to be read back to him—often to his amazed astonishment.

Thousands of people were—or believed themselves to be—cured by the sleeping visionary. The percentage of his successes is still being furiously debated. Some, like his biographer Jess Stearn, credit Cayce with a batting average close to 100 percent—ascribing failures to patients not completing their treatment or switching physicians. Others maintain that he was effective about half the time and also point out that a great many of his healings were actually performed by the osteopaths he had directed patients to.

But from the observer's viewpoint it doesn't greatly matter whether Cayce cured a hundred or ten thousand patients. The paranatural mystery lies in his method.

Cayce worked for a time as a bookseller and could no doubt have read a great many medical texts. Yet in his sleeping state his descriptions of the human anatomy and its problems were so extensive and his terminology so concise that they would have required at least a couple of terms in medical school. And even if he had somehow, somewhere, taken a secret study course, it should still have been necessary for him to at least see the patient before making a diagnosis.

Besides, no medical tome extant contained the kind of remedial concoctions Cayce prescribed, with—in many cases—wonderful results.

As the readings went on, however, they reached further and further afield; acquiring a theme of mysticism that had nothing to do with the physical facts of healing.

Cayce augurized on future events, he gave "life readings" that delved into past incarnations—his own and those of others—he described the vanished continent of Atlantis, interpreted dreams, answered questions about the human aura, discussed astrology and Karma, and elaborated on techniques of dowsing.

He touched on virtually every aspect of occult thought, compiling the most universal record on the subject ever produced in one lifetime.

From the strict Christian fundamentalist beliefs of his youth, Cayce seemed to have veered into a Christianized version of several ancient Oriental mystery religions, combined with a form of spiritualism that was all his own. From this grew what can only be called the Cayce Creed—although his present heirs rather dislike the term.

Parts of this creed, however, are so amorphous, couched in

such convoluted language, that they are open to any degree of misinterpretation. And this is where their danger lies.

Cayce, who was modesty personified, never claimed infallibility, or anything approaching it. His own reaction on hearing his pronouncements read back to him after awakening was usually: "Well, I wonder where that came from, and if there's anything to it?"

But a great many of his disciples—avid for a dogma crutch to support their spirits—now insist on turning him into God's mouthpiece. What Cayce produced as thoughts and surmises, they take as decrees. What were vague, nebulously worded probes into the future, they mold and twist into concrete prognostications. And if later events don't happen to bear them out, they quite happily alter facts until they appear to.

Cayce was often and unequivocally wrong in his prophecies, especially when dealing with developments beyond his American horizon.

In 1943 he predicted that China would lean toward the Christian faith "in the next twenty-five years." Toward the end of World War II he warned that neither a defeated Germany nor Japan would prove co-operative with the victors after the peace. On the other hand he divined that the hope of the world would come from a de-Communized Russia. To which he added: "By what will Russia be guided? By friendship with that nation which hath even placed on its monetary unit 'In God We Trust.'"

All these prophecies show that Cayce let himself be influenced by the editorial opinions of the small-town newspapers he read almost as thoroughly as the Bible. The above forecasts were exactly what the more upbeat and less analytical journals were then handing their public.

This may also account for the fact that he foresaw the discovery of a death ray—or "super cosmic ray"—by 1958. The Hearst Press Sunday supplements had been predicting and illustrating such a weapon for a good twenty years.

In other respects, too, the Sleeping Prophet proved vulnerable to the foibles of his background. He once informed an elderly lady invalid that she had delayed marriage until she was thirty-nine because of her "secret sin"—his term for masturbation. The lady confessed to it and duly convinced herself that this was indeed the cause of her delayed wedlock. If masturbation were responsible for prolonging spinsterhood we would have very few marriages in the under-forty group.

As might be expected, the medical establishment either ignored or attacked Cayce. Nor did he impress the more scientific psychic observers.

He produced a medical reading for the small daughter of Dr. J. B. Rhine, head of the famed parapsychology laboratory at Duke University and originator of the term ESP. It turned out to be a misdiagnosis and elicited some scathing comments from the world's leading parapsychologist. Later—and perhaps in consequence—Cayce withdrew from a controlled test arranged by one of Rhine's associates.

But nobody who met Cayce, not even Harvard's skeptical investigator Hugo Munsterberg, doubted his personal integrity. However they judged his gifts, they found the man unpretentiously honest.

Cayce could have made several fortunes during his career, but his business methods were such that he died a very long way from wealthy. It was almost a miracle that he didn't go bankrupt every year. His normal fee was twenty dollars a reading, but he insisted on treating poor patients free of charge. When some people complained that his recommendations hadn't helped them, he wrote long and apologetic letters and returned their money. This despite the fact that his trances exhausted him and he had to restrict his readings to preserve his strength.

Cayce died in January 1945 at his home in Virginia Beach. He had founded the ARE fourteen years earlier, but at the time of his death it had less than seven hundred members.

"It was a pretty dismal picture," remembered his son, Hugh Lynn, who took over the organization on returning from war service. "All we had, really, was our home to serve as headquarters and a colossal pile of my father's transcribed readings.

"They were stuffed all over the place. In one stack I found a nest of mice." He chuckled. "They must have been the most psychic mice on record."

Hugh Lynn was faced with the problem of what to do with this mountain of transcripts. He decided to have a few of them

printed, mainly in the hope of finding out what had become of
the patients for whom they were given (see Figure 16).

The response was startling. People wrote in from every part
of the country testifying for the results of the prophet's pre-
scriptions. One of the most encouraging reports told the aftermath
of a medical reading Cayce had done for a local girl aged three.
The child had scalded herself hideously with a pot of boiling
water and her parents were afraid she would be scarred for life.
Cayce recommended rubbings with a particular blend of various
oils—which has since become known as his Scar Tissue Lotion.
The girl not only healed perfectly, but had recently been elected
Miss Virginia Beach.

The upshot of this was that the ARE undertook the
herculean task of sorting, filing, indexing and duplicating the
15,000 or so accumulated transcripts—14 million words on
90,000 typewritten pages!

Gladys Turner, the prophet's secretary since 1923, had faithfully recorded every word of his readings. But she hadn't divided
them into subjects or headings. They were traceable only through
the case numbers.

Miss Turner and an assistant set about breaking down the
collection of readings into 8,976 Physical, 2,500 Life, 799 Business, 677 Dream Interpretations, 401 Spiritual, 24 Home and
Marriage, and 879 Miscellaneous. The process was only completed in 1970. It made for a library of 333 volumes and over
200,000 index cards.

This library is the dynamo that generates the power of the
Cayce movement today. It is the source for the 50,000 pieces of
literature turned out every month by the ARE Press. It provides
the themes for Hugh Lynn Cayce's lectures. It attracts hundreds
of independent researchers who are fascinated by what one
parapsychologist called "that great white whale in the psychic
field." And it supplies the inspiration for the outside study groups
now forming at an average rate of five a week.

Home of the library and headquarters of the ARE is the old
Cayce Hospital in Virginia Beach, Virginia, which the prophet
lost during the Depression and his heirs purchased back (see
Figure 17).

Virginia Beach, allegedly "The World's Largest Resort," has the nondescript and decidedly forgettable appearance of so many beach towns that have outgrown their natural attractions without adding enough artificial ones. But the old hospital, set on a lawn hill, is a cool, white and rambling three-story structure whose charm is not even spoiled by the concrete press building next door.

Hugh Lynn Cayce, ARE managing director, has a simple office upstairs. Rosy-cheeked and white-haired, with twinkling blue eyes, a softly precise voice and easy sense of humor, he looks the epitomized small-town family doctor. Actually he majored in psychology at Virginia's Washington and Lee University.

He obviously adored his father, though he recalled that being the son of a psychic had certain drawbacks.

"When I was eleven we were living in Alabama," he told me. "Dad had forbidden me to swim in the Alabama River— it was dangerous there. But it was also awfully tempting. So one spring afternoon I went along for a swim with a lot of other kids— way upstream, where we wouldn't be watched.

"But when I got home my father told me exactly what I'd done—the names of all the other boys—also that one of them had cut his foot on a piece of glass. It was that last bit that really got to me. I knew then that I had a dad who couldn't be lied to. And for a boy my age that was . . . well, pretty terrible."

Did he try and interpret his father's writings?

"Of course, I'm bound to. People ask me what I think about them and I tell them. But"—his voice became very firm— "I always add that this is merely *my* idea, not some kind of gospel.

"What we really want is for people to test the readings, try them out. Not just be inspired by them. That's why we call in specialists to go over the various subjects."

He thumbed at the library downstairs. "For instance, we've had psychologists look into what Edgar Cayce had to say about dreams. When we come to the medical readings, I try to get MDs. On schizophrenia, psychiatrists. And so on. And what they get out of them is entirely their business. Because, you see, we are a study group—not a religious cult."

Hugh Lynn is certainly anything but a cultist leader. He

entirely lacks the blinkered single-mindedness essential for that role. He smiles when you ask him about his religious beliefs. "I guess you could call me a Confused Presbyterian."

The ARE staff now includes Herbert Puryear, Ph.D., a former assistant professor of psychology at Trinity University, Texas, who conducts research into the Cayce readings in a thoroughly orthodox, professional manner.

One of Hugh Lynn's main concerns is to keep his father's work from being tarred with the spiritualist brush. "Edgar Cayce was not a spiritualist," he insists. "He had no 'guides' or 'controls' and we never noticed any change of voice during his trances. I think I must have attended more séances than I have hairs on my head, and I never found any similarity between them and my father's readings."

Yet, regardless of his views, the ARE does have spiritualist overtones. This tendency comes from the lower ranks rather than the leadership, but it flavors the atmosphere. And Hugh Lynn admits that he has been collecting reports of "communications" from his late father. "Not very successfully so far," he added.

"Do you have certain signs by which you could recognize genuine contact?" I asked him.

He nodded. "Yes. We set up some signals, so to speak, before his death. Most of them are secret, of course, but I will tell you about one. This has already been—revealed."

He sat quietly for a moment. When he spoke again his voice dropped so low that I had to bend forward to catch his words.

"My mother was given what is called a 'life seal' in one of her readings by my father.

"It had symbols in it; among them two red roses—they were supposed to stand for me and my brother. Now, she died shortly after my father. And a little later a woman friend of hers had a dream. In that dream my mother had appeared and she said, 'Tell Hugh Lynn from me—tell him when I communicate with him I will give him two red roses.'"

He gazed out of the window before he went on: "Years passed. I had put this out of my mind, more or less. And then one day a man called on me. He asked me to talk to his wife on the telephone. She was a very troubled woman—in fact, she'd been in a mental institution. She kept on hearing voices. Terrible voices.

"Well, this woman talked to me and she told me about those voices—they were deviling the life out of her. It was a kind of chaotic nightmare gabble: strings of obscenities—the filthiest stuff I've ever heard—then some snatches of poetry—some prophecies —and more obscenities, more filth. It just went on and on in her head, and she related it to me as she heard it.

"And then—all of a sudden—she stopped. And she said, 'Mr. Cayce, your mother says . . . to give you . . . two red roses. . . .'"

Just across the road from ARE headquarters lies the motel in which nearly all visitors to the Cayce Foundation stay. For most of them "visitors" is the wrong word. They are pilgrims—and as far as they are concerned the white ex-hospital is a shrine. Their object is not so much study as inspiration. Their aim not an expansion of knowledge but a panacea for all their worldly ills.

As author-playwright Noel Langley put it: "Many people come here feeling this is the pool of Bethesda, and that if they read a reading, take out a membership, or for all I know set foot in the building, the angel will come down and settle the troubled waters and all will be well."

This deification of his father's work is precisely what Hugh Lynn Cayce is trying to avoid. But my impression was that he is entirely too kind and mild-mannered to put a stop to it. It would mean squelching too many fragile egos.

Over breakfast at the motel a lady with an agitated Adam's apple and vibrato voice held forth about auras: "All disease symptoms are plainly visible in the coloring of your aura. Only to those who can see auras, naturally. And that's why"—she poured milk over her Rice Krispies—"that's why Edgar Cayce taught us only to consult those doctors who are capable of seeing auras."

"Excuse me," I interjected. "Where did he state that?"

She looked at me in astonishment. "Why, in his reading on the human aura, of course! We've all seen it."

The six people along our table nodded in chorus. They had all seen it.

Later that morning I went to the library and checked the reading in question—Vol. XI, No. 1. It said nothing of the kind.

But just as certain people can read anything they fancy into and out of the Bible, so do others extract whatever they wish from Cayce's readings. Even if it happens not to be there.

This tendency has reached epidemic proportions among the hundreds of "Search for God" groups. They can be launched by anyone at all, and they function with only the barest minimum of supervision from the ARE.

I attended one held in the home of a New York business woman. It began with a free-style prayer and a brief dip into a Cayce reading on reincarnation. Discussion was to follow.

Instead an elderly male medium in the group performed a single-handed *coup d'etat* and seized the soapbox. He talked for two uninterrupted hours, during which I grew acutely aware of every spring in the settee beneath me. He talked about *his* interpretation of the reading and halfway through any connection with Cayce became purely coincidental. Among other things he had discovered that most cases of cancer were caused by "nests of dead souls" in the body.

Afterwards I quizzed the other members of the group. All but one were convinced that the mediumistic gentleman had quoted Cayce with exactitude. The solo exception consisted of an architectural student who had gone to sleep.

I watched variations of the same scene in several other group meetings. In each instance the gathering was taken over by some high-powered and numbingly loquacious crank who utilized the Cayce tag merely to project pet bees from his or her own bonnet.

The Cayce legend also helps in a purely commercial field. Currently millions of ornamental copper bracelets are being unloaded on the public on the strength of a totally fictitious rumor that the late prophet recommended them against arthritis. Nobody knows how or when the rumor started, but those copper bands are going at prices ranging from $3 to $100, depending on whether you buy them from an occult corner store or Cartier. And with copper selling at 61 cents a pound wholesale, it leaves a peachy profit margin for both.

Do they work? According to a rheumatologist: "About as well as a dirty sock worn around the wrist."

But the Arthritis Foundation has a more illuminating simile: In a study conducted at a Cook County Clinic, Illinois, a number of arthritis sufferers were given a plain sugar pill.

Fifty percent of them claimed they felt "definite improvement." Those who failed to respond to the sugar pill were given injections of salt water. And 30 percent of that group "improved."

That dirty sock could, conceivably, have had the same effect.

VI
A CREED
CALLED ECKANKAR

IF THE SANCTIFICATION of Edgar Cayce is under way, that of Paul Twitchell may be said to be nearing completion. The significant difference lies in the fact that Cayce is dead and Twitchell very much alive.

The legendry and lore spun around him goes considerably beyond the mere walking-on-water stage. According to a typewritten article sent to me by the secretary of his organization, there is a "raging controversy" going on as to whether or not Mr. Twitchell has replaced the "eminent figures of religion, Buddha, Christ, Moses, St. Paul of Christian fame and Mohammed."

The article, written by one James Walker, also has it:

—That Twitchell casts no shadow when he walks in the sun and many times no footprints.

—That the gigantic meteor which exploded in Siberia in 1908 was in reality not a meteor but Paul Twitchell's temper.

—That his powers caused the electricity failure in New York City and parts of the East Coast in 1965.

—That a few years ago, after a Catholic priest annoyed him in Seattle, Washington, he informed the priest that from that day on the Church would no longer be a power in the world. "Then strangely it began to collapse."

In the November 1968 issue of *Search* magazine another writer, Charles Daniel, declared that Twitchell was actually the product of an immaculate conception.

"The miraculous birth took place just below the city of Natchez, Mississippi, near a stock farm, only a few years after the original thirteen colonies had become a nation. At the time of his birth a great earthquake shook the Mississippi valley, forming a vast body of lakes in western Tennessee."

To quote a third author, Charles Walters, Twitchell received a telegram on May 11, 1965, asking him to aid a woman dying of cancer in Bristol, England. He was then attending a conference in California.

"Twitchell bilocated—his soul immediately leaving his body and making the trip to England faster than any jet plane could ever hope to go.

"When he materialized, Twitchell was standing beside the bed of Claudia Rhinemann.

"He recognized the angel of death which had entered the woman's body.

"Gently, Paul Twitchell placed his hand on the woman's pale forehead.

"With his other hand he reached toward heaven—and God took his hand.

"God sent his spirit and holy spark through Twitchell and into the dying woman's pain wracked frame.

"The angel of death was forced from the woman's frail shell of a body.

"Twitchell had done what he was asked to do—Help."

This report, which appeared in the periodical *Candid Press*, was followed by a direct statement from Mr. Twitchell, offering some additional details:

"I have been blessed with the ability to see all—know all—help all. I must use this ability and power to help as many people as I can.

"I myself have no real power, but I am an instrument of the Lord. He has chosen me to do His work on earth and in the worlds of this universe.

"I can only serve Him by serving you."

The main purpose of this remarkable reportage was to introduce Paul Twitchell's forthcoming readers' advice column in the journal. The column bore the modestly impressive title, TALK TO GOD.

All of the above material—plus several manila envelopes more—I received in response to an inquiry directed to his headquarters in Las Vegas, Nevada. It sounded sufficiently intriguing to warrant further research.

The first thing I discovered was the astonishing dichotomy of Twitchell's public image. Unlike, say, Jeane Dixon, L. Ron Hubbard or Edgar Cayce, he is an almost total cipher in non-occult circles and gets little coverage in the general press, radio and television. Not a single one of my numerous contacts in the communications field had even heard of him.

But within the metaphysical realm he looms large indeed. With an estimated 500,000 followers worldwide, fifteen centers in the United States and four overseas, and a weekly mailbag of some 10,000 letters, he ranks among America's most successful cult leaders (see Figure 18).

He is also one of the newest. His movement began—with three devotees—in 1965.

The creed's official name is ECK, Inc., derived from the word *Eckankar*; accent on the first syllable. As he explained to both Webster's Dictionary and myself, the word comes from the Tibetan Pali language and means "all-inclusiveness with God." It is, as he further pointed out, neither a religion nor a philosophy, but the direct path to God as revealed to Paul Twitchell.

But Eckankar's particular fascination lies in its practical formula for "soul travel." This is based on a very widespread human experience, somewhat akin to levitation dreams. Many people have had—at some stage between consciousness and sleep—the sensation of slipping out of their skins and moving elsewhere; *seeing* their physical frame lying inertly in bed.

Hundreds of patients, after emerging from anesthetics, recalled how their mind had floated off and actually watched the entire operation being performed on their bodies—usually with great compassion, but quite devoid of fear or pain. For those who remembered this phenomenon it seemed magically wonderful—a touch of pure spirit existence before returning to physical life.

Until recently psychologists have classed these out-of-body excursions simply as a form of half-dream, with no more significance than other types of semiconscious imagery. Now, however, at least some sleep specialists are probing at an entirely different concept. Could it be, they ask, that there exists a hitherto unexplored level of real consciousness—not a dream world, but an actual stratum of cerebral being in which time and space as we measure them have no meaning?

Eckankar not only confirms this, but takes it several giant steps further. It teaches that those dreamlike out-of-body trips are rudimentary beginnings of soul travel. With instruction and practice they can be repeated at will and in any desired direction.

More than that. After prolonged study and exercise sessions the journeys need no longer be confined to this earth. The soul—the immortal consciousness of man—can actually be sent wandering through infinity, it can "visit the realms which one will inhabit forever after leaving the physical body behind."

The essence of Eck, therefore, is the promise of excursions into the next world while still dwelling in this one.

The same basic theme can be found in a number of Eastern religions, and Twitchell lays no claim to being its originator. The difference lies in its application. Whereas Hinduism, Buddhism, and Sufism consider soul travel the prerogative of a small group of ascetics willing to mortify their flesh and forego worldly pleasures, Eckankar offers it to anyone capable of absorbing a study course. And without interfering with either their terrestrial work or enjoyment.

Soul travel is merely a part of the Eckankar creed, though

undoubtedly the most universally fascinating. But it cannot be separated from the rest of the framework, which concerns "expansion of consciousness" and "proper spiritual unfoldment."

The "chela" (student) has to go through three series of lessons, each consisting of twelve discourses sent to his home at the rate of one a month. Each series, therefore, takes about a year and costs sixty dollars. There is also an additional series of "Eck Satsang" discourses, at forty-two dollars a set, plus supplementary books such as an Eck dictionary, a *Diary of Spiritual Healing*, and a much sought-after *Spiritual Aid in Reducing Weight*.

The historical background of Eckankar is as nebulous as that of most mystery religions. For although it carries the subtitle "Secret Science of Soul Travel," its propagator is doing his level best to reveal the secret to the largest possible multitude.

Twitchell calls Eckankar the oldest religion in the world. It was, in his words, "imported here from Venus by an unknown race who are living in Agam Des, and whom we know as the Eshwar Khanewale, or simply as the God-Eaters." Agam Des, incidentally, is a "spiritual city" not listed on our maps. Few people have been there, because entry is by invitation only and confined to spirit bodies. Twitchell's own visit was arranged by his mentor, a Tibetan lama, reputedly five hundred years old, named Rebazar Tarzs—a curiously un-Tibetan name.

Twitchell's position in the Eckankar hierarchy is likewise a trifle unclear. He constantly refers to various masters and teachers whom he holds in great awe and who are obviously his superiors. Yet Eckankar brochures invariably call him the Mahanta—the present living Eck master—entrusted with the mission of spreading the message of the creed throughout the world.

Although much of this message is delivered with almost impenetrable obscurity (as befits a mystery creed) the instructions on soul travel are as clear as a calisthenics drill. They come in the form of six basic techniques, depending on where you wish to go and whether alone or accompanied by a master.

One of them involves lying flat on your back in a dimly lit room, staring—without blinking—at a colored disk placed between your eyebrows. Starting with five minutes, you increase the staring period by one minute every night until eight minutes are reached.

At this point you relax, cease staring, and merely gaze at the disk. Then, according to the instructions, "the environment will start fading away and in its place you will find an altogether different type of landscape, usually with someone like the higher Eck master giving an explanation of where he is and what is happening."

Others necessitate chanting the word *Sugmad* in two distinct syllables while simultaneously touching your feet with your fingertips. This has to be kept up (with rest periods in between) until the soul is projected into the upper worlds.

None of these mind trips require any kind of drug, though some are based on methods of self-hypnosis. And there is no doubt that the techniques given have enabled several thousand people to go "tripping" without swallowing LSD.

Their letters—vast files of them—are on evidence at Eck's Las Vegas headquarters, some of them written in almost ecstatic terms. Since I suffer from an inherent distrust of testimonial correspondence, I did some private checking, which more than confirmed the contents of the letters.

A lady filing clerk in Washington, D.C., told me that Eckankar had cured her of her panic terror of dentists. "I couldn't bear the Novocain injections—just the thought of the needle gave me the creeps. But now I simply project my soul out of my body beforehand, and I don't feel a thing. I'm somewhere else."

A middle-aged New York realtor claimed that Eck had saved him from alcoholism. "Instead of hitting the bottle I take soul trips," he confided. "I used to have suicidal tendencies, too. Now I wouldn't dream of doing away with myself."

A Miss Violet Halsey, who lives in North Carolina and gave me permission to mention her name, told me that Twitchell visited her several times a week when she chanted *Ma-han-ta* for five minutes or so in front of her mirror. "He suddenly stands beside me and talks to me," she said. "Oh, I know his body is somewhere else—but his spirit is right there in my room. It's just wonderful. Now I don't get to feeling so lonely anymore— who would, with someone like him to talk to?"

There were others who insisted that Twitchell's apparition had saved them in moments of dire peril, that he materialized at the bedside of sick relatives, and that a simple letter from

him had relieved one sufferer from maddening migraine headaches. A Philadelphia woman assured me that she finally passed
her driving test—at the fourth attempt—because the Mahanta
sat between her and the tester and whispered encouragement
in her ear.

By then I was getting extremely curious to meet the miracle
man in the flesh. It proved quite simple, despite the fact that
Twitchell keeps his home address a secret and his telephone
unlisted. I made the necessary arrangements through Helen Baird,
Eck's staff artist and general representative in Los Angeles.
Twitchell himself lives in San Diego, about 120 miles down
the coast. The movement's headquarters is in Las Vegas only
because of Nevada's low company taxes.

Miss Baird, a talkative, lively and energetic blonde, had
come to Eckankar via the White Brotherhood, Scientology, and
several other more or less occult creeds, none of which—she
explained—had given her fulfillment. Working for Eck not only
satisfied her spiritually but also kept her frantically busy; which
she obviously enjoyed.

The Twitchell homestead turned out to be an airy Californian prototype, replete with hi-fi gear, tape recorders, sofa
dolls and electric typewriters. On the walls shone rainbow-hued
seascapes of the kind sold in souvenir stores; all looking as if
they had been painted by computer.

Twitchell is small and bony, with graying hair, thin lips,
and bright blue eyes set deeply in their sockets. For a man
purportedly born just after the American Revolution he is remarkably well preserved. He doesn't, in fact, look a day over
fifty-five.

He speaks slowly and with a strong Southern drawl, pronouncing most of his "yous" as "yers." He has an unusual
habit of keeping his hands flat on the table before him as he
talks, moving them as if spreading the pieces of an invisible
jigsaw puzzle. Occasionally he illustrates his words by drawing
geometrical designs on a note pad he keeps beside him.

I had some difficulty pinning down his background. He
stated that he was born (his disciples say reincarnated) on a
Mississippi riverboat, but refused to give a date. Later he wrote
me a letter claiming that his real name was Peddar Zaskq, that

he never knew his actual parents and that Twitchell was merely the name of the family that fostered him.

On other points he was more forthcoming.

It seems that he learned basic out-of-body movement from an older half-sister before he could actually walk. Rebazar Tarzs, his Tibetan lama guide, first appeared to him aboard a U. S. Navy vessel in the Pacific in 1944, at a moment of extreme nervous tension while the ship was being tracked by a Japanese submarine.

After the war, Twitchell put in a stint as a free-lance writer for pulp magazines, "doing about five hundred dollars a month out of it. That was pretty good, but I tell you, I was really knocking maself crazy."

Following a brief visit to India, however, Rebazar Tarzs began to appear to him regularly, dictating a series of books which today form the literary basis of Eckankar.

"This Rebazar—is he a spirit?" I asked.

Twitchell shook his head. "No, he's not. He's a natural man like you and me. But he can make his appearance anyplace in the world."

"Supposing you pricked him with a needle—would he feel it?"

"Well, I've never tried that. I guess I'm too much in awe of him."

Twitchell gave his first public lecture in Long Beach, California, to an audience of three. Afterwards all three asked him for a study course, which he obligingly typed out for them. This was Eckankar's modest beginning in 1965.

For three years he ran the movement single-handed, producing books, tapes, records and discourses for a steadily swelling throng of disciples. Occasionally he received a boost from outsiders, such as one clergyman in Georgia, who read an Eckankar book and preached an entire sermon against it—thereby whetting the interest of his whole congregation.

Twitchell also lectured in Europe, talking in London, Copenhagen, Amsterdam and Zurich. Gradually he began to pick up representatives, who formed little Eck groups on both sides of the Atlantic.

"By 1968 we had so much business coming in that I had to get an office," he related. "I had to get CPAs, lawyers, everything.

I formed a corporation of this thing—Eckankar, Inc.—because they told me I could save on taxes."

What made people flock to his creed?

"That's a very strange thing." He drew a large circle on his note pad. "We've come to the point when we're a great deal like it was in Athens just before Percules [he meant Pericles] and the Golden Age went out. People had affluence, they had everything they wanted in life, you know. But they found out there was one thing in their life they didn't have." He paused. "They didn't have that very mysterious thing which stood back there and directed all of life. They didn't have the knowledge nor did they know how to make contact with it. So—they formed the mystery cults."

He shaded the circle. "And this thing is existing today in our world here. People now are finding the point that the mystery of life doesn't end with comfortable living, but that there's something beyond that. So out of curiosity they come in, and sometimes they get hooked on it, sometimes they don't. It's something—something they're looking for. And it's breaking the social structure, because this common denominator—or this thing called God—is making everybody equalized, see?"

I didn't, quite. "Then why don't these people turn to the already established religions?"

"Because," Twitchell said firmly, "they go to an established church and here is a man standing on a platform every Sunday and he gets into talking about the social issues of life, you see. And—well, man is interested in *mystery*."

Eckankar certainly offers enough arcanum to satisfy even the most ravenous demand. Twitchell's books on the subject are written with a certain poetic flair, but minus any structuring to speak of. Most of them deal with the author's excursions into the soul regions, which renders their geography somewhat hazy. To add to their opaqueness, he rarely reveals whether the exotic names he quotes belong to Homo sapiens, departed spirits or assorted Oriental demigods. This also precludes any attempt to check on his sources.

Twitchell works at tremendous pressure and with conveyor-belt speed. Sometimes he produces two manuscripts simultaneously, swinging between two electric typewriters without—apparently—getting his texts confused. When not on a lecture tour he rises at four in the morning, works till coffee at seven, then until lunch at midday. After an hour's nap he goes on working till midnight—seven days a week.

He eats very lightly: special purée-type soups and fruit; meat only rarely. He doesn't drink ("I never set foot in a bar") and has a positive abhorrence of smoking. His strongest aversion is against what he terms "carousers" of every shade.

"Ah suppose you could call me a moralist," he said, "because, frankly, I don't like this moral liberalism we're getting into. Man is a social animal and needs discipline. Not the looseness of morals championed by *Playboy*'s philosophy."

He blames moral laxity for most revolutions since the time of ancient Egypt and added the warning: "There are forces now trying to build the same looseness of morals in our society here that will bring about similar results."

Twitchell himself is married to a very wholesome-looking young woman named Gail, whom he met in the Seattle Public Library in 1963. He was then, according to his own count, going through twenty books per night—a reading speed possibly unmatched in the annals of human literacy.

His official biographer, Brad Steiger, had also mentioned security-shrouded meetings with various government officials. I asked Twitchell to give me an example. He obliged immediately:

"First time I was in England I had this call from George Brown's secretary. He was something like Secretary of State."

"He was the British Foreign Minister."

"Yeah—something like Secretary of State. He asked me questions about—like what did I think the future of their policy was. Like—they had a big debt to the Zurich bankers at the time. Did I see any future of this thing clearing up? And, I tell you, he had me on a spot. When people ask me questions like this—a man in that position—I can't say to him, 'Oh, everything is gonna be just fine, your Excellency.' I have to sort of lay it on the line. So I told him, with the banking situation, I said, 'I don't see how you're ever going to get out of this situation during your administration.'"

I thought it best to shelve further investigation into Mr. Twitchell's encounters with governmental figures.

There seem to be grave perils attached to being an Eck Mahanta. During our conversation, Twitchell referred to "people coming after me with guns." In his subsequent letter he was more explicit. He had, he explained, not been feeling too well at the time "because somebody tried to poison me in Madrid, Spain, and I barely escaped death."

"I never travel alone anymore," Twitchell wrote, "because some people disagree with my Doctrine quite bitterly. This seems to be the burden of anyone today who becomes a public figure!"

I asked the knowledgeable Miss Baird who these potential assassins might be.

"The same kind of people who killed JFK and Robert Kennedy," she said warmly. "Negative people. They see someone with a mission to help mankind and they want to destroy him. They just can't bear to see anyone doing so much good."

At the conclusion of our talk Paul Twitchell escorted me out into the white Californian sunshine. He cast a clearly discernible shadow. I can't vouch for footprints.

13. Lafayette Ronald Hubbard, founder of the Scientology movement, perhaps the most controversial creed of its kind.

14. Group meeting at the Church of Scientology in New York (PHOTO: CHURCH OF SCIENTOLOGY OF NEW YORK).

15. Edgar Cayce, the "Sleeping Prophet," an almost legendary figure in occult circles today.

16. Hugh Lynn Cayce, son of the prophet, who administers his father's heritage as head of the Association for Research and Enlightenment.

17. The old Cayce hospital in Virginia Beach, now headquarters of the Association for Research and Enlightenment and Mecca for thousands of student-pilgrims.

18. Paul Twitchell, head of Eckankar and currently America's foremost exponent of "soul travel," lecturing his disciples.

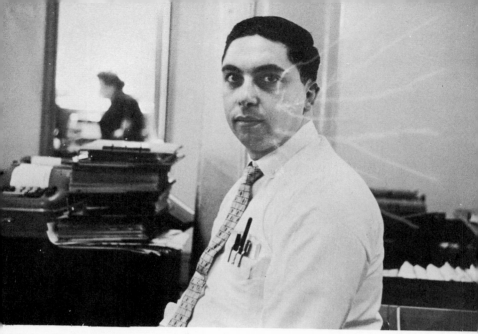

19. Irwyn Greif, Brooklyn reader of the "Great Akasha" by which he reveals his clients' past incarnations, often going back thousands of years.

20. Benn Lewis, a professional artist of Washington, D.C., who preaches "Soulcraft" and maintains that he is the Apostle John returned to earth.

21. Dr. Daniel W. Fry, one of the earliest saucer "contactees," who claimed to have taken a ride in an extraterrestrial vehicle back in 1950.

22. One of Gabriel Green's election leaflets. He was running for senator in California, allegedly on the advice of a four-foot-short man from the planet Alpha Centauri.

23. "P. K. Man" and wife. Ted Owens, who claims to be representative of "Space Intelligences" on earth, poses affectionately with Martha.

24. Global map showing supposed location of the sunken continent of Atlantis, a legendary land first mentioned by Plato.

VII

A PATTERN
OF PSYCHICS

THE ROUND-FACED young man with the full lips, blue eyes, and long blond sideburns smiled into the telephone receiver.

"What—he hasn't called you yet?" His voice sounded gently concerned. "Well, I think he's having trouble with that other woman. But don't worry, dear, you'll hear from him. Yes, I'm quite sure—I feel it." His smile became stronger. "All right, I'm absolutely certain. Let me know when he contacts you. And—keep faith. G'bye now."

He turned back to me with a little apologetic gesture. "Sorry about this. These calls . . . ! Now—where were we?"

We were in the midst of a much-interrupted interview with one of this country's most promising "sensitives." His name is Ron Warmoth, and he represents a new breed of psychics that is part of America's occult upsurge as well as her Affluent Society.

Their role is easier observed than described. They are, in a sense, private spiritual counselors, but elevated to a degree of intimacy and sophistication that makes them resemble metaphysical psychoanalysts. Except that their functions also include business guidance and occasional stabs at crime solving.

Ron Warmoth is typical of this group, though considerably more successful than most. His clientele reads like a register of those who have made it in the movies or are making it in society.

His mobility reflects that of his clients; a kind of four-way pendulum swing between New York, Florida, Hollywood and Palm Springs. Our conversation took place in his Manhattan studio, which has a shocking pink rug on the floor and a "trance painting" of Warmoth with his spirit masters on the wall.

His personal approach, however, is quite unmystical. You could call him a practical interpreter of human vibrations.

"I believe that people emit thought waves rather like radio waves—through the air—and that my brain is a particularly sensitive receiver," he explained. "I can tune in on them—and without trying very hard."

"Do you get precognition the same way?" I asked.

"Yes." He stroked his forehead. "Every individual casts his future before him like a shadow. It's a matter of cause and effect. So what I pick up from a person is like observing that shadow— seeing what has already been planted. That's why I never predict further than about six weeks ahead."

"And do you have to be near someone for that?"

"Not at all. I can pick it up from a voice on the telephone. Or from letters—I get about a thousand a week. But I don't analyze the handwriting—I get it from the feel of the letter itself. And it works even more indirectly than that—"

He paused for a delicate smile. "For instance, I have a client who's having an—er—illicit love affair. Now I'm able to pick up —through her—whatever the man involved is doing and where he is. And I can usually tell her what day he's going to call her."

Ron's psychic sessions are as casual as the sweaters he wears. No lighting effects or meditation and a minimum of props. He spreads a deck of Tarot cards but—as he admits—more for the client's benefit than his own.

"I let them shuffle the cards to put them at their ease. I found it has a relaxing effect. Personally, I don't need anything. I could be just as psychic in the middle of Grand Central Station. And they don't have to ask me questions. I tell *them* what it is they want to know."

"Such as?"

He chuckled. "Oh, I'm very blunt. If a man comes to me with marital troubles and I can feel what his wife is like, I'll say to him, 'Look, she's a bitch on wheels. Get rid of her!' And I'll tell him the approach to take—based on what I know *she* is going to do. I'll tell him where he should be careful. I'll say, 'Here is where she's going to get you on money,' and I'll tell him ways to prevent her from getting it—where to invest it and things like that."

Ron's practical touch has given him an enviable reputation in southern Californian racing circles. When the wife of a well-known —and highly illicit—bookmaker came to see him, he told her abruptly, "Go home, take your husband's money from its hiding place, and hide it somewhere else. He's going to be arrested today." She did—and he was. The bookie went to jail, but he saved his wad.

Bookmakers, however, aren't usually in his line. He caters chiefly to show-biz folks and their entourages, especially those resting cozily on past laurels.

It began with a reading for the former comic star Judy Canova. In her wake followed a comet's tail of celebrities, including Alice Faye, Hedy Lamarr, John Conte, Eddie Albert, and Sally Fields. This apart from society empresses like fashion designer Tiana Pittelle and millionairess Dorothy Fields.

Occasionally he gets celebrities of a different stripe. One of them was Jack Murphy, alias "Murph the Surf." Since Mr. Murphy is currently serving a life sentence for homicide, I had to take Ron's word for what happened between them:

"I told him he would be implicated in a murder he hadn't committed. I also told him to stay away from the Hilton Hotel." Warmoth shrugged. "Well, he didn't stay away from the Hilton —he was arrested there. And I still think he took the rap for a murder someone else did."

All of which is rather strange for a man who didn't want to be a psychic in the first place.

"Oh, I had psychic leanings, even as a child," he remembered. "But I wanted to go on the stage. So I studied acting, and later dancing under Katherine Dunham. But one season in summer stock convinced me that I wasn't cut out to be an actor. I had absolutely no ability."

Instead Ron began to spread the Tarot cards in various Hollywood coffeehouses. His clients were mainly hippies and his readings were always gratis. But his reputation for accuracy (he claims 90 percent) traveled by grapevine across that shadowy borderline that divides—and sometimes links—the movie capital's subworld with its top stratum.

In 1967 Judy Canova came to him for a session, and left deeply impressed. It was Ron's first professional sitting—insofar as he received a fee—and it marked the end of the gratis ones. From then on he was "in" with the movie colony.

What do they come for? Warmoth contemplated a soft white palm. "Their concerns are the same as other people's. Marriages, love affairs, business ventures . . . sometimes I get the unexpected, though."

Ron does not consider himself a "psychic crime buster," but he has done a certain amount of mental detective work. I was able to check out the case of one ex-star (no name, please) whose two small daughters disappeared from her garden.

She informed the police first and Ron Warmoth shortly afterwards. But the psychic zeroed in on the children considerably faster than the cops.

"Your children are in such-and-such a house in a street running down a steep hillside," he told the mother. "Does that sound familiar to you?"

The lady breathed a deep sigh of relief. "Yes, it does," she said. "Thank you."

The house belonged to her ex-husband. He had lost the girls in the divorce settlement and tried to get them back by staging a kidnaping. The mother pressed no charges.

Warmoth obviously prides himself on his outspokenness. Like most of his colleagues, however, he admits to holding back really grim revelations; such as impending death. "If you tell someone he's due for a heart attack, he's liable to get one from sheer anxiety."

Ron Warmoth can serve as an example of what—for want of a better term—might be called the purely cerebral psychic.

Meaning those sensitives who perform no *visible* feats of super-naturalism. This category is fast replacing the more traditional spirit mediums, who rely on ghost materializations, floating objects and disembodied phantom voices.

Psychics of Warmoth's stamp are more intellectually subtle in their technique and therefore more appealing to an audience whose capacity for wonder has grown callous through massive contact with video miracles. After watching a man slow-motioning over moon rocks, the sight of a levitating kitchen table is pretty thin beer.

But their very subtlety and the strict "personalness" of their performance also make them extremely difficult to assess. They print no general prophecies that can be checked. They rarely submit to controlled laboratory tests, for the—possibly valid—reason that such conditions tend to detract from their "psi" abilities. And the only witnesses you can question about their efficacy are those to whom the reading applied in the first place.

Contrary to what one might expect, such witnesses can prove far from reliable.

At an occult forum held in New York, a spiritualist lady reverend gave a demonstration of her alleged psychometric powers. Psychometry is the art of gaining information about another person by holding an object—preferably metallic—belonging to him. The data is supposed to flow from the vibrations adhering to it. Our spiritualist, a formidably stout matron, collected objects from all of us, fondled them briefly and then proceeded to announce our "prime character features."

She rapidly recited ten things about me, of which two were accurate, one dubious, and seven so patently wrong as to be humorous. Most of them, incidentally, were on the positive side. I quite enjoyed being called "modest to the point of self-effacement," even if it happened to be sadly untrue.

The lady next to me got her points at equal speed. When the mediumistic matron had passed out of earshot she nudged me and whispered, "It's uncanny! How can she describe me so perfectly after just holding my keyring?"

Of course, it *is* possible that the psychometrist was as correct about my neighbor as she was inaccurate about me. Possible, but highly unlikely. Chances are that the lady accepted the characteristics bestowed upon her as true because she *wanted* them to be true.

This does not explain the psychic accomplishments of certain sensitives. But it says a great deal about the veracity of the witnesses you have to depend on in any attempt to gauge them. Many of them, apart from being intensely impressionable, harbor a great craving for the miraculous, the supernormal. They want the psychic to be right because this affirms their own desire for such powers to exist. And they will—quite unconsciously—reshuffle facts and sequences in order to make the clairvoyant appear triumphantly so.

If it is difficult to measure the effectiveness of psychics dealing with present lives, it is virtually impossible to form any conclusions about those who concentrate on past existences. And this is precisely the specialty currently enjoying the greatest vogue.

Past lives can be perused by various methods, but by far the most impressive is insight into the "Great Akasha"—the Divine Consciousness. The Akashic records are said to be imperishable archives stored in the Fifth Plane—the Soul Plane—of the mystical universe, containing every thought and deed that has occurred since time began.

They can be read by the initiated by means of "soul projection" and then revealed to their students or clients. The scope of these revelations is limitless, but I found that Akasha readers tend to dwell only on the more glamorous or dramatic of their disciples' previous incarnations. Nearly all of the Akasha students I questioned had been temple dancers, crusaders, inventors, priests, monarchs, courtesans, artists or religious martyrs in their bygone days. The peasants, herdsmen and laborers and their wives, who formed 90 percent of the past population of the globe, hardly seem to crop up at all.

The whole reincarnation cycle is an integral part of Hinduism, and other Eastern faiths, together with the tenet that actions taken several lives ago may strongly influence our present existence. But only in recent years have large numbers of Americans accepted this view. And with it, naturally, came the desire to find out what these past incarnations were like.

One way of learning about them is to take sessions of

"Comprehensive Psychic Analysis" with Irwyn Greif. Mr. Greif, who lives in Brooklyn, New York, works as a claims examiner during the day, but holds classes and receives private clients at night. He is a very intense, short and plump man of forty, who makes tape recordings of every one of his clients' analyses (see Figure 19).

He can frequently trace current difficulties to involvements dating back a couple of thousand years. One of his clients, for instance, was a girl much given to sexual promiscuity, but far from happy about this tendency. Greif discovered that this was due to her having been a follower of John the Baptist. "Now," as he explained to me, "her sex life had become an unconscious search for religion—for another John the Baptist."

These sessions, costing ten or fifteen dollars each, are held in the Greifs' uncarpeted living room, surrounded by children's toys. Mrs. Greif supplies an additional touch of homeyness. She is a delightful Momma type, who does everything but say, "Eat, eat, *mein Kind*," to her husband's visitors.

There is nothing detached or aloof about Greif's analyzing methods. "Sometimes my eyes get hot and electricity pours from me," he said. His knowledge comes from ethereal beings—"You could call them angels"—from outer space, who gave him extensive training in the mysteries of the universe. Part of this training consisted of slide projections showing Greif as a kind of muscle-bound moron—to demonstrate how he looked to *them*.

Most of his lessons were whispered to him in dreams, but occasionally his teachers contacted him in broad daylight. Once, in the middle of Lexington Avenue, he found himself in touch with the crew of a flying saucer hovering two hundred miles above Manhattan. They communicated with him, he told me, via an invisible ray aimed at the back of his skull.

Later I talked to one of Greif's clients, a practicing psychiatrist named Bernard Rosenblum. "You may be dubious about this," said Dr. Rosenblum, "but Greif has quite remarkable therapeutic powers."

I thought of those angel creatures and the invisible ray from the flying saucer and tried to dead-pan my voice. "Has he?" I asked. "How?"

"Well, it's not easy to explain," said the doctor, "but when I first came to Greif, I had this strange fear of being struck on the head. A totally irrational dread that haunted me.

"I never told him anything about that—as a matter of fact, I'd told nobody." He cleared his throat and sounded faintly embarrassed. "Then Greif informed me that in my next-to-last life I had been an English seaman. And one day I was walking along the docks of Liverpool when a loading net above me broke loose and dropped on my skull and killed me.

"Well—do you know—after that this phobia about my head being busted left me. And it never returned. What do you make of that?"

I didn't know what to make of it. I still don't.

Mediumship of this sort—that is, divorced from spirit manifestations—came to the United States almost exactly a century ago. It arrived in the person of Helena Petrovna Blavatsky who, among her other accomplishments, was the first Russian female ever to become an American citizen.

Madame Blavatsky, who liked to be called H.P.B. or Jack, was one of those outsized personalities so completely at odds with her period that she seemed to be battling the entire nineteenth century—and very nearly holding her own. Some of her genteel biographers have since tried to whittle her down to ladylike proportions, but only succeeded in turning her into a lifeless cardboard figure.

For you can no more make a demure Victorian matron out of H.P.B. than you can change the flat-chested, fanatical Joan of Arc into a busty Christian Amazon. Both have been attempted at regular intervals and with comparably dismal results.

Helena Petrovna was born in 1831, as the daughter of a German nobleman who had emigrated to Russia and become an officer in the Czar's army. She grew into a difficult child and an impossible young woman. Her favorite playmates were the bearded artillery troopers of her father's regiment. She detested feminine frills, perfumes and needlework and once stuck her foot into a vat of boiling water to avoid having to attend a ball.

Her appearance may have colored her attitude. She was a painfully husky girl, broad-faced and broad-shouldered, with embarrassing muscular development. Physically and intellectually she rather resembled Sweden's seventeenth-century Queen Christina, who could—and did—knock down a cavalryman with a blow of her fist.

She was also given to screaming tantrums, convulsive fits during which she saw visions, and sudden states of trancelike rigidity. When her mother lay dying her final words were, "At least I will not live to see the suffering in store for Helena."

The suffering seemed about to start when Helena turned seventeen and was married off to one Count Blavatsky, who was more than four times her age. Other girls of her era would have pined; Helena simply upped and ran out on her husband, on Russia, and her entire feudal background. This happened before the old boy had a chance to consummate the marriage—providing this lay within his capabilities.

The most obvious cause of her flight from wedlock became publicly known at a later date. She had a deformation of the womb that would have rendered normal intercourse exceedingly painful. But there were other—more significant—reasons. Helena simply wouldn't accept matrimony on the then customary terms. She wanted to dominate men, not humor them. As she once declared to a newspaper reporter, "I wouldn't be a slave to God himself, let alone a mere male!"

Madame Blavatsky (she stuck to her married name) then began a life of restless wandering that took her four times around the world. She had a certain amount of money and a colossal amount of courage and curiosity and poked her frizzy head into every underexplored region on earth. Sometimes with an armed escort and often alone she roamed through central Africa, the Middle East and India, and may even have entered the then forbidden Tibet. She claimed to have actually studied there—but then she frequently and admittedly pulled her disciples' legs.

During her travels she delved deeply into what interested her most—the occult. She always seems to have had certain paranormal abilities, which she reinforced with a whole bag of Oriental *jadoo* tricks gleaned from the repertoire of Hindu and Arabian fakirs. By the time she was forty-two and arrived in America it was impossible to tell how much of her power was genuine, as distinct from parlor magic.

The impact of her personality alone left Americans dumbfounded. She smoked incessantly, rolling her cigarettes with one hand, cowboy fashion, and sealing them with a flick of her tongue without breaking her conversation. She carried a knife in a fold of her dress and frequently slapped it, remarking, "That's for any man who molests me. He'll be a man no more!"

By then her money had gone, which didn't worry her, and she was forced to live in one of the roughest sections of New York; which bothered her even less. What did disturb her was the state of America's occultism. It was entirely dominated by spirit mediums and given over to the wholesale production of table raps, ghost trumpet voices and luminous apparitions.

Not that Madame was skeptical of spirits. She encountered them constantly, was pestered by them at night and frequently had to brush them aside when they interfered with her writing. But they had nothing to do with her *message*—the creed with which she intended to enlighten the world.

This creed was based on the Hindu doctrine of reincarnation and the dual existence of astral and physical shapes. She herself claimed to be a reincarnation of the ancient Greek scientist Pythagoras, and she distributed famous reincarnation labels among her friends as she went along.

She announced that there existed in Tibet a secret brotherhood of masters (to which she belonged) who had acquired powers far beyond the abilities of ordinary men. Some of these powers she demonstrated (such as clairvoyance), others she merely hinted at. She declared that mankind was part of five "root races," each with seven "subraces," which again have seven "branch races." Some of these races (with two more yet to come) were invisible, another had barely visible astral bodies. Some lived on the lost continents of Atlantis and Lemuria, others on earth. These races would come and go in cycles. When the present earth cycle was completed, another would start on the planet Mercury; and so on, ad infinitum.

It is hard to overestimate Madame Blavatsky's influence on the American metaphysical scene. Portions of her teachings have been incorporated into virtually every occult group extant—though mostly without giving her a credit line. Over and over again I have listened to cult leaders expounding the Blavatsky gospel to their flock—as their own uniquely original discoveries or rather revelations. Sometimes I had the feeling that the ghost of the Russian woman was hovering over the audience; slapping her massive thighs and laughing her head off.

Unfortunately Madame suffered from a dichotomy in her talents. She was a spellbinding raconteur and an execrable author. The kindest thing one can say about her two voluminous works, *Isis Unveiled* and *The Secret Doctrine*, is that, after all, they weren't written in her native language. Some of her subsidiary outpourings were even more stupefying:

"In order to become the *knower* of *all-self* thou hast first to be the knower. To reach the knowledge of that *self*, thou hast to give up Self to Non-Self, Being to Non-Being, and then thou canst repose between the wings of the *great bird*. Aye, sweet is rest between the wings of that which is not born, nor dies, but is the *aum* throughout eternal ages."

To make matters worse, we have absolutely no way of knowing how much of this purple blah she meant seriously. For in her own later confession—which she retracted, reaffirmed, and retracted again—she recorded: "What is one to do, when in order to rule men, it is necessary to deceive them?"

However, she was the deceived at least as often as the deceiver, for Madame's powers of observation did not match her curiosity. Thus after witnessing a performance of the Mango Miracle—in which a mango tree is apparently made to grow before the eyes of the spectators—she proclaimed it "one of the genuine wonders of the East."

But the Mango Miracle happens to be a routine trick of India's *jadoo-wālās* ("magicians") and rates about as highly with them as our sawing-a-lady-in-half stunt. I have described the technical details of the trick in a previous book (*This Baffling World*) and can only say that it's quite simple once you know how it's done.

Madame Blavatsky may have been celibate, but she was no man-hater. She found an ideal companion in the person of Colonel Henry S. Olcott, an eccentric, courageous, enterprising and highly intelligent Civil War veteran, who minded neither

her chain-smoking nor her combativeness nor her house ghosts. He had a few of his own. Together they formed a platonic but very effective team.

In 1875 they founded the Theosophical Society in New York, the title formed by the Greek words *theos* (God) and *sophia* (wisdom). Theosophy was what Madame called the synthesis of her creed, and it attracted celebrities like Thomas Alva Edison and General Abner Doubleday.

Today the Society is an international order, with 1,500 world-wide branches and about 40,000 members. Theosophists are remarkably undogmatic, devoted to principles of universal brotherhood, and among the very few occultists who actually encourage the study of comparative religion. Nor do they seem to mind everybody else helping themselves to the more spectacular portions of their credo.

Madame Blavatsky left America in 1879, and continued her perpetual globe-trotting. She lived her last years in London, almost penniless, racked by various ailments, but as pugnacious, hard-working and convention-defying as ever. She died in 1891, sixty years old and at least half a century ahead of her time.

H.P.B. was the Liberated Woman long before Women's Lib existed. If one word could describe her it would be the French expression *cran*—which means guts, but more elegantly so. Although she undoubtedly lied, hoaxed and hoodwinked on occasions, there was a basic honesty in her fierce uncompromising independence. She was, in Chaucer's words, her "owne woman, well content." Neither her charisma nor her charlatanism were ever displayed for financial ends. She had all the magnetic flamboyance of Aimee Semple McPherson and could have waxed just as prosperous. But she despised money and refused to become an acceptable "lady medium." Unlike most of her colleagues in the occult she never stooped to pander to the tastes of the great mass of well-heeled spirit seekers—and she cheerfully paid the price of that attitude.

But there was one striking similarity between Madame Blavatsky and many of her fellow psychics—her sexual ambiguity. As far as is known she showed no physical manifestations of lesbianism, although emotionally she was certainly a borderline case.

And there is no doubt that a quite unusual proportion of

sensitives tend toward bi-, if not outright homosexuality. One of the strongest impressions I gathered during my research in the field was the pronounced effeminacy of many male mediums and the equivalent masculinity among women psychics.

I don't put this down as a random generalization. The late Eileen Garrett, an outstanding medium in her own right, remarked on the same phenomenon in her book *The Sense and Nonsense of Prophecy*, and added: "It can be understood, I think, only if we examine in some detail the origins and histories of the prophetic and divinatory gift."

Havelock Ellis, one of the founding fathers of clinical psychology, noted that sensitives were drawn mainly from the ranks of uncombative men and undomesticated women in ancient times. People whose energies found different outlets than those prescribed for the majority of their tribe. "Thus it is that from among them would, in some degree, issue not only inventors and craftsmen and teachers, but sorcerers and diviners, medicinemen and wizards, prophets and priests."

Leo Martello, New York's best-known and most outspoken witch, wrote: "The man who possesses the soul of a woman in the body of a man is inherently 'one up' on his fellowmen. He can intuitively understand women much better than the average man, and at the same time identify with this same man. Without any sexual expression whatsoever the bisexual person elicits the most intimate of friendships from other men who cherish his understanding, tenderness, noncompetitiveness. At the same time women sense a silent sympathy in him and intuitively can enjoy his male companionship without having to play the part of a woman and can confide in him without fear of betrayal."

Which sums it up nicely, though merely from the social point of view. It would be interesting—and certainly worth some research—to discover whether there is such a thing as a *mental* parallel between dual sexuality and psychic talent.

Few contemporary psychics emulate Madame Blavatsky's claim to being the reincarnated shape of a past notability. But at least one has gone several steps beyond her and maintains that he has received no less than twenty-two confirmations that he is John the Apostle.

Benn Lewis is a professional artist living in Washington, D. C. Several of his paintings hang in the Pentagon and the White House. But his studio home is also a church—the Washington Cosmic Center—where he preaches a gospel known as Soulcraft. The basic theme of the creed is to prepare man for the Second Coming of Christ. These preparations, however, are guided entirely by sudden messages Mr. Lewis receives from departed spirits like George Washington, Nostradamus, and an obscure but persistent Mr. Dudley (He actually received communication from Benjamin Franklin while talking to me—the impact gave him a kind of mild spasm.) (see Figure 20).

These messages frequently come in the form of prophecies, which Lewis distributes in neatly typed, haphazardly spelled bulletins. The one I have before me reads:

"*Come ye apart now!* You literally as well as figuratively, *are about to enter your Noah's Ark!* Take the attitude with your fellowman, 'This all was meant to be; would you not take a peak [sic] through the window of my *Ark* and see what we have to offer?' "

His disciples, mostly elderly Washingtonians, strongly affirm his identification with the best-loved of the Apostles. One lady, on meeting him for the first time, allegedly stood awestruck at the sight of him. She had, he told me, witnessed the Crucifixion while under hypnosis and reported that the man standing next to Jesus looked identical to Benn Lewis.

I am not familiar with the Apostle's appearance, but Lewis is short, rotund, red-haired and clean-shaven. He talks volubly and with a slight lisp, accompanied by sweeping theatrical gestures.

For an occultist his background is unusual. He worked in the art department of Warner Brothers in Hollywood, and as a movie extra. Since then, however, he has been ordained as a minister (by a lady medium) and received a doctorate (from a metaphysical college in Kansas City).

His art subjects have changed along with his attitudes. From magazine cover type productions of romantic and military scenes to somber allegorical canvases depicting visions like "Modern Civilization." He enjoys a solid local reputation as an arts teacher, and his twice-weekly classes are well attended.

In 1970 Lewis published a book (at his own expense) which

told the story of his life in fictionalized form. Although the hero of *I, John* is named Robert Coleman, he made it clear that it actually dealt with Benn E. Lewis.

"When you write about me," he admonished me in parting, "don't use phrases like 'He claims to be John the Apostle.' Stick to the facts. I *am* John the Apostle!"

I did not have an opportunity to observe Lewis's alleged healing powers. In any case, they fall into the traditional spiritualist or faith-healing pattern. But in this field there has recently been a startling new development: psychic surgery. At the moment it is performed only in the Philippines and Latin America. But —God and the AMA willing—we'll probably get it in the United States in the near future.

Psychic operations have apparently taken place in the Philippines for decades before they attracted much outside attention. But over the past few years American observers—mostly with a metaphysical bent—brought back eyewitness reports that were mind-boggling.

The "surgeons" in question are members of the Union Esperitista Cristiana de Filipinas, Inc., and ply their art in Baguio, Quezon City, and occasionally Manila. The account that first whetted my interest came from a Pittsburgh chiropractor who watched a series of these operations from only a few feet away and described them as "nothing short of miraculous."

His voice shook with emotion as he described the scene:

"The doctor—or healer—walked through a primitive room crowded with perhaps fifteen patients. He wore no gloves and carried no instrument of any sort—I watched closely. The people he treated were the poorest folks I've ever seen; some of them literally in rags.

"The patients were brought before him one by one. He told each one to lie down and said a quick prayer over him or her. Then—using only a finger as a scalpel—he cut into their bodies and pulled out some afflicted organ *in front of my eyes!* I saw him remove gallstones, nasal polyps and several huge tumors. He placed everything in a glass jar with alcohol, so I was able to inspect them closely. Sure, there was lots of blood—spurting all over the place. But when I looked at the patients' skins afterwards, not the faintest trace of an incision could be seen.

"I don't mind telling you—I knelt down right there and then and prayed. Because I'd seen one of God's miracle workers in action."

Two weeks later I had an opportunity of viewing some films taken of these operations. They were preceded by a somewhat overwrought address from a spiritualist woman tourist, but the actual films were soundly professional. You saw the young healer —apparently using his stiff forefinger as a knife—slice into his patients' flesh. You saw the welling blood staining the white sheets in which the patients were partly covered. After each removal the healer held the raw organ or tissue in front of the camera before storing it in his jar. It was uncanny . . . unbelievable. . . .

And I was suddenly seized by a powerful bout of déjà vu. I had the overwhelming feeling of having watched all this before, somewhere. And then the chair I was sitting on began to feel like a hard wooden pew and something like a fingersnap clicked in my brain: Of course—the Grand Guignol!

About fifteen years ago there existed in Paris a theater that had no replica anywhere on earth. The Grand Guignol was actually a small converted church, where the audience sat in the pews. The theater performed nothing but specially written horror plays. They featured probably the most gruesome scenes ever enacted on a stage—as distinct from actuality. It attracted a few morbid-minded Parisians and a great many tourists; General Patton was a regular there while stationed in France. The place folded sometime in the mid fifties; a victim of television and a real estate deal.

Among the one-acters I saw there was a piece entitled The Mad Surgeon. It showed a gaga nineteenth-century physician performing hair-raising operations on conscious, screaming captives tied to a table. He carved out hearts, livers and brains, wound intestines around his wrist, and removed several eyes.

I sat in the front row and can attest to the steaming realism of the action; I could have sworn the man was excavating in earnest. He had an unnerving way of gloating over each blood-dripping morsel before depositing it in—a glass jar. No one fainted that particular night, but several people made hurried exits.

Since I was writing an article on the theater, I went backstage afterwards. I found surgeon and victims amiably snarling at each other through clouds of Gaulois smoke. The surgeon turned out to be an ex-comedian down on his luck. He willingly demonstrated to me how the whole thing was done.

The extractions were slipped to him by the ghoulish nurse at his elbow. They were genuine pork giblets, only the intestines came in plastic. He palmed them, then used the same hand to knead his victim's flesh. In doing so he squeezed a plastic bubble of blood hidden in the organ and—*voilà!*—it spurted. The deftness of the performance would have made any movie camera lie its lense off.

I remembered all this while watching the Filipino healers. Later I had my thoughts pretty well confirmed by another eyewitness; a slightly more hardheaded and less miracle-minded M.D. from Indianapolis.

"At no time did I see any actual opening in the patients' skins. The healers always kept their hands over the incision spot," he told me. "And they never removed any outwardly visible growths. People with lumps or goiters were merely rubbed and prayed over. And their afflictions were still firmly in place when they left."

As inspirational hocus-pocus these sleight-of-hand operations are probably harmless enough. They may even cure patients with psychosomatic ailments. But they could be indirectly dangerous, especially if imported into Western countries. For somebody who believes that his or her gallstones have been extracted by magic may postpone their actual removal until it is too late, or nearly so.

If I came upon psychic surgery with my guard down, so to speak, the very mention of "thoughtography" brought all my mental defenses into play. I had seen enough "ghost photographs" to plaster several walls. I knew how they were manufactured; as a matter of fact, I know a man who sells the equipment for making them.

It took a while before I realized that the "thoughtographs" in question were something altogether different. That they represented the latest—and perhaps most bewildering—step in the history of psychic phenomena.

Since 1955 or thereabouts, a former Chicago bellhop named
Ted Serios had been trying to find "takers" for an altogether
fabulous gift he claimed to possess, but couldn't explain. He
was able to "think" photographs, or rather to project mental
images into the camera so that they showed up in the picture
taken.

Both Serios and his alleged talent had a number of strikes
against them. Serios was a heavy drinker, extremely moody and
temperamental, inclined to get excited and loud when faced
with disbelief, unpunctual, forgetful, and a most unreliable performer. His gift had a deplorable habit of failing when he needed
it most. On occasions he would get five "hits" with six pictures.
At other times he would take thirty pictures without managing
to even fog the film. He frequently cried after such failures.

His feat also suffered from the handicap that it was—literally
—unprecedented. It sprang from no discernible creed and fitted
into no available pigeonhole. And in this respect both occultists
and scientists think alike: both prefer their miracles neatly labeled
and equipped with some kind of theory.

To make matters worse, Serios used a rolled piece of cardboard—he called it a gismo—to peer into the camera lens as
the shutter clicked. He said it merely helped to concentrate
his powers, but it aroused a lot of suspicions. Even when inspec-
tion showed it to be completely hollow, there was always the
chance that a smooth switch could substitute a loaded gismo
for the empty one.

But in 1964 Serios at last found a backer of considerable
weight. This was Dr. Jule Eisenbud, Associate Clinical Professor
of Psychiatry at the University of Colorado. Eisenbud wrote a
book about the erstwhile bellboy that attracted worldwide attention. What was more important—he gave Serios the chance
of performing in front of genuinely qualified researchers and
under laboratory conditions. He also got him to abandon the
gismo occasionally; which didn't seem to affect the results.

Those results continued to be highly erratic, ranging from
the fantastic to the negative. But at least people were paying
attention to what *might* be the psychic conundrum of our
century.

When I went to see Serios in action in Chicago, I carried enough reservations for a diplomatic mission to Moscow. I had boned up on "ghost pea-lamps" and "ghost stamps," on radioscopic salts, transparent celluloid film, double exposure, X rays, sodium thiosulphate, and half a dozen other means of doctoring spook snaps.

Ted Serios was about fifty, a thickset man with a craggy face and a voice like George Raft in a "Public Enemy" movie. He seemed nervous and intense and very unsure of himself.

A magazine photographer had brought a Polaroid camera along. This ruled out about half the possibilities for photographic trickery. No darkroom involved, and the pictures could be peeled off in front of us a few seconds after being taken. The films used were supplied by myself and two other people, all in unbroken packages.

Serios walked around the room, then positioned himself in front of the cameraman. His fists clenched—his whole body tautened—his face flushed purple with the sheer physical effort of concentration. He let out a hoarse bellow: "Now!" and the camera clicked.

There was nothing on the resultant picture but his contorted face.

Then began what seemed a torture session for Serios. Five, ten, twelve times he repeated the effort, sweat streaming from his face and neck, his speech growing breathless. A few times he snapped the camera at himself, mostly the photographer did it. All we got was his face—over and over.

And then there was no face, but something that should—by all the laws of logic—not have been there. The blurry, badly focused, but recognizable shape of a building. Some office building somewhere, but certainly not within view of our Polaroid. Serios relaxed, heaved a sigh, and broke out a grin. The rest of us stood around, gazing at the photo, shaking our heads.

I have been told that Serios can—on occasions—produce images by arrangement, that he has projected pictures of selected buildings or historical scenes. I also learned that he has no consistent control over his gift and no way of making it useful.

As far as I'm concerned, it couldn't matter less. All I know

is that, while staring straight at the camera, he somehow eliminated his own face and substituted a building, and that this single
feat will haunt me for the rest of my life.

Ted Serios has no theory with which to rationalize his
gift. He proclaims no message and belongs to no spiritualist
movement or metaphysical group. He may just be the living,
sweating proof of what *they* are seeking.

VIII
THE SAUCERIANS

IN JANUARY 1969, the United States government released a 965-page report entitled A *Scientific Study of Unidentified Flying Objects*. The study had been commissioned by the Air Force, took fifteen months to complete, cost $500,000, and was directed by Dr. Edward U. Condon, Professor of Physics at the University of Colorado.

Most of the project, which became known as the Condon Report, was devoted to the analysis of a huge number of flying saucer sightings. It found nearly all of them attributable to standard or experimental aircraft, weather balloons, stars, flocks of birds, marsh gases, insects, atmospheric phenomena, optical illusions, and plain fantasies.

The key statement summarized:

"Our general conclusion is that nothing has come from the study of UFOs in the past 21 years that has added to scientific knowledge. Further extensive study of UFOs probably cannot be justified in the expectation that science will be advanced thereby."

Almost every newspaper in the nation featured the Report and commented on its conclusion, although few commentators read even a fraction of it. The gist of editorial opinion was that it constituted a burial hymn of the "saucer mania."

The Condon Report may be open to argument. But the conclusion drawn from it by the press was quite undisputably false. The so-called saucer mania may get rather less publicity than of yore, but it remains a flowering branch of America's occult growth.

What the Report probably and the newspapers possibly failed to notice was the profound metamorphosis of the entire saucer syndrome. It is no longer a matter of somebody sighting something in the sky. UFOs have become a cult, a philosophy, symbols of faith, tokens of menace or salvation, and an integral part of national folklore.

The debate over their mere *existence* is as passé as the pros and cons of Evolution.

The only comparable development in modern times was the growth of the "Cargo Cults" in the South Pacific area. There, among the Micronesian and Melanesian islanders, exists a widespread belief in the coming of a kind of marine Santa Claus: a ship loaded with an immense cargo of goods that will make the entire island rich and happy. The cult is directly traceable to the arrival of the first whalers and explorers around the turn of the eighteenth century. They did bring loads of trading trinkets (along with rotgut liquor, tuberculosis and VD) and the cult merely predicts that next time the cargo will be considerably larger—and free.

Around this optimistic prophecy an intricate system of prayers, sacrifices and rituals has sprung up, with the original theme elaborated almost to the point of oblivion. The central totem figure, however, remained intact—a carved likeness of an old-time wind jammer.

In the same year the Condon Report was released, a gentleman named R. E. Dickhoff published an illustrated volume advertised as *Behold—The Venus Garuda*. In it he revealed the presence in space of twelve-feet tall, winged humanoids named

Garudas, who regard Earthlings as food and are currently plotting to enslave—and devour—the race of Homo sapiens.

Among my saucerian acquaintances, Mr. Dickhoff is regarded as a somewhat dramatic but by no means negligible author. The general tenor of their opinion was: "How do we know what's on Venus?"

None of them felt moved to ask: How does *he* know?

For this would be contrary to what might be termed the basic tenet of saucerianism. Once you accept flying saucers as (*a*) real, and (*b*) from another world, you are free to weave around them any sort of fabric you fancy. Nobody within the fraternity will question your motives, your sources or your mental stability.

We've come a long, long way since the days UFOlogists argued about whether or not flying saucers could turn at right angles.

The change that has occurred is not so much of certainty as of perspective. The accent has shifted from observation to participation, from being a sighter to becoming a "contactee."

The first recorded sighting in the United States took place in June 1947. A young businessman named Kenneth Arnold, piloting his own plane above Mount Rainier, Washington, reported spotting nine silvery disks flying in formation. In his statement to the Yakima airport authorities he used the phrase "saucer-shaped" to describe the objects. Reporters pounced on the story, and the term "flying saucers" was born.

For three years America—and most of the Western world—was then inundated with reports of other sightings, involving—according to Gallup Poll—some 5 million people. It was not until 1950, however, that the first account of personal contact cropped up.

It came from a former technician at the White Sands Proving Ground named Daniel Fry. While taking a stroll in the New Mexico desert, Fry claimed to have come across an "oblate spheroid about 30 feet in diameter at the widest part, and about 16 feet in height, silvery in color . . ." He reached out to touch it, when a voice said, "Better not touch the hull, pal, it's still hot!"

The voice, Mr. Fry discovered in due course, belonged to an

invisible spaceman called Alan, who was actually conversing with him by telepathy. The result of their conversation was that Fry received a ride in the saucer, plus a lesson in extraterrestrial history. The flight took him over New York within half an hour, which meant they were flying at about 8,000 m.p.h.—a regular horsecart speed compared to later saucer accounts. Nothing much happened on the trip, and Fry was deposited back on earth safe and sound (see Figure 21).

He described his experience in a book, *White Sands Incident,* which sold fairly well. Today Dr. Fry (he holds a Ph.D.) lives in Merlin, Oregon, heads an organization called Understanding, Inc., and brings out regular bulletins proclaiming universal brotherhood. His current contact, he told me, consists of a member of an "alien race" who resides in Cario, Egypt, and operates under the guise of an import-export agent. His real aim, however, is to prevent nuclear war.

Dr. Fry may have achieved a historical first, but he was soon overshadowed by a much more spectacular contactee. For in 1952, there burst upon the scene one George Adamski. And with him arrived the age of the "Message from Outer Space," the totally rearranged planetary system, and the sexy Venusian. All three have been with us ever since.

Adamski related that he was picked up at his Los Angeles hotel by a Martian and a Saturnian. They led him to a saucer-shaped scout ship, which then flew eight miles up and into a cigar-shaped, 2,000-feet long mother ship. Which in turn transported him 50,000 miles into space.

In the course of this trip and several subsequent ones he met a couple of gorgeous Venusian gals (one blond, one brunette), plus an ancient sage. The damsels did little but smile, but the sage gave Adamski the blueprint of the universe that has since become one of the standard charts of sauceriana.

According to Adamski, there are thousands of populated planets in space, most of them immeasurably superior to our globe not only technically but morally. They are grouped in systems of twelve, each whirling around an individual sun, and twelve such systems form an island universe; twelve island universes . . . and so into infinity. Man, Adamski learned, was the only creature in cosmos capable of evil. The space people's sole reason for approaching earth was to help us; though in a rather vague and undefined fashion. This, too, has become part of the Saucerian creed.

In his books and lectures, Adamski offered "decisive proofs" of his encounters. These consisted of UFO photographs and pencil sketches of space beings, who looked strikingly like long-haired flower children dressed in Eisenhower jackets.

His evidence of having taken a saucer journey from Missouri to Iowa came in the form of an uncanceled rail ticket from Kansas City to Davenport, for which he had requested a refund.

Although Adamski's prose rarely ascended above pulp magazine levels, his books were top sellers in the UFOlogy field, his lectures invariably packed. By the time of his death in 1965, George Adamski was widely recognized as the Marco Polo of the saucer world.

He had ushered in the era of the contactee; the earthling who was friend, confidant and message bearer of the creatures manning those silver disks. Contactees emerged in swarms throughout the country, several of them gathering knots of followers and establishing organizations for the purpose of disseminating their particular message. It was just a question of time before one of them would venture into politics.

The man who did was an ex-photographer named Gabriel Green. And he took the step at the behest of a four-feet-short individual called Rentan, who hailed from the planet Alpha Centauri. In 1962 Green ran for the office of senator in the Californian Democratic Primary and rolled up 171,000 votes (see Figure 22).

"I ran as a peace candidate, opposed to nuclear testing in the atmosphere," he reminisced. "This was before we'd signed the treaty banning such tests. And from the beginning the extraterrestrials have stressed how detrimental those tests were."

"Did the extraterrestrials ask you to run on that ticket?" I inquired.

"Well—originally they wanted me to run for President," said Green.

"By 'they' do you mean this person Rentan?"

"Yes, but you see he was acting as representative of the Universal Confederation of Planets."

I looked nonplused, and he obligingly filled me in:

"All the local planets are members of that Confederation. This is as opposed to the Universal Alliance of Planets, which also comprises several hundred planets. And then there are something like"—he calculated rapidly—"85 such confederations within this galaxy alone, composed of from 150 to 7,500 planets each. It does get rather mind-staggering. At the moment the Alliance people are trying to get the Confederation to merge with them—trying to form a world government. It would mean standardization in space and would probably be an improvement. But—" he sighed, "it's not easy. Nobody likes to change."

"Sounds pretty complex," I said. "Is this something you've written about?"

"Oh, no." Green waved depreciatingly. "That's common knowledge."

We were sitting in the living room cum office of his small, charming Hollywood house, surrounded by books, charts, filing cabinets and superb blowups of UFO photographs. The Japanese mobile hanging outside the door tinkled melodiously in the warm Californian breeze. The office serves as headquarters of Green's Amalgamated Flying Saucers Club, which currently has 110 units with 5,100 registered members.

Green is tall and slender, dresses conservatively, wears horn-rimmed glasses, and looks like an eminently dependable accountant. He has a low voice and a gently unassuming smile, that must have been serious handicaps at political stump rallies.

"How was all this information communicated to you?" I asked.

"Well, I don't speak any foreign languages," Green said modestly, "so they had to talk to me in English."

In due course, it appears, these communications became snappier than long-distance telephone calls.

"One time I was with my associate, discussing problems of the movement," Green remembered. "And we thought it would be a good idea to get Rentan's opinion. My associate said, 'Just a minute, I'll get him on the line,' meaning telepathically.

"About ten, fifteen minutes later there was a knock at the door, and there was Rentan, big as life—all four feet of him.

And I said, 'Gee, Rennie, how'd you get here so fast?' Because I knew that in a spaceship the trip from Alpha Centauri takes two hours—which is a four and a half light year journey, approximately.

"And he said, 'Well, since I was in a hurry, I teleported.' Which is instantaneous, or thereabouts."

Green explained that he knew about teleportation, since several of his associates had been transited in that fashion. "You get into a kind of cabinet, they press a button, and you wind up in a cabinet somewhere else."

Apart from his short stature, Rentan looked like an ordinary human. But Green easily accounts for the sharply differing descriptions of space inhabitants rendered by his fellow contactees.

"That's because they come from different planets. You take earthlings—they don't look exactly alike. So, of course, you'll find different appearances among people from, say, Mars or Venus or Clarion or Alpha Centauri. In any case," he added, "Rentan wasn't typical. I met others who looked quite unlike him. There's his age, for instance. He mentioned that he was at least two thousand years old. That he was actually in the same body when Christ walked this earth. That would make him unusual to begin with."

These personal contacts, Green remarked a trifle sadly, faded out about eight years ago. He rather suspected, though, that he was still meeting extraterrestrials without being aware of it. "For all I know you might be one of them; putting me on," he smiled.

I assured him that I was neither.

"Yeah, but you know, from time to time there are those real odd people who come to give me information. I often wonder about them . . ."

The Amalgamated Flying Saucers Club of America is only one of the dozen or more contactee organizations that dot the country. They amalgamate and disintegrate, change titles and leadership, fizzle out in one place to spring up at another, and sometimes shift the accent of their activities.

One of the veterans in the field, for instance, is George van Tassel's outfit. Based on a remote restaurant and airport in California's Yucca valley, this group currently devotes its energies to the construction of a thirty-five-feet-high silver dome, which is—to quote its full character—an "electro-static magnetic generator for basic research into rejuvenation anti-gravity time travel conducted by the College of Universal Wisdom."

Van Tassel, who began his quest with a simple saucer ride back in 1953, hoped to have the dome in operation by the end of 1970. "Then as many as 10,000 people a day will be able to be rejuvenated by the Integration."

Most contactee groups feel bitter about various spiritualist cults, whom they accuse of stealing both their ideas and their members. But this is nothing compared to how the more practical-minded UFO researchers feel about *them*.

As one UFO buff told me in tones close to hatred, "Every time we try to get at the facts of some interesting sighting, up they pop from the woodwork with their little green men. It's like trying to solve a murder case with a thousand gibbering nuts dancing around you, obscuring the traces."

I could understand some of his anger from the example of NICAP. Founded in 1956, the National Investigations Committee on Aerial Phenomena embraced ten thousand members and included top aircraft, naval and rocket specialists among its Board of Governors. It was simultaneously the most dedicated and competent private organization ever set up for the purpose. Headquartered in Washington, D.C., it is currently headed by Major Donald E. Keyhoe, a former flying officer in the Marine Corps and highly reputable aviation writer.

NICAP began simply as an investigative body, whose sole object it was to discover what—if anything—lay behind those tens of thousands of unidentified "things" reported in the sky. But within a few years it found itself embroiled in a hopeless, nerve-grinding war on two fronts.

On the one hand, NICAP's hierarchy became convinced that the United States government in general and the Air Force in particular were covering up concrete evidence of the UFOs' extraterrestrial nature. This caused its spokesmen to launch shrilly emotional attacks on official bodies, accompanied by sensational charges they could never substantiate. Which, not unnaturally, resulted in grim governmental disfavor.

On the other hand, NICAP did not believe that anyone

on earth had actually met with UFO crews, and that all such reports were either fantasies or commercial fiction. This led them into sharp conflict with contactee kings like Adamski and Fry.

Because Major Keyhoe insisted that UFOS were not of this earth, officialdom gleefully dunked him in the same bucket as all those exponents of "little green men" he detested. He lashed out furiously at both sides, and in consequence NICAP landed between two chairs with a fairly resounding thud.

Today the Committee has lost much of its former spark. And it finds itself in the unenviable position of being denigrated by establishment and saucerians alike.

But the Committee also bears a heavy burden of blame. For by accusing the government of UFO hush-ups it watered the latent seeds of the paranoia which now spreads over the entire saucerian landscape like a prickly cactus growth.

The saucerians, true to form, went a few dozen steps further offbeam. With them it became a question not of witnesses being silenced, but being murdered! And the plot involved not merely the United States government, but a score of other earthly authorities, plus several in outer space. The only outfit not rung in on the conspiracy so far have been the mythical Elders of Zion—though no doubt they'll arrive in due course.

Each contactee organization currently boasts its own pet villain, who is held responsible for everything from lost letters to cerebral hemorrhages. At a recent Space-Craft Convention in Berkeley, California, a taped message warned humanity to beware of the planet Zeno:

"Adolf Hitler was a Zenonian. All those who advocate fluoridated water, pasteurized milk, and compulsory vaccination of children are Zenonians. They control all government officials on your planet. They control the Communist world plot. Beware of the Zenonians!"

This stridently manic tone has become quite customary in saucerian communications. Listen to enough of them and you get to take cannibalistic Garudas in your stride.

The quintessence of conspiratorial terror, however, are the "Men in Black." These updated bogeymen so permeate saucerian thinking that they rate the standard abbreviation MIB.

There is considerable divergence of opinion as to whether

they work for the FBI, the CIA, the Soviet Secret Service, Red China, an extraterrestrial authority, or perhaps all of them combined. But it is accepted saucerian gospel that the MIB will shadow, interrogate, sabotage, kidnap and occasionally kill folks who have contacted space inhabitants.

For a more detailed survey of their activities, here is an extract from a recent saucerian publication:

"Among their objectives are the absolute control and regulation of political, financial, religious and scientific institutions and information. They're ordered to seize, by force if necessary, all new devices which parallel or threaten their technological supremacy. They will harass, coerce, and steal from inventors, researchers, and scientists whom they consider dangerously meddlesome, along with every piece of information leading to the exposure of their furtive deeds and doings. . . . They have been seen, spoken with and photographed—the evidence is irrefutable. We could expose much of what our own and many other governments are covering up, and their design to keep all citizens in absolute ignorance under the guise of protecting them from mass chaos in the face of the truth about flying saucers. It is an old plot."

The bit that interested me most in the above was the "irrefutable evidence." I spent the better part of a year trying to find it, but despite my crime reporter's training—with meager results. These amounted to various saucerians telling me how they had been watched, pursued, questioned (and on one occasion spat at) by the MIB. But since my informants were also in the habit of observing levitating silvery giants or taking impromptu excursions to Jupiter, I felt somewhat reluctant to accept their testimony as "irrefutable."

However, the Winter 1969 edition of *Saucer News*—one of the most widely read UFOlogy publications—also offered "photographic evidence" of the MIB's reality. It featured two pictures of them. One showed the rear view of an (empty) Cadillac, in which they had allegedly arrived. The other had captured a plump, bespectacled gentleman wearing an undeniably black overcoat standing in a factory doorway in Jersey City, New Jersey.

The only irrefutable evidence presented by these photos was of the existence of plump, bespectacled gentlemen in Jersey City.

The same edition of *Saucer News* also ran a reader's letter (whose name, it stated, was being withheld for "security reasons") which revealed the full extent of the persecution mania currently gripping saucerians.

The letter related how a Dr. George Russell and William R. Sewell had visited Mars, Clarion, and various other planets in 1962. It told of Dr. Russell's death—of "brain fever"—and his burial on one of the planets.

Sewell returned from space alone and handed the scientific information they had gathered over to the United States government. He was subsequently sent on a secret mission to Australia, where he was fatally injured by an assassin. I'll quote the rest of the missive in full:

"A Mr. Cole, who was in on the secret, was found slain in his hotel room. Virginia Russell [Dr. Russell's widow] was found dead in her apartment and death was attributed to a heart attack. President John F. Kennedy, who was cognizant [sic] of the facts, was assassinated.

"Why is the truth withheld from the people?

"Wake up citizens of the U.S.A.—wake up I say!!!"

It takes no medical training to recognize a fully fledged psychotic behind these lines. Yet the letter was widely and earnestly quoted in saucerian circles and solemnly read to me as yet another example of the perils surrounding UFOlogy. Despite the fact that the quoters admitted they'd never heard of any of the names mentioned, except the late President's! This they put down to the fiendish perfection of the government's hush-up policy.

The sad crux of the matter is that saucerians believe they are being murdered in something like wholesale fashion. At regular intervals UFOlogy publications print the roll of martyrs, which gets longer every season. The coroner's finding in each case is brushed aside as irrelevant—something akin to the infamous Gestapo stereotype of "shot while attempting escape."

The classic example was Dr. Morris K. Jessup, one of the few astronomers seriously involved in UFOlogy. In April 1959 Dr. Jessup committed suicide by inhaling the exhaust fumes of his station wagon. The medical examiner stated exactly that. Whereupon the saucerian legend grinder went into over-

drive. Within months they had the unfortunate doctor linked
with information about a United States Navy experiment in
which a destroyer was teleported from Philadelphia to Norfolk,
then made invisible, and half its crew rendered insane! It was
this information, saucerians hinted, that marked Jessup for "liquida-
tion."

Several writers suggested various means by which this was
accomplished. My favorite one came from UFO scribe Richard
Ogden and was sent to the editor of *Saucer News*. It held
that Jessup fell victim to a tape recording employing hypnotic
self-destruction orders, "superimposed on music and mixed with
white sound. No one can resist being hypnotized by sound waves."

Mr. Ogden elaborated: "Do you realize that someone could
simply call you on the phone and when you answer, you are
given a dose of white sound that puts you into a trance before
you could even hang up. Your subconscious would be given suicidal thoughts and then you would go out and destroy yourself.
Of course, first you would be told to write a letter to someone
suggesting that you were about to commit suicide. This is what
happened to Jessup. It is cold-blooded murder!"

How can any coroner, with his humble forensic training,
compete with *that?*

Since then the scroll of "victims" has grown apace, each
accompanied by a network of surmises suggesting dark deeds.

It runs from author and radio personality Frank Edwards,
who died of an "apparent" heart attack, to the obscure saucer
passenger Barney Hill, who "apparently" succumbed to a brain
hemorrhage. Saucerians see the "Men in Black" behind all these
demises and dozens more. Listening to them leaves you with
the impression that there hasn't been a natural death in UFO-
logical circles for the past fifteen years.

But if you prod further you step into a gray cloudland,
darkened by the sinister atavistic concept of "them." Chinese
peasants half a century ago used the term in the same gloomily
generic fashion—"them" meant the cause of all their mis-
fortunes and could denote the gods, the warlords, the Foreign
Devils, the landowners, or all of these together. To saucerians
it spells an equally all-embracing combination in which their
own government is somehow in league with sundry others, plus

private bodies, plus interplanetary forces to suppress . . . well, what? On this point they aren't quite sure, but whatever it may be that is being suppressed, it's the TRUTH.

And if this sounds enigmatic, here is what John A. Keel, one of saucerdom's leading authorities on the depredations of the MIB, has to say by way of enlightenment:

"The subject is most complicated. A simple and brief explanation is not possible. You must prepare yourself to understand the complex 'Big Picture'; a knowledge of history is more important than a knowledge of astronomy. Science has been stalemated for twenty years. This situation is beyond the reach of science. All mankind lies at the core of the mystery. Man's past and his future are directly involved and will be effected—seriously effected [sic]."

What "Big Picture"? Whose history? How is science stalemated? Mr. Keel doesn't say, but he knows that "all mankind" lies at the core of it. Somehow.

The saucerian concept does not necessitate belief in tangible space creatures. At least one top UFOlogist insists that they have no visible shapes at all. Yet he claims to be the representative on earth of what he calls the SIs—meaning "space intelligences."

The SIs' earthly ambassador is much given to sending letters and cables to high administrative figures (including Presidents Johnson and Nixon). The following he dispatched to George Clark of the CIA, on October 26, 1965:

A rare warning: SIs in fury. See copy letter NASA before Gemini Six shot. Keep in mind vanishing Agena rocket. Unless U.S. Govt. complies with SI wishes, they will unleash terrible U.S. catastrophe within ten days. Don't know what they have in mind. But let the Govt. be warned.

P. K. Man (Owens)

The United States government did not comply with the SIs' wishes (being, perhaps, unaware of them) and in consequence a power failure blacked out much of seven Eastern states fifteen days later. That, at least, is how Ted Owens sees it.

Owens is probably the most unusual contactee in the country. He has never laid eyes on a space creature, never taken a ride in one of their craft, never visited a foreign planet. He merely states that they have altered his brain to convert it into a perfect receiving set for their telepathic messages, which he is ordered to pass on to "whom it may concern." He is astonishingly humble about his mission. "They just give me orders and I carry them out as best I can," he told me. "They don't reveal much to me about their own world."

At fifty, Owens is a massive chunk of a man with the forearms of a wrestling instructor, who chews rather than smokes cigars. But his hair is silvery white, his voice brightly persuasive, and his vocabulary remarkable. He frequently bestows affectionate pats on his shy little wife, Martha (see Figure 23).

At the moment the Owens family inhabits a very modest house in Virginia Beach, Virginia, where Ted works at an office job he is loath to discuss. His list of past occupations is bound to establish some kind of record—he has been a court reporter, hypnotist, jazz drummer, legal secretary, bodyguard, dancing teacher, boxer, fortune-teller, lifeguard, jewelry designer, and the active part of a knife-throwing duo (Martha providing the target).

The "P.K." he frequently affixes to his signature stands for "psychokinesis"—his alleged ability to move objects by mental power alone. This—like a great many other talents—he ascribes to the influence of the SIs.

"How does this influence operate?" I wanted to know.

"Well, it began after an encounter my young daughter and I had with a cigar-shaped UFO in Texas," Owens said. "Now, up to this point I knew nothing about flying saucers. But after that I began to get a flood of ideas—on mental imagery, on hypnosis, and a lot of other things—until I collected a great, big, fat, thick notebook full of them." He indicated the bulk of the book with his powerful fingers.

"Frankly, I think they must have held us captive that night without my realizing it, to get all that knowledge into me."

"And who, exactly, are 'they'?"

"Ahh." He chuckled through his cigar. "At first I believed—I actually thought I had come in contact with the intelligence behind nature itself. That was when I discovered that I could actually cause thunderstorms—with or without rain—by using a form of mental imagery on the sky."

Owens shook his head. "It was only when we were living in Washington, D.C.—and UFOs began appearing all around the area—that I realized the SIs were responsible. Later I found that we had a sort of two-way hookup going—they could talk to me, I to them."

"But without seeing them," I put in.

"That's right." He nodded. "Because the SIs are just pure energy—invisible. And don't let anyone tell you different!"

In order to prove their existence, the SIs produced blackouts, hurricanes and torrential rainfalls, either allowing Owens to command them or telling him beforehand, so that he could predict them. Over and over he contacted newspapers, radio stations and government officials with his prophecies—only to be ignored after the announced event had occurred.

What, then, was the ultimate purpose of it all?

"The ultimate purpose," said Owens, placing a loving arm around his wife's waist, "is for me to make contact with world authorities on their behalf. They can't do it, you see, not having physical shapes. But if I can arrange for them to obtain a base here in the United States, they'll help us get rid of all our present problems—war, hatred, famine . . . the lot!"

He grinned ruefully. "It hasn't done *me* much good, personally. But—I'll keep trying."

One of the constantly quoted by-products of UFO appearances is a substance we call "angel hair." These are glistening clouds of fine threads which come floating from the sky on bright days—often accompanied by a flurry of UFO sightings in the area. Saucerians have long tried to connect the two; each group according to its own lights.

The scientific-minded prefer to regard it as the ionization of the atmosphere produced in the wake of a spacecraft moving in a force field. The more mystical hold that it may actually be the hair of planetary beings—perhaps angels. One lady writer in the magazine *Chimes* speculated that it could even be the nourishing manna from Heaven mentioned in the Old Testament.

But all these factions agree that the substance has been put

through every imaginable laboratory test and "defies analysis."
The latest such test report came from Houston, Texas, where
an (unnamed) chemist allegedly went over the stuff in the
laboratory of an (unnamed) petroleum company in November
1969. He subsequently announced himself unable to determine
what the substance was; or at least was so quoted.

All of which leads me to assume that either no such tests
ever took place or that they were conducted so amateurishly
that the anonymity of the mystified chemist was a safety precaution for the sake of his continued employment.

There is no mystery whatever attached to "angel hair."
Those gossamer threads are spun by millions of baby spiders,
who annually leave their nests and are carried aloft on rising
air currents, sometimes to over ten thousand feet. Eventually
they drift to earth, the spiders move off to build their own
nests, and the filmy strands are left lying for saucerians to weave
mysteries with.

While some UFOlogists are thus manufacturing new legends,
others concentrate on preserving the old ones. Although a glance
at the names involved usually shows that the same lot are doing
both.

When mankind's machinery began edging toward the moon,
most astronomers believed that the ancient tales of "moon inhabitants" were about to join the fable of the unicorn. But
they had reckoned without the saucer fraternity.

The late George Adamski showed the way. He had reported
a personal observation tour over the far—the hidden—side of the
moon, during which he not only discovered huge cities but
actually saw people strolling along the streets.

Then came the Russian satellite photos of the moon's hidden
half, which revealed nothing but a crater waste. Lesser men might
have flinched, but Mr. Adamski had his answer pat. The Russians,
he explained breezily, had retouched the pictures before releasing
them, eliminating every sign of the flourishing civilization he—
George Adamski—had observed.

When Apollo 11 accomplished the first actual landing on
the moon, the situation became somewhat more difficult for
those wedded to the myth of lunar creatures. Difficult, but not
insoluble.

About two months after the feat, a steady trickle of letters began to reach the press and TV media, announcing that Mission Control in Houston had staged a phony transmission failure, cutting off the astronauts just as they were starting to describe *an armada of spaceships* parked on the surface of the moon! What were said media going to do about this outrage?!

As source of this sensational exposé the correspondents cited the September 29, 1969, edition of a Montreal newspaper called *National Bulletin*.

I determined to track down the issue in question—no easy task, as it turned out. No United States or Canadian list of publications carried such a title. The Montreal Chamber of Commerce denied all knowledge of it. I finally pounced on a copy at a Times Square newsstand, where it had languished between one periodical devoted to stamp collecting and another dedicated to nude, hip-booted ladies.

Now, by no stretch of the imagination could the *National Bulletin* be termed a *news*paper. It is a weekly tabloid concentrating on the racier aspects of life. The edition at the time of writing, for instance, fronts headlines like FATHER OF 182 GIVES UP SEX AT AGE OF 99, and FOLK SINGER IN HOT WATER OVER GIRL, 14. The center spread features LOVE SPELLS OF WORLD'S LOVELIEST WITCH, and deals with Louise Huebner (see Chapter III) while consistently misspelling her name as "Heubner."

The article I was after had been penned by one Sam Pepper, who assured his readers: "I was able to lay hands on a top secret tape transcript of the return to the [Apollo] spacecraft. This transcript was received back on the Earth as the words were uttered, yet Mission Control kept them secret from the public at large, by a delay tape technique, that allows monitors on Earth to censor video and audio tape two or three minutes before it is transmitted to your home television."

Mr. Pepper then quoted from his transcript, allegedly verbatim, what moon walkers Armstrong and Aldrin said that caused Houston to cut them off:

"What was it, what the hell was it? That's all I want to know . . ."

"These—(garbled) babies were huge, sir, they were enormous . . ."

"No, no, that's just field distortion—Oh, God, you wouldn't believe it . . ."

"What—what—what the hell's going on? Whatsa matter with you guys, wha . . ."

"They're there, under the surface . . ."

"What's there? (garbled)—malfunction—Control calling Apollo."

"Roger, we're here, all three of us, but we've found some visitors . . ."

"Yeah, they've been here for quite a while judging by the installations . . ."

"Mission Control, repeat last message . . ."

"I'm telling you, there are other spacecraft out there! They're lined up in ranks on the far side of the crater edge."

It went on for a column or so more—an UFOlogical dream come true. The question was only; where and how did Sam Pepper obtain this supersecret transcript? And why—with the world's press to choose from—did he pick the pretty obscure *Bulletin* in which to unfurl his sensation?

The whole story obviously hinged on those questions. In order to solve them I wrote to the *National Bulletin* in Montreal. My letter was returned marked "Undeliverable." I wrote to the paper's given New York office. And I wrote to Mr. Pepper in care of both offices. No reply was forthcoming from any of them.

Unable to get enlightenment from the source, I asked one of my saucerian contacts why he thought Mission Control would censor the astronauts' fantastic discovery.

"Well," he said patiently, "the government can't admit that there's a technically advanced race of people up there. Maybe a superrace. It would cause a panic—send Wall Street into a tailspin."

"Okay. But then why didn't Mr. Pepper release his material abroad?"

He gave me the indulgent smile reserved for the uninitiated. "They wouldn't publish it either. The CIA would stop 'em. And then, there are the churches, too. And the international financial powers."

Then I knew. It was "them" again.

With most of the normal mass communications media closed to UFO lore, saucerians have to rely chiefly on their own specialized publications. These consist of enormous numbers of paperback books, mountains of mimeographed pamphlets (some so fabulously spelled and syntaxed that they read like satires on the subject) and a small group of periodicals.

These journals blossom and fade rather rapidly, but they boast a couple of indestructible personalities who can be relied upon to launch a new project the moment the old one withers on the vine.

One of them is Gray Barker, head of a miniature empire called Saucerian Publications, and himself author of several UFO-logical volumes. Barker runs his organization from his hometown of Clarksburg, West Virginia, thus refuting the rumor that saucerdom is a county in southern California.

His main vehicle currently is the already mentioned *Saucer News* which prints virtually *anything* connected with the topic, with a splendidly seigneurial disregard for details like style, technical accuracy or sources.

It hasn't always been like that. *Saucer News* was started in 1954 by a young ex-Princetonian named James W. Moseley, who brought to it not only education, taste and some capital, but also a high degree of genuine intellectual curiosity.

For several years the magazine presented a well-balanced picture of the UFO scene. It faithfully reported sightings, interviewed eyewitnesses, featured various—sometimes conflicting—interpretations and took considerable pains trying to identify those swarming, zooming, hovering whatsits in the sky.

Moseley learned the hard way that this was the last thing his readers wanted. What they demanded was confirmation of their faith; analysis merely irritated them. UFOs were symbols of a developing religion, contactees its enlightened prophets. To doubt—or even closely scrutinize—either meant becoming identified with those learned skeptics in the observatories who refused to see the splendors of lunar civilization simply because it didn't show up on their telescopes.

The saucerians, who accounted for the vast majority of his

public, grew distinctly miffed at Moseley's rationalism. Since he wouldn't supply their monthly dose of unquestioned miracles they turned to other periodicals that did.

In due course, Moseley lowered his standards, but never enough to reconcile his lost readers. Somehow his critical faculties always showed through and ruined the starry-eyed acceptance of the impossible, the true Alice in Wonderland flavor most saucerians insist on.

Moseley eventually sold his publication to Gray Barker, but he remained an important writer and lecturer in the field. He holds by far the most original views of any UFOlogist I spoke to.

A lean, well-groomed man, who wears business suits and executive glasses, Moseley admits that he has changed some of his opinions drastically over the years.

"I used to think that all people who claimed to have met space beings and ridden in their craft were simply profit-seeking yarn spinners," he said in his quiet professorial voice. "But that's not necessarily so."

"You mean those accounts might be true?"

"I mean they might be true to *them*—or some of them, anyway. They might never have taken a saucer trip in their lives and yet be telling the truth *as they know it*."

He gave an odd kind of half-shrug. "It's difficult to explain —but there is a strange consistency in most contactee stories, a distinct pattern. If they rest on delusion then it's a real mass delusion, cut to a standard measure. Almost as if it were imposed by some outside force. I think," he added cautiously, "that the solution of the whole UFO mystery might lie in our correctly interpreting these contactee reports. Not taking them at face value, but rather reading the symbols that keep recurring."

"And have you deciphered any of those symbols?" I asked.

He laughed. "I've been trying for twenty years, and I haven't managed it yet. Maybe I never will. Maybe none of us will."

The enigma of the flying saucers actually contains two mysteries wrapped in one package. The first is the nature of the objects themselves. For although the Condon Report seems to have explained the majority of sightings, there remains an unidentified rest still defying analysis. Could these be the result of some hitherto unknown natural phenomenon? Or extraterrestrial spacecraft probing our planet just as we probe theirs?

But the second riddle has perhaps more immediate significance. It is the reaction—or rather overreaction—of a huge number of people toward the mere possibility of such spacecraft existing. Their response was not so much curiosity or fear, but frantic attempts to incorporate them into their own frame of reference, no matter on how infantile a level. To turn them into parts of a miracle creed not so very different from the accustomed fare pumped out by television and comic strips.

In this they behaved exactly like those cargo cultists of the South Pacific, who had to make a totemistic religion of the white man's coming in order to absorb its impact.

This reaction is neither new nor confined to any particular portion of mankind. It was evident in sixteenth-century Europe, whose citizens were forced to rearrange their entire concept of their place in the universe as a result of Galileo's and Copernicus's discoveries. Their rearrangement took the form of hundreds of new religious movements—some lasting, some ephemeral—and violent rebellions against their temporal and spiritual masters.

But in one respect our contemporary saucerians differ sharply from previous movements. Whereas the Renaissance rebels were determined to help themselves, our UFOlogists expect help from beyond this earth.

The mystery lies in their trauma of helplessness, their obsession that all governments have entered an immense conspiracy against them. There is something curiously un-Occidental in their passivity; a fatalistic resignation quite alien to their social heritage. In all the incidents involving the "Men in Black," for instance, I did not hear of a single one of the alleged victims attempting to fight back!

Aid is to come solely from the space creatures—and then only if mankind were willing to surrender its sovereignty, to grant them bases, abide by their rules, join their confederation as decidedly junior members. Then—and only then—will they descend and solve the problems of this planet in their own fashion. Most saucerians seem to derive positive pleasure from the idea of our subjugation.

The fact that such an attitude should be widespread in an

age of unprecedented human power is perhaps the real core of the conundrum.

For it may be that UFOlogists are appealing for relief from human strength, not weakness. For respite from the scientific-mechanical juggernaut that has grown beyond their comprehension and is pushing them further and further into realms in which they cannot find their bearings.

If such is indeed the case, then the saucerian movement will gain fresh adherents every time man conquers another inch of the expanding, timeless, incomprehensible universe.

IX
LOST WORLDS AND SECRET CITIES

THERE IS A definite overlap between this chapter and the previous one. The kinship does not lie in the subject matter, but in some of the personalities involved. For a great many of the people now embracing saucerianism hold—or held—equally fervent convictions regarding the existence of fabulous hidden realms right here on earth.

It makes for a curious synthesis of very new and very ancient beliefs. UFOs, after all, date back only to the late 1940s. But the concept of Shangri-la or its equivalents seems to be as old and widespread as human society.

The Scandinavians had the legend of a tropical island paradise called Ultima Thule somewhere in the far north. Pre-Norman England produced King Arthur's magical court of Camelot, which, characteristically, came to grief over a moral lapse of its queen.

The Spanish conquistadores explored and ransacked South America in search of the golden El Dorado. Half a dozen nations of Asia Minor, as well as the Persians, believed in the mystical city of Shamballah which some held to be the actual Garden of Eden.

In one instance a reputedly legendary site turned out to be a historical fact. This was the Troy of Homer's *Iliad*, destroyed by the most famous ruse in military annals. For over two thousand years the city and the entire Trojan War were considered a classical fairy tale, until an eccentric millionaire proved otherwise.

Heinrich Schliemann, the son of a German clergyman, grew up obsessed with the vividness of Achilles, Paris, Odysseus, the Wooden Horse, and all the rest of Homer's poetry, which his father read to him as a bedside story. It was too detailed, too realistic, he convinced himself, for a mere legend.

Schliemann made a huge fortune in the California gold rush. He determined to use every cent of it, if necessary, to prove the reality of Troy. Using Homer's epic as a guide map, he decided that the site of the city had to be at Hissarlik, a Turkish village on the Asian shore of the Dardanelles strait. He began digging there in April 1870, and kept on for four years.

He found not one Troy, but nine of them! Nine cities buried on top of each other, ranging in size from small towns to mighty walled capitals. They were all unmistakably Troys— but which was *the* Troy? Schliemann decided that Troy VIIA— the second largest—was King Priam's stronghold, immortalized by Homer. It was destroyed by the Achaean Greeks some time around 1180 B.C., a deed probably quite unconnected with the abduction of the beauteous Helen of Sparta and more likely the result of commercial rivalry between the Greek city-states and the Trojans.

The example of Troy is cited over and over by the champions of mythological geography, most of whom regard Schliemann as their patron saint. But there are two decisive differences between his convictions and theirs.

The first is that Schliemann never invested his dream city with supranormal qualities; he regarded it as an ancient town like any other. And secondly he did not try to establish that it wielded a mysterious influence over our present world.

But these are precisely the points thousands of contemporary occultists are striving to make. For them it isn't enough to prove the past existence of some legendary realm. It has to either *still* exist or at least mold the fate of mankind in some metaphysical fashion that reaches out from the past.

Take Robert Ernst Dickhoff, who gave us the twelve-foot Venusian Garuda man-eaters mentioned in the last chapter. Mr. Dickhoff, described by his ads as a "Man of dedicated Honesty and Truth," also discovered that vast portions of the globe were once colonized by Martians. In his astonishing book *Agharta* he presents a graphic picture of the network of tunnels they created, radiating out from Antarctica and surfacing in the western United States, Brazil, Tibet, and several Pacific islands. According to his estimates, they went back to Mars about eighty thousand years ago, but left behind one secret metropolis called Rainbow City, which still serves as an interplanetary space port. That, apparently, is where it all ties in with UFOs.

Milinko S. Stevic, a Yugoslav-born engineer currently lecturing on the United States parapsychological circuit, advances an even more startling theory. He holds that there are entire subterranean towns situated beneath such large surface centers as Tokyo, Leningrad, Buenos Aires, Sao Paulo and New York.

These underground cities are connected with each other by a system of tunnels. It was via these tunnels, Mr. Stevic explains, that Adolf Hitler reached America, where he now resides in New Jersey.

Stevic is a short, balding man with glittering spectacles, who usually dresses in sober black. He speaks with tremendous animation, but with such a powerful Slavonic accent that it is sometimes difficult to decide whether he is addressing you in English or his native Serbo-Croat.

"The access of churches—many churches—have been built over the secret entrances of the subterranean city," said Stevic, pointing at the floor. He lowered his voice and revealed: "One of those churches is St. John the Divine at 103rd Street and Amsterdam. All churches which are marked as 'Monuments' —meaning you cannot tear them apart—all such buildings are hiding secret entrances with push-button elevators."

I don't know about those push-button elevators, but Mr.

Stevic was definitely wrong about St. John the Divine. It's at
112th Street—not 103rd, in New York City.

The underground towns are part of the Atlantean empire
on earth; but only a minor part. The major portion is housed
in hermetically sealed cities at the bottom of the Atlantic Ocean.

"There are about twenty of these cities, covered with giant
domes made of fiberglass," explained Stevic, waving his arms
to illustrate the huge size of the domes. "There are three such
layers of glass, and the thickest is about fifty meters—" He
mumbled some rapid calculations and added, "That is 164 feet.
The domes are not exactly semispherical, but more like egg-
shaped."

Mr. Stevic's Atlantean theory is also linked with flying
saucers. Some of them originate from Atlantis. Others from the
moon, from Mars, Venus, Mercury and Jupiter. One of their
functions is to deposit extraterrestrial visitors in the United States
of America. Stevic estimates the number of such visitors living
here now as "above 5 million."

Whatever the strength of Stevic's theory, it is a perfect
example of the juxtaposition of antique and contemporary
beliefs which permeate America's occult demographic imagery.

The legend of Atlantis dates back to Plato. The Greek
philosopher introduced it in two of his dialogues, written in
the fifth century B.C. He described it as continent, "larger than
Libya and Asia put together," and the heart of a great and
powerful empire.

"But afterward there occurred violent earthquakes and floods,
and in a single day and night of rain all your warlike men in
a body sank into the earth, and the island of Atlantis in like
manner disappeared beneath the sea. And that is the reason
why the sea in those parts is impassable and impenetrable, because
there is such a quantity of shallow mud in the way; and this
was caused by the subsidence of the island."

We have since learned, of course, that the central Atlantic
Ocean is neither impassable nor impenetrable, but this the
Atlantean theorists explain by the mud having sunk much further
beneath the surface. They still place the location of the lost
continent as roughly in mid-ocean, between America to the west,

Europe and Africa to the east, and Greenland to the north (see Figure 24).

It was somewhat harder to explain just where and how Plato received his information. He quoted no sources of any kind, and most of his contemporaries seem to have regarded the story simply as philosophical symbolism. But it is quite possible that he was referring to the Minoan empire of Crete, the world's first maritime power, which, though situated in the wrong ocean, was almost certainly devastated by a colossal earthquake or series of volcanic explosions.

But regardless of his sources, Plato's account of the lost continent aroused an echo that is reverberating through the world to this day. More than two thousand books have been written on the subject, the authors ranging from earnest geophysicists to equally earnest crackpots of every hue and persuasion.

Before delving any further, it should be stated here and now that no scientific proof—either geological or archaeological—has ever been found to support the existence of Atlantis. Historically the situation is even more nebulous, since Plato dates the destruction of the empire island as around 9600 B.C.—that is well before chronicled history began.

The most recent geological findings, in fact, point the other way. According to Dr. Robert S. Dietz and John C. Holden of the Environmental Science Services Administration laboratories in Miami, Africa and South America were once a single continent (their outlines still fit if you place them together) but were pushed apart by a massive subterranean flow—which is still running and pushing continents at the rate of up to four inches a year. With Africa and South America united in one land mass, there simply would have been no room for Atlantis to exist—at least not as a continent.

However, if there is no scientific evidence that Atlantis ever existed, neither do we have decisive proofs that it *didn't* exist. Which may be a lopsided way of arguing, but one valid enough for a colossal number of researchers. The most spectacular of them was undoubtedly Ignatius Donnelly, United States congressman from Minnesota during the 1860s.

Donnelly based his conviction on the striking similarities

between certain cultural features of ancient Egypt and the Indian civilizations of pre-Columbian South America. Both constructed pyramids, both knew the art of embalming the dead, both used a 365-day calendar. Ergo, he reasoned, they must have learned these accomplishments from an even older culture thriving on a continent situated about halfway between their regions—Atlantis.

Donnelly wrote before the raft voyages of Thor Heyerdahl demonstrated that such cultural exchanges could also have occurred by mass migration over very long distances.

In any case, Donnelly's surmises were much too worldly to satisfy the esoteric groups who have since taken over Atlantis lock, stock, and legend. For in more recent times the Lost Continent has become the virtual preserve of the mystics, who are quite uninterested in the geophysical side of the question. Madame Blavatsky's theosophists, Rudolf Steiner's Anthroposophists, the Rosicrucians, and a dozen other bodies simply take Atlantis for granted and proceed from there.

Their method is more or less that of Edgar Cayce, who did more than anyone else to make Atlantis part of the occult upsurge. Cayce gained his knowledge of the continent—like he gained everything else—through his trance readings. With his usual honesty he quite frankly admitted that he had no explicit proofs for his theories, and didn't twist himself into knots trying to manufacture some.

Cayce taught that the Atlanteans boasted a civilization several thousand years ahead of their times, possessing a form of laser beam and flying machines. Just before the final castastrophe swallowed up their empire, waves of Atlanteans dispersed in all directions. They took with them some of their advanced technology and thus accounted for the emergence of superior—and strangely similar—cultures in Peru, Mexico, Guatemala, Mesopotamia and Egypt.

It is this part of the Cayce creed that has captured the imagination of occultists throughout America. They introduced a few alterations, such as Atlantis being destroyed by a series of *atomic* explosions unleashed in a terrible continental war. They also insist that all of mankind's great inventors, artists and religious leaders were actually Atlanteans who—throughout history—have acted in

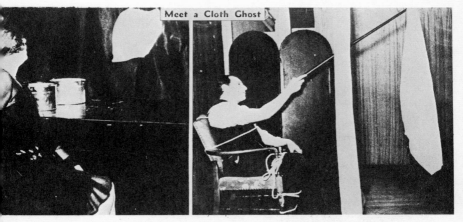

25. Joseph Dunninger producing a "spirit apparition." Tied to chair inside curtained booth, fake exposer frees his hand, brings out stick concealed in sections and white cloth tightly folded under his vest. Dangled from stick, ghost cloth looks effective in darkness (PHOTO: *Look* MAGAZINE).

26. Blowing a "ghost." Rose Mackenberg, former assistant of Harry Houdini, manufactures ectoplasm by filling her mouth with mixture of soap, egg white and gelatin in water, then blowing a bubbling cascade that glows in the dark (PHOTO: *Look* MAGAZINE).

Ghost From a Bottle

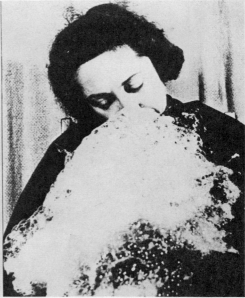

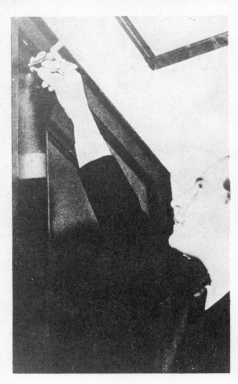

27. Mechanical spirit rapper fastened to wall produces ghost knocks by means of clockwork. Rappers retail at $4.75 (PHOTO: *Look* MAGAZINE).

28. Spirit message on slate. Dunninger demonstrates how fake medium can write message even though his hands are held in the dark (PHOTO: LA TERZA).

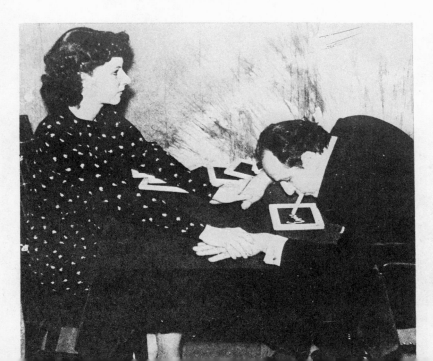

29. George King, president of the Los Angeles Aetherius Society, working on his invention—the "spiritual energy radiator."

30. Edwin John Dingle—Ding Le Mei—holding class in his Institute of Mentalphysics, a movement headquartered in California's Yucca Valley.

31. Anton LaVey, high priest of the First Church of Satan. A former lion tamer, carnival performer and police photographer, he now heads sect of more than 7000 Satanists.

32. The ESPATEACHER, an apparatus specially designed to test an individual's extrasensory powers by registering correct guesses as to the sequence of lights flicking on and off.

33. This and next picture show experiment conducted by ASPR (American Society for Psychical Research). "Receiver" behind curtain faces twenty-five tiles. She is to touch them in a prearranged order not known to her.

34. "Sender" watches "Receiver's" hand on closed circuit TV several rooms away. She must try to "push" subject's hand toward prearranged tile by thought waves alone.

35. One of the assistants of the American Society for Psychical Research (ASPR) conducting a pendulum test.

36. Dr. Karlis Osis, ASPR's director of research, showing range of long-distance experiment with ESP. Participants were stationed in New York and Tasmania, Australia.

small, closed groups and still continue to do so. The titles of these groups may vary, they may be called the Masters, the Brothers, or the Wise Ones, but their heritage and purpose are the same.

The Atlantean cult is frankly elitist, based on the conviction that a hidden handful of superior men and women secretly guide the world's destiny. I only met one self-professed Atlantean who, however, told me that I had probably met many others without becoming aware of it.

She was a middle-aged Philadelphia nurse named Angela Newbrig, who heads a small circle of believers calling themselves the Silver Choir. The choir part, I was told, is strictly symbolic. They don't sing.

"Are all Choir members Atlanteans?" I asked their leader.

"Oh, no," said Miss Newbrig. "I'm the only one in the group."

She waved an elbow at the four men and seven women shoe-horned into her two-room apartment. "They simply add their psychic vibrations to mine when I communicate with my Atlantean brothers and sisters. We do it by mental radio, you know, and they"—she waved again—"help to increase my range."

"How many Atlanteans are there in this country?"

"That's one of our secrets." She bent her graying head close to mine. "I'll give you just one of their names, so you'll know that I'm telling the truth. Mr. Billy Graham!"

Unfortunately it proved almost impossible to disentangle Miss Newbrig's "pure" Atlanteans from another group—the Lemurians. This decidedly upstart breed only appeared on the occult scene about eighty years ago, but they effectively trumped the Atlanteans by revealing themselves as *their* ancestors.

Whereas Atlantis harkens back to antiquity, the Lemurians' pedigree goes no further than to a nineteenth-century English zoologist. Phillip Lutley Sclater pondered on the distribution of a little simian animal called lemur, found mainly in Madagascar and Southeast Asia. He suggested that a land bridge might once have existed in the Indian Ocean, which might account for their present habitats.

From this premise—and no other—sprang the vision of Lemuria.

Madame Blavatsky promptly adopted Lemuria as the home of one of her "root races"—four-armed giants, who were sexual hermaphrodites to boot.

But the true prophet of Lemuria was a retired British cavalry officer. Colonel James Churchward, formerly of His Majesty's Bengal Lancers, was seventy years old and living in Mount Vernon, New York, before he began to write down his Lemurian manuals.

The Colonel had served in India and become friendly with the high priest of a monastery. This priest led him to a collection of clay tablets hidden in a cave and helped him decipher the hieroglyphics with which they were covered. From these tablets, Churchward maintained, came his detailed knowledge of Lemuria, which he preferred to call Mu (pronounced Moo).

It should be noted that no one but the Colonel has ever seen a single one of these tablets and that they had a habit of becoming more graphic as time went on. The Colonel's first book, *The Lost Continent of Mu*, appeared in 1926. This was followed by three others, each more detailed than the previous, and more were promised before Churchward died in 1936—all or mostly drawn from those mysterious tablets inscribed with Mu letters.

It is to Churchward—or rather to his tablets—that we owe what concrete statistics exist on Lemuria.

For a start Mu was not merely a continent, but the biblical Garden of Eden as well as the cradle of *all* humanity. Man was created there—by a single act—200 million years ago. The continent was an immense stretch of rolling country, over five hundred miles long and three hundred miles broad. It extended from north of Hawaii to the vicinity of the Fiji Islands, thus straddling between the North and South Pacific Ocean. At its population peak—some twelve thousand years ago—it harbored 64 million people in nearly perfect amity. The people of Mu were both highly civilized and peaceful, but Churchward stressed that the dominant race of the continent was white and ruled—gently but firmly—over their black, brown and yellow brethren.

This paradise perished through the explosion of a subterranean gas belt, leaving only the Pacific islands sticking above the surface of the ocean. And, of course, those clay tablets.

The Colonel was no great shakes as a stylist. He employed

what might be termed "parade ground prose,"—that is he made up in repetition what he lacked in expressiveness. He also reached for occult means when he ran out of scientific ones; using telepathy and trance visits to previous incarnations to fill in the considerable gaps in his knowledge of geology and archeology.

His books did fine in their original hardcover editions. Later, when our occult resurgence made Mu a red-hot topic, they were reissued as paperbacks and are now selling like—well, reasonably warm cakes. Lemurian aficionados quote them as textbook classics. One of them, a student of U.C.L.A., assured me gravely that Churchward had won a Nobel Prize (he wasn't certain which) for his works.

The American revival of Lemurianism predated UFOlogy by several years. It could, in fact, be described as the dawn of our occult renaissance, and coincided with the closing years of World War II. And here we come upon one of the guiding lights of United States mysticism, the man whose name runs like a red binding thread through the annals of Lemurianism, saucerianism and several subsequent developments of related themes.

He is a small man with an impish expression named Raymond A. Palmer. At present he lives on a dairy farm in Amherst, Wisconsin, while simultaneously running a remarkable bundle of publications, which include *Flying Saucers*, *Search*, a swelling library of occultist books, plus a mail-order business for prayer-inscribed tiles, religious desk sets, chili seasoning, and hair restorer.

Before founding his own publishing outfit, Palmer edited the Ziff-Davis Company's science-fiction magazines, *Amazing Stories* and *Fantastic Adventures*. Early in 1945 he received a manuscript—perpetrated rather than typed—entitled "A Warning to Future Man." It came from a Pennsylvania welder named Richard B. Shaver, and was of a quality that made Palmer's fellow editors wish to consign it instantly to the reject basket.

Palmer, however, showed the unique instinct for the wants of his reading public he demonstrated over and over again in later years. He did what very few editors ever do—sat down and rewrote Mr. Shaver's outpourings in acceptable pulp prose. He also sent the original author a check for a hundred dollars.

The piece—rechristened "I Remember Lemuria!"—appeared in the March 1945 issue of *Amazing Stories*. It created what *Life* magazine termed "the most celebrated rumpus that rocked the science fiction world." And it added fifty thousand copies to Palmer's circulation.

The story was told in form of a "racial memory"; series of images flashing through the author's mind, which *could* have been actual remembrances of a primeval past.

According to Shaver, all mankind are descendants of a race of giants who once inhabited the earth and departed for distant planets around twelve thousand years ago. Humans have lost all memory of them, except for vague legendry about Atlantis and Lemuria. But the heritage of those giants is still thriving under our feet.

There, in an immense world of underground caverns, live the "abandondero"—the Abandoned Ones—who had been left behind when the giants migrated into space.

They have degenerated into a legion of dwarfish cretins, as vicious as they are stupid, known as the "detrimental robots" or "dero" for short. The dero are malevolence personified, their chief pleasure comes in form of sexual orgies of such unspeakable depravity that they end in hideous physical deformations of the participants.

Their secondary pastime is the constant harassment of human surface dwellers, which manifests itself in anything from tripping folks who are running for a bus to feeding them suggestions of rape, arson or murder while they're sleeping. The dero, in fact, are the "devils" that have plagued mankind since history began.

Unfortunately for us, the magnificent giants abandoned much of their machinery underground, together with the "abandondero." Which means that the dero have access to such marvels as tele-portation gadgets, rock-piercing long-distance rays, space rockets, rejuvenating apparatus, and devices capable of projecting dreams, illusions and mental suggestions.

All these wonders are now being used to bedevil and hamper us Homo sapiens. But they could, Shaver suggested, be wrested from the hands of the dero and utilized for our benefit. It was simply a question of penetrating the netherworld in the right places and getting hold of this gadgetry.

The reaction of the science fiction public to this story seems to have flabbergasted even Palmer. He was, after all, putting out a fiction magazine, and no one had hitherto regarded *Amazing Stories* as anything else.

But the deluge of letters he received in response struck a new —almost alarming—note. Thousands of people began to *Remember Lemuria!* In more or less dead earnest.

As described in the story, the dero frequently come to the earth's surface and can pass as moderately unattractive humans. Now a multitude of readers wrote in describing encounters with them. Several suggested that the Japanese—then the wartime enemy—were actually dero and that Pearl Harbor had constituted the start of the general attack on humanity Shaver had predicted. A frightening number of people confessed to being under telepathic influence from the dero, who were trying to goad them into anything from bomb-planting to multiple homicide.

For the next four years the Lemurian stories appeared regularly and kept Palmer's magazine at its peak 185,000 circulation—a record in the science fiction field. The pieces became known collectively as "The Shaver Mystery," although style and treatment were indubitably Palmer's. The real mystery about the series is how much of it was actually written by Shaver. Palmer claimed to have visited the arc welder in his Pennsylvania home and to have convinced himself that the man was really in touch with the cave people. They spoke to him, he related, in loud and strident voices, informing him of the latest horrors committed by the dero. On that particular occasion they had torn a woman into four pieces only a few miles from the Shaver house.

The series ended—by order of the publisher—in 1949. There is some difference of opinion as to the reason for their termination. Palmer insists it was because they "contradicted Einstein" —one of those enigmatic statements for which he is famous. The publishers maintain that readers got tired of them; which is certainly only partly true. The genuine science fiction buffs were indeed protesting against the Shaver saga being presented as fact. But the mystical fringe was a long way from saturation point.

Judged strictly by the standard of their peers, the Shaver (or Palmer) stories were minor masterpieces. Leaving aside their alleged factuality, they glowed with a sinister incandescence that conjured up every reader's latent childhood terrors, with a few adolescent sex traumas thrown in for good measure. They worked along decidedly atavistic lines, stirring hobgoblin memories lying dormant in most of us. The very word "dero"—with its instant devilish association—was a semantic bull's-eye.

They were to fantasy pulps what *Treasure Island* was to pirate novels—irresistibly vivid pictorializations of a basically remote theme. There is a direct parallel between Blind Pew with his stick tap-tapping over fog-moistened cobblestones and the malformed dero hobbling through cavernous tunnels: both are the original stuff nursery nightmares are made of. And it takes real talent— perhaps even a soupçon of genius—to weave it.

When the Shaver series ended, Palmer immediately gave further proof that his finger rested firmly on the nation's occult pulse. In the very first issue of his new magazine, *Fate*, he published Kenneth Arnold's history-making article, "I Did See the Flying Disks," and thus launched saucerology upon the world.

Palmer was the pioneer plugger of the UFOs interplanetary origins—for which he printed a staggering array of material. But just as it was impossible to determine how much of the copy he wrote himself, so it remained a moot point how much of it he meant seriously. He had—and still has—a singular knack of putting statements in the form of oblique questions; planting the thought while seemingly leaving the decision to the reader.

You can go through volumes of his output without ever being able to nail down his convictions. Every key statement seems to end in a question mark. It may be his way of allowing himself room to maneuver which—by the run of things—might be essential. He is definitely not overburdened with consistency. After years of expounding on the extraterrestrial nature of flying saucers, for instance, he veered to the opinion that they come from inside our hollow earth!

It is at this point that the UFO syndrome gets inextricably tangled with a row of underworld themes, bringing in earth gods, dwarfs, giants, subterranean serpents, and the whole kingdom of Pan, complete with the fauns, centaurs and satyrs of classical mythology.

A number of spiritualist organizations hold that these crea-tures—plus others undreamed of by the ancients—are alive and exceedingly active in the bowels of the earth. The Borderland Sciences Research Associates of Vista, California, specialize in describing encounters with them; sometimes via psychic projection, occasionally in person.

But with the coming of the UFO, a new dimension was added to the picture. One set of beliefs merged with another, so that today we have the cavern creatures increasingly identified with outer space beings. Often to such an extent that the term Venusian, for example, could denote an inhabitant of sub-Antarctica as easily as a planetary dweller—simply according to who uses it.

The merging process began simultaneously with the appearance of the Shaver series. While Lemuria was being projected from Chicago, a Mrs. and Mrs. Hefferlin were releasing their version of the underworld from Livingston, Montana. In their preamble, Gladys Hefferlin made a point of telling readers that their material bore no connection with the Shaver Mystery—a somewhat superfluous statement.

The Hefferlins held that the focal point of the global maze of caverns and tunnels was Rainbow City. Situated aboveground in the Antarctic, warmed by hot springs and protected by ice walls ten thousand feet high, the city was built 2½ million years ago—of plastic. Its population figure is uncertain but, to quote the authors, "no one is a freak of any sort."

Far from being in the grip of depraved dero, Rainbow City and the subterranean passages that radiate from it are the realm of a highly benevolent trio of rulers called the Ancient Three. Their forebears originated on Mars, but the present triumvirate were born on earth. Which may account for their preoccupation with global politics.

As the Hefferlins told it, World War II was virtually won by the Ancient Three on behalf of the Allies. Thus Rommel's drive into Egypt was not stopped by General Montgomery and his Eighth Army. "The Ancient Three stepped in there and caused Rommel to run. They laid down the law to Rommel and scared him so much that he dared not take another step into Egypt."

Similarly it was not General MacArthur who halted the Pacific drive of the Japanese at the northern gateway to Australia. "The Ancient Three stepped in and stopped the Japs in their own way."

This much is history, but from there the Hefferlins seem to

have perused some hitherto unknown textbooks. According to
them:

"The Arabian States united into a federation by act of the
Ancient Three. And the strength of the federation as a unit is
greater than the combined strength of the individual states.
They organized according to the pattern of the United States,
which is the pattern that all the world will follow when the time
is ripe."

The Hefferlin revelations must have come as a dizzying surprise to American, British and Australian war veterans alike. Also
to whatever Israelis that might have chanced to read them.

But for our purposes it is more important to note how the
theme of a hidden polar metropolis keeps cropping up on the
occult atlas. Rainbow City (remember Dickhoff's Agharta) is
just one name for it, and the Martians merely one race of many
credited with its creation. Others include Venusians, Atlanteans,
Lemurians, earth trolls, the spirits of lost spelunkers and—
according to a Norwegian resident of California named Olaf
Jansen—the twelve-feet-tall forebears of man himself.

Opinions likewise vary as to which pole houses the mystery
town. Most mystics plunge for the Antarctic, since the South
Polar area boasts a solid land mass as large as the entire American
continent. It remains partly unexplored—a white, empty expanse
on the map. The fact that it has been flown over many times does
not disturb the Rainbow City theorists. For the fabled site is either
(a) so well camouflaged as to be invisible from the air, (b) underground or (c) frequently spotted, but the reports invariably
hushed up by the governments concerned for reasons similar to
those causing the official silence on UFOs.

The North Pole is rather less inviting to legendry, mainly
because it consists of ocean several miles deep and covered for the
most part with eternal ice. That, at least, is the picture handed
out by explorers and geographers. Since it lies surrounded on all
sides by known regions like Siberia, Canada, Alaska, Greenland,
Iceland and Scandinavia the official version is pretty generally
accepted.

But not by the mystic minority who have selected the million
or so square miles of Arctic Ocean between Alaska and the
magnetic pole as the location of their particular lost continent.

They received a tremendous moral boost from a remark which Admiral Richard E. Byrd made before setting out on his polar flight in 1947: "I'd like to see that land beyond the pole. That area is the center of the great unknown."

Coming from the then greatest living polar explorer, this was electrifying. We still don't know whether Byrd meant his statement to be taken literally or as a romantic figure of speech. But to the occult-oriented it spelled only one thing: the Admiral was off to find their fable land!

From that moment on the rumors began to descend like confetti. Stories of radioed messages reporting fantastic sights (promptly censored by U. S. Naval Research). Of warm, densely wooded regions surrounded on all sides by icy seas. Of amazing plants and animals spotted by Byrd both in the north and south polar regions. One writer even stated that the Admiral had actually watched a prehistoric mammoth shambling through thick undergrowth.

The only item missing was confirmation by the explorer himself. And it remains missing to this day. During his lifetime Admiral Byrd refused to let anyone go over his private diaries and charts. And after his death his Boston family stuck to the refusal.

This, however, has not prevented the appearance of more than a dozen books, brochures and magazine articles vividly describing the hidden wonderlands Byrd allegedly discovered around both poles.

Then—in December 1959—the indefatigable Raymond Palmer launched the theory that UFOs came from *underneath* the polar caps.

He did so in the publication *Flying Saucers,* and with his customary sphinxlike aplomb. He began by marshaling an impressive arsenal of proofs against the interplanetary origin of spacecraft (which he had propagated with equal dexterity for the preceding nine years). He proceeded to demolish the image of a "perfectly round Earth" (which scientists abandoned decades ago) and instead drew attention to the Van Allen radiation belt around our planet. Then came the gist of the message—as usual accompanied by question marks:

"What if the Earth is not spherical, but actually doughnut

shaped, exactly as its surrounding Van Allen Belt? Whatever makes the belt thusly shaped, might it not also be responsible for shaping the Earth similarly?"

And if, he concluded, the earth is also hollow, "then we no longer need look for the saucers from outer space—but rather from 'inner space'!"

The idea of such a hollow globe actually dates back to a veteran of the War of 1812 named John Cleve Symmes. After retiring from the United States Army, Captain Symmes authored a manifesto, which he dispatched to five hundred schools and universities throughout America and Europe, declaring: "The earth is hollow. Habitable within; containing a number of concentric spheres; one within the other. It is open at the Pole 12 or 16 degrees."

Symmes, however, took the precaution of attaching to each of his manifestos a notarized certificate confirming his sanity.

Palmer had a harder row to hoe than the gallant captain. In Symmes's age both poles were uncharted regions and therefore open to any kind of speculation—including holes several thousand square miles in diameter. But today's aerial surveying, at least, would presumably notice such gaps in the earth's crust.

Palmer had an answer: it was that official conspiracy once again. Several governments (if not all of them) were fully aware of the earthly origin of flying saucers, he explained. They considered this knowledge top secret. If revealed it would bring public demand for action which would "topple governments." Why? Because the "inherent nature of the flying saucers and their origination area is completely disruptive to political and economic status quo."

He certainly had a point there. For if UFOs from outer space were considered too unnerving for mankind's feeble psyche, how much more so were saucers coming from right under our feet!

However, this still left the actual "hole in the pole" unproven. It remained so for quite a while. Eventually Palmer produced photographic evidence in the July 1970 edition of *Search*. (He has an intriguing habit of carrying on his polemics in both his magazines alternatively or simultaneously.)

The photograph was a blurry reproduction of the globe's

north polar region. In the center could be seen a dark, circular blob, described as the controversial hole. No such blob appears in any other photo of the area, making it a matter of speculation as to how it got on Mr. Palmer's particular copy.

In the November issue of *Search* appeared an article by Ray Palmer entitled "Don't Laugh at Me." It covered three closely printed pages requesting people not to laugh at him. . . .

In northern California's Siskiyou County, near the Oregon border, rises the cone of an extinct volcano. Looming 14,162 feet above a foot carpet of pine forests, Mount Shasta is both awesome and inspiringly beautiful. To a great many people it is also a great many other things.

No other mountain in the world has inspired so vast and varied a collection of occult attributes. Shasta is—according to whom you consult—the headquarters of America's witches, the earth base for several fleets of spacecraft, the home of the last surviving Lemurians, the hunting ground of the monstrous Big Foot, the lair of the magical Green Cat (actually a disguised goddess), the site of a nameless but well-hidden Oriental city with marble palaces and golden roofs, the main entrance of this continent's cavern world or, alternatively, the revealed vantage point from which to observe the Second Coming of Christ.

To the shopkeepers in nearby Weed it is something else again. As one of them expressed it, "That mountain is a goldmine. Brings in hordes of tourists every season. Sure, a lot of 'em are straight from the funny farm, but who cares! We never have no hassle with them, and they sure help business."

Among the groups who make a Mount Shasta pilgrimage every summer when the hiking is safe are the "Celestials." They number around forty (not counting children), come mainly from the Midwest, and are currently headed by Joe and Margaret Fonella. The Fonellas are a youngish couple, soft-voiced and courteous, who seem to live in a perpetual state of mild astonishment. The annual pilgrimage is their holiday. The rest of the year they run a stationery store in Chicago.

The Celestials are unique insofar as their entire purpose is based on the occult significance of Mount Shasta. Different members seek different things on, around and inside the mountain. They agree only on the geographical location of their quests.

I asked the Fonellas whether the same people come every year. They both shook their heads in unison.

"Oh, no. We get a large turnover every summer. We've only been going since 1968, and at least half the members have changed since then."

"And what exactly do *you* expect to find there?"

Joe smiled in a puzzled fashion. "Well, we read something in a magazine. About a man. He was looking at the mountain through this telescope and he saw a—well, a kind of . . . er—"

Margaret helped him out: "A town. With temples and golden houses like in India."

"Did you find that town?"

They looked at each other, then turned back to me. "No." After a moment Joe added, "It's probably there someplace. But that's a big mountain."

Was it just that city they were seeking?

Margaret smiled at the question. "There's lots more up there. It's a fantastic place, really. Flying saucers landing on top sometimes. And real way-out animals."

"And those strange people in robes," Joe put in.

His wife nodded. "Yes. A man who has a shop in Weed told us about them. People in robes. They come in and buy canned stuff from him. They talk in a language nobody knows. And they pay in gold dust."

"Do you have an idea who those people might be?" I asked.

Both Fonellas nodded. "They come from Lemuria," explained Margaret. "When we were still with the Rosicrucians we knew a lady who'd been inside the mountain—way deep inside. She met them in there, and they were real nice to her. They'd come here—oh, thousands of years ago. And they'd been living inside that mountain all the time. They showed her all that fantastic machinery they had—thinking machines and rockets and rays and like that. She told us all about it."

I clicked my ballpoint. "What's the lady's name?"

It was Joe's turn to answer, "Her name was Mrs. Moylan. But she's dead. She was kind of old."

I must have looked disappointed because Joe gave me an encouraging smile. "Well, anyway, we *know* about those people. From Mrs. Moylan—and then from the guy at the grocery store;

the one who'd told us they pay him with gold dust. That proves it, doesn't it. So—when we meet up with them—we'll let you know immediately."

"I could take notes," said Margaret. "I do shorthand."

I thanked them and left the stationery shop. I was already in the plane back to New York before I remembered that gold dust is no longer legal tender in the Golden State.

X

THE SPIRIT SEEKERS

IN THE FALL of 1959 I had my first encounter with what is generally known as a haunting. It does not rank among my favorite memories.

At the time I was working for an Australian press combine in Fleet Street, London. Our editor had heard stories about ghostly activities in—of all places—a cooperative dairy. Consequently a photographer and myself were dispatched to nearby Kent with orders to "spend the night and find out what the bloody hell's going on there."

We spent the night but we never did discover what, exactly, was going on.

Our equipment consisted of a camera, two flashlights, a tape recorder and one (unlicensed) .32-caliber pistol. With this gear we moved into the administrative building, a sad, naked little cement cube festooned with milk production charts and warnings against hoof and mouth disease. We drank black tea from a thermos flask and waited for things to happen.

What happened was mainly footsteps. Sometimes soft and shuffling, like carpet slippers. Then a series of rapid thumpety-thumpety-thumps, rather like a child skipping rope. Occasionally a measured, hobnailed tread, like a sentry pounding a beat up and down, down and up. At intervals this continued from about 12:30 A.M. until just before dawn.

The curious feature about these noises was that they seemed to come from nowhere in particular—they could have been made in the middle of the room, along the walls or above the ceiling; they had neither direction nor source.

Once—shortly after three—there was an unearthly crash outside the door. We rushed out and found that a row of empty metal milk containers had been flung across the yard skittle fashion. Some were still rolling when we arrived. There was nobody in sight. After that, for the rest of the night, it was just those footsteps again.

It didn't make much of a story. We had the sounds on tape, but that was about all. We had seen no levitations or apparitions, heard no moans or spirit voices, felt no mysterious chills. But the sweating, unnerving, totally irrational terror of that night stayed with me for a long time afterwards.

This was perhaps the oddest part of all. Because nothing that occurred had been in the least menacing or even especially eerie. The fright arose from the sheer inexplicability of the thing, from our utter helplessness in the face of it.

Theoretically, of course, it could have been the work of a prankster; but I'm willing to swear that it was not. We were both young, alert and pretty fast on our feet. And in the hygienic bareness of that dairy building there was absolutely no place for anyone to hide. And I can think of no known physical causes that might have produced the footsteps or scattered the milk cans.

I learned a lesson that night that stood me in good stead while researching this chapter. Simply this: the volume of fear engendered by a so-called "ghost manifestation" is out of all proportion to the event itself.

My encounter had been with a poltergeist—the most common and least esteemed of spirit phenomena. The word is German and means "racketing ghost." The German label has stuck chiefly because the first documented case of such a disturbance came from Bingen-am-Rhein in A.D. 355.

Poltergeists are rather a glut on the market; a dozen or more are reported each year in the United States alone. Psychic researchers hold them in about as much regard as film critics have for Popeye the Sailor. They are utterly pointless and undignified, they can crop up anywhere, any time, and they seem as devoid of rhyme or reason as they are of purpose.

Most parapsychologists, in fact, don't consider them spirits at all. Their term for these outbreaks is RSPK, which stands for "recurrent spontaneous psychokinesis." According to their theory the manifestations are caused by an unknown form of energy which emanates from a living person (usually an adolescent boy or girl) and transmutes itself into sounds or movements. This energy—a kind of concentrated anger or frustration—lingers on the premises even if the person producing it is not present. This tallies with the fact that nearly all poltergeist visitations occur in places housing either children close to puberty or adolescents; age groups in which anger and frustration levels are notoriously high. In our haunted dairy almost half the staff consisted of juveniles.

Poltergeists can be incredibly destructive—they have been known to hurl crockery, furniture, bricks and ornaments, smash windows, fuse lights, start fires and flood out entire basements. But there is no record of anyone being physically injured by them.

The accent here has to be on *physically*. Their emotional impact is quite another story.

Which brings us to the crux of the entire ghost syndrome or what passes as such. Leaving aside the welter of unsubstantiated legends, no investigator has yet unearthed a single instance of people getting hurt through a haunting per se. The damage is inflicted by our own psyche, which cannot accommodate the presence of "spirits." We have no means of coming to terms with such an experience.

An equivalent shock would be to look into a familiar mirror and suddenly notice that the glass is not reflecting the room it hangs in but . . . another room. By itself this discovery would be harmless. But it would be a cold, dry finger reaching into our brain, shifting something, altering our whole concept of the nature of things around us. And afterwards nothing would ever be *quite* the same.

The modern mind is particularly defenseless against phantoms. Our forebears had life patterns that included witches, ghosts, devils, leprechauns, basilisks and large assortments of demons. They were frightened of them, of course, but not substantially more so than they were of wolves, robbers or the plague. It is only since we have excluded such apparitions from the realm of the possible, since we have shed the protective armor of superstitions, that madness touches us when we believe ourselves confronted by them.

The naked horror they arouse is such that most of us are willing to accept *any* explanation for them, rather than cope with the reasonless, mindless nothing they would otherwise represent. It is no coincidence that the spiritualist movement had its formal start in the middle of the last century—during the very period when philosophical rationalism reached its peak.

A surprising number of occultists assume that spiritualism was imported to America from England. Actually it happened the other way around. The British merely took to it with grim enthusiasm and made it their own to such an extent that today the only worthwhile periodicals on the subject come from London.

The movement began in 1848, sparked by poltergeist manifestations in Hydesville, New York. The scene was the home of the Fox family, and the occurrences centered around the two young Fox daughters, Catherine and Margaret. The haunt—which came in the form of loud knocks—was unique, insofar as the children learned to communicate with it.

Little Cathie would clap her hands three times and command, "Do as I do, Mr. Splitfoot!" Whereupon three sharp knocks would ring out from somewhere. Margaret would raise her hand and ask in a childish singsong voice, "How many fingers, how many, how many?" And back came four slow raps.

The knocking spirit followed to whichever place the girls were sent. Neighbors, clergymen, newspaper reporters and medical committees came and marveled. Mrs. Fox and her daughters gave a string of public demonstrations, during which the girls played alphabetical question and answer games with their spook.

The poltergeist actually revealed its identity: he was the ghost of a man murdered in the Hydesville house.

The message audiences took from these performances became the doctrine of spiritualism: ghosts were the restless spirits of the dead. They could be communicated with, reasoned with, and coaxed into dispensing news from the beyond about other departed souls.

Some forty years later Catherine confessed that the whole business had been a hoax. She and Margaret had produced the rappings by cracking their knee joints and big toes. Witnesses swore that the sounds came from walls and ceilings.

But by then few people cared about what the Fox sisters said. Spiritualism had swept America and Europe. Introduced in England in 1850, it had become a fashionable passion among the Victorian middle and upper social strata (the only subsequent parallel was to be contract bridge). The French adopted it all the way down from the Empress Eugénie. In Germany—or rather Prussia—it gave rise to the immensely dignified Spiritualistische Studiengesellschaft (Spiritualist Study Society), which counted nine professors as members.

In the United States the movement achieved its zenith around the 1850s. The number of Spiritualists were then estimated at 1½ million (from a total population of 25,000,000), offering employment for 20,000 professional mediums and readership for 12 newspapers and magazines devoted exclusively to the creed.

The astounding spread of the movement was due to several factors acting in combination. Together they went far beyond the mere curiosity aroused by a poltergeist.

By giving spirits something like personalities, by contacting them and listening to their messages, spiritualism removed most of the dread attached to the phenomenon, turning it into a sociable, almost cozy thing. At the same time it presented participants with a comforting sense of continuity after death. Since spirits could, apparently, return from the grave and rejoin the living, however tenuously and briefly, it meant that death need not involve total loss of one's ego.

While thus offering a much more immediate assurance of afterlife than the established religions, spiritualism did not denigrate any orthodox faith. On the contrary, the movement insisted on its devoutly Christian framework and only opposed—as it still does—the lack of mysticism in most churches.

Yet after its initial flowering, spiritualism slid downhill on its native soil. It is, in fact, the only metaphysical creed that did not share in America's occult renaissance.

Today the National Spiritualist Association embraces four-hundred separate units, ranging from Arizona's Harmony Chapel to Wisconsin's Morris Pratt Institute. Total membership hovers at slightly above 150,000 (as against 50,000 in Great Britain, which has less than a quarter of our population).

The blame for this decline rests largely on the so-called "physical mediums"; meaning those sensitives who specialize in the production of visible and audible phenomena. For the general public they have become synonymous with spiritualism, and to say that their reputation is spotty would be putting it benevolently.

Starting with the Fox sisters, their history has been so permeated with fraud that the phonies have almost obliterated the honest practitioners. They are a living proof for the validity of Gresham's Law, which holds that an inferior currency will always drive good coinage out of circulation.

Perhaps the most celebrated medium around the turn of the century was an illiterate Neapolitan named Minervino Murge, who changed her name to Eusapia Palladino. She combined the dexterity of an acrobat with the morals of a barnyard fowl, and for thirty years left a trail of awed spectators and rumpled beds around the globe.

Her forte was phantom hands—which either plucked at people's clothes or strummed guitars—and wildly levitating tables. These hands would make themselves felt and heard even though Eusapia's own were firmly clasped by other sitters. They supposedly belonged to her spirit guide, a deceased Englishman named John King.

Palladino's triumphant career fizzled out during an American tour in 1909. There one of her séances was attended by Harvard psychologist Hugo Münsterburg. The Harvard investigator managed to conceal a black-clad assistant under the table. He watched Eusapia slip a bare, prehensile foot out of her shoe, pluck at coats with her toes and nimbly run them over guitar strings. Whereupon he grabbed hold of her leg. The séance ended with a bloodcurdling scream—"as if a dagger had stabbed Eusapia right through the heart."

If Münsterburg was a menace to spirit mediums, Harry Houdini was their nemesis. Houdini (actually Erich Weiss of Appleton, Wisconsin), the most fantastic magician and escape artist in human memory, made a special hobby of exposing the "spook swindlers," as he called them, wholesale. His motivation was mainly artistic vanity. He took tremendous pride in his stage trickery and became livid with rage whenever spiritualists declared that he used supernatural powers to aid him. (He broke his long friendship with Sir Arthur Conan Doyle when the illustrious author announced that Houdini's walking-through-walls stunt was achieved by dematerialization.)

Houdini would travel hundreds of miles at his own expense merely to torpedo some obscure operator. His method was lethal. He would attend a séance, and afterwards repeat every "phenomenon" that had occurred—but with the lights on. In that fashion he wrecked the careers of well over a hundred "sensitives."

The mediums got even with him in their own way. After his death in 1926, they set the psychic world aquiver with a stream of reports of how Houdini's ghost had contacted them and abjectly begged their forgiveness. He was either blindly groping around limbo or actively frying on brimstone, according to the particular medium's taste.

The avenger's award must go to a Mrs. Wickland, whose body the late magician allegedly entered during a séance held in Los Angeles in 1930. Speaking in Mrs. Wickland's voice, Houdini wailed: "Since my passing I have gone to many, many mediums but the door is closed to me. When I was on earth I closed the door with double locks by ridiculing psychic phenomena and mediums . . . I lectured and charged money—for what? To blind the eyes of people. They would pay to hear me lecture and run down poor, honest mediums. Oh, it is awful."

And here, her husband noted, Houdini's agitation was so deep that he covered his face (Mrs. Wickland's) with his (her) hands.

The spiritualist movment reacted to the endless string of

fake medium exposés in the silliest possible fashion. They claimed "malice and persecution"—often without having investigated the case. In many instances the sensitives weren't even members of any spiritualist church. Yet no matter how blatant their fraud might have been, the spiritualists felt obliged to rush to their aid, at least verbally.

Judging by their statements there never was such a thing as a crooked medium. The most they will admit is that some of them might have used trickery "when they felt their powers weakening." Which sounds remarkably like a girl conceding that she may be just a little bit pregnant.

While this practice may show touching loyalty, it also helped to cripple the movement over the years. By their automatic defense of every spook merchant extant, the spiritualists became automatically identified with them and suffered accordingly in public esteem. They never attempted a housecleaning, and their organization still makes no effort to control the activities of those on whom they bestow their "Doctor" and "Reverend" titles.

The victims, most frequently, are the spiritualists themselves. They are essentially simple people, and by this I don't mean stupid. They are unsophisticated insofar as they find it hard to believe that what is a sacred mystery to them may be good business to others. They have a great desire and need for faith which is much more important to them than the exercise of their critical faculties. They also have—in many cases—a curious humble arrogance; an inordinate pride in having fathomed something that is hidden from the great mass of humanity. All these features, plus a generally low level of education, tend to make them the epitome of both good will and gullibility.

At one charming and stylish spiritualist resort hotel in the Midwest I watched a ghost materialization that I didn't think could have impressed a child. Yet all around me elderly, well-dressed men and women caught their breaths as the luminous strip of cheesecloth unfurled outside the performing sensitive's tent. A heartless reporter from a Pittsburgh newspaper ended the show by squirting a water pistol filled with ink at the textile phantom (see Figures 25a and 25b).

Later we entered the tent, found the ink-soaked piece of cloth, and handed it to the guests, who had paid up to six dollars each in "donations" to witness the wonder. They were somewhat saddened, but not in the least indignant.

As one frail and gentle little lady from Millville, Pennsylvania, put it to me, "Mr. B may have slipped on this occasion. But I'm sure the spirits of our loved ones came to him many times before."

Not a word about this incident appeared in the spiritualist press. And Mr. B continues to do the rounds of spiritualist resorts and summer camps, collecting donations and unfurling ghosts. He had been similarly caught in Miami Beach and Long Island without any noticeable dent in his psychic repute.

Cheesecloth, however, is not the standard material of phantom apparitions. They customarily appear in the form of "ectoplasm," which supposedly exudes from the medium's nose, ears, nipples, mouth and genitalia. Ectoplasm is a sort of solidified white mist, which occultists claim denotes the presence of a spirit and can sometimes take vaguely human shape. It has been photographed on hundreds of occasions and—with a little retouching—can pass as the traditional white ghost figure. I've seen it manufactured from a mixture of peroxide and toothpaste blown up into a bubbly cascade that glows in the dark. But, as one spiritualist spokesman pointed out, this merely proves that it can be imitated. *He* had seen the real stuff (see Figures 26a and 26b).

This attitude—which seems to positively beg for deception—rather bewildered me. At least it did until I read the sentiments expressed by the Archbishop of Rheims in Bernard Shaw's *Saint Joan*, on the subject of miracles:

ARCHBISHOP. A miracle, my friend, is an event which creates faith. That is the purpose and nature of miracles. They may seem very wonderful to the people who witness them, and very simple to those who perform them. That does not matter: if they confirm or create faith they are true miracles.

LA TRÉMOILLE. Even if they are frauds, do you mean?

ARCHBISHOP. Frauds deceive; An event which creates faith does not deceive: therefore it is not a fraud, but a miracle.

This is pretty well how most spiritualists seem to feel on the matter. They *know* spirits exist. Therefore any performance which graphically demonstrates this, demonstrates the truth. If, on certain occasions, such demonstrations have to be aided by artificial means they nevertheless still express a basic truth. And in creating and spreading faith in that truth they perform a praiseworthy function, regardless of the means employed.

The trouble is that no spiritualist I've met had even the haziest notion of the ingenuity of those means. They smiled with unconcealed disbelief when I mentioned the existence of people like Robert Smith.

Smith (this is not his real name, since I promised not to print it) makes a fair to splendid living out of supplying psychic phenomena to those who have difficulties creating them otherwise. Some are manufactured by himself, some imported to order, most are suitably modified stage gadgets used by magicians and fun fair entrepreneurs.

Ghosts, which can be rolled up and down like window shades, retail at around $50, depending on size and mobility. Luminous spirit faces painted on the inside of special robes go for $12.50. Free-floating and with movable features (choice of young or ancient, serene or horrific), they cost around $18. Ghost knockers with an echo effect that makes the raps appear to come from several directions at once are $4.75 each. (But they wear out quickly.) Then there are trumpet voices (whispering or booming) for $5, levitating tables in four sizes, floating vases, lamps, daggers and firearms, and a twitchy little phantom hand that can wave for $11 (plus tax) (see Figure 27).

I have attended spirit séances in seven countries on three continents, and I think I've seen every one of the above gadgets used at some place or another. I've also seen mediums do quite nicely without them.

A Los Angeles specialist in "ghost writing" had me sit opposite him at a small table on which lay a slate and chalk. He let me grip both his wrists before the light went out. After a few minutes I could hear the chalk scratching over the slate. When his assistant turned on the light, there was my name on the slate—wrought, he assured me, by his spirit guide. The only trouble was that he had flakes of chalk sticking to his lower lip. He had picked up the chalk in his mouth and scrawled the words while I held his wrists (see Figure 28).

In New York a kindly spiritualist minister took me to a séance at the home of a portly gentleman who describes himself as "the foremost Trumpet Medium of the Universe." Five of us sat around in a tight circle, touching hands and touching each other's feet, so that no one present had a limb free. The spirit trumpet stood in the center.

When the room darkened I felt our stout medium slip his hand from mine for a moment to scratch it, then put it back again. In due course the trumpet spoke up stentoriously, delivering greetings from the Great Beyond to two ladies in our circle. We could see the faint glow of the luminous instrument hovering in the air slightly above our heads. Our messenger from the spirit world, it appeared, was an erstwhile Confederate artillery sergeant by name of Lesley or Wesley (his voice was a trifle unclear).

It was a neat enough trick, but unfortunately I'd seen it demonstrated at a magicians' gathering years earlier.

Our medium had disengaged both his hands in the dark when he scratched them. But instead of putting both back he merely placed one of them on his knees, allowing me and his other neighbor to touch either side of it. This was to give us the impression that we were touching one of his hands each, while actually leaving one free. One was all he needed to lift the trumpet from the floor to his mouth. The sound and directional distortion produced by the metal funnel did the rest.

The irritating part about this widespread occult conmanship is that it obscures a very real issue. For there *are* things "going bump in the night" which we cannot, as yet, explain rationally.

You can call them "hauntings" or "manifestations," but either word merely serves as a cover for a shoulder shrug. We have psychics galore probing into them, we even have ghost hunters of sorts, but none of them have produced anything better than reams of facile jargon supporting whatever theories they happen to hold. And so far none of their theories fit the facts.

There is no evidence—other than wishful thinking—that these occurrences are caused by the spirits of the dead. The same applies to the version that they may be "astral projections" of the living. Scientific researchers, who abhor the term "ghost" and prefer "phantasm," tend to regard them as self-induced hallucinations. This, however, fails to explain how several people manage to hallucinate the same image simultaneously. It also cannot account for the extremely physical pandemonium attributed to poltergeists.

Perhaps the best proof for the futility of our theories lies in the failure of these manifestations to respond to them. They refuse to be attracted by any method yet devised—except those on Robert Smith's mail-order catalog. And, once present, they equally refuse to be turned off by the means now at our disposal.

The most publicized recent example of this was the haunting of the Beverly Hills house belonging to author Joe Hyams and his blond actress wife, Elke Sommer. The couple moved into the villa—a modern, quite unmacabre structure—in July 1964. They fled from it in March 1967. And according to my latest information the activities that made them leave are still going on.

They took a variety of forms. People visiting the house, including delivery men, kept getting glimpses of a husky middle-aged man with thinning hair and a bulbous nose. No such person was living there.

Night after night, while the Hyamses listened from their upstairs bedroom, doors below them opened and slammed shut. But the most persistent effect was the noise of scraping chairs from the dining room; exactly as if a group of people were pushing their chairs back after a meal.

Hyams set about systematically trying to cope with the disturbances. He cut off all tree branches near the windows. He got the original blueprints of the house and searched every corner of it. He called in termite inspectors, had carpenters check doorframes, and consulted a geologist about possible fissure movements in the subsoil.

He marked the position of the chairs on the dining room floor, installed a sensitive microphone and connected it with a tape recorder. The scraping sounds came the same night. They were clearly audible when he played back the tape. But the chairs had not moved a fraction from their marked places.

Hyams contacted the Southern California Society for Psychical Research, which then investigated the building for three years. He also contacted several private detectives who did the same. The combined results of their investigations were zero—

except that the SPR granted the phenomena "full scientific cre-
dence"; the only house ever to enjoy that distinction.

A total of seventeen mediums and psychics visited the place.
All of them either saw or felt numerous ghosts on the premises,
some of them as many as three or four. They all reported exceedingly bad vibrations. One, Jacqueline Eastlund, exclaimed
dramatically, "Nothing can get me to remain in this house. I am
frightened."

Lotte von Strahl, possibly the most reputable sensitive in
Hollywood, was made of sterner stuff. "In the name of Jesus
Christ," the gray-haired lady intoned, "I command you to leave
this house at once. Leave these good people alone and stop
disturbing their house!" Then, after listening intently, she announced, "He's leaving."

The same night the chairs in the dining room were scraping
again.

Hyams wrote an article about his haunt in the late *Saturday
Evening Post*. From then on he was inundated with advice on
how to get rid of his spook; most of it from self-styled experts
at the business. It added up to a fascinating collection of spirit
lore, but none of it stopped the doors from slamming or the
chairs from scraping.

Finally an unexplained fire broke out in the dining room.
After that Joe and Elke decided that they'd better move out.
By then the house had become a local legend and went up for
sale at a very low price. It was bought by Diahn Williams, a
former model turned movie actress, who knew all about the drawbacks of her bargain.

The ghost—or whatever it is—remained in residence. As Miss
Williams told an interviewer, "He drops things and slams doors.
A lot of specialists have insisted on coming in and studying it
and Hans Holzer wanted to exorcise it. But I prefer my privacy . . ."

Exorcism, of course, is the Church's traditional method of
tackling such phenomena. This is a lengthy and elaborate ceremony and bears hardly any relation to Mme. von Strahl saying
"shoo" to the spirit. The full ritual, which includes the recital of
the fifteen Gradual Psalms and the sprinkling of every part of the
house with holy water, is rarely performed nowadays.

The special Conjuration—*Exorcismus domus a daemonio vexatae*—runs:

> I adjure thee, O serpent of old, by the Judge of the living and the dead; by the Creator of the world who hath power to cast into hell, that thou depart forthwith from this house. He that commands thee, accursed demon, is He that commanded the winds, and the sea and the storm. He that commands thee, is He that ordered thee to be hurled down from the height of heaven into the lower parts of the earth. Hearken, then, Satan and fear. Get thee gone, vanquished and cowed, when thou art bidden in the name of our Lord Jesus Christ who will come to judge the living and the dead and all the world by fire. Amen.

It's an impressive procedure and always has an encouraging effect on the unfortunate occupants of the house. But there is no record of it ever having stopped the manifestations.

"You see, exorcism wasn't actually designed for that purpose," a Catholic priest in Boston told me rather wryly. "If you read the words carefully you will notice that they're aimed at Satan and his demons—not at spirits. Because, strictly speaking, we don't recognize ghosts and spirits as such."

This is the general attitude of all orthodox Christian churches, as well as Judaism. While accepting the scriptural teachings that demons can take control of persons, they note that no biblical reference exists to the haunting of premises. As far as demoniacal possession is concerned, today's clergy steps aside for psychiatry. And regarding phantoms and poltergeists they appear just as politely skeptical and bewildered as the laity.

But simultaneously with this country's upsurge of occultism, something resembling a spiritualist rebellion took place within several Church establishments. Protest movements arose in opposition to the rationalism of the hierarchy.

Typical of these movements is the Spiritual Frontiers Fellowship (SFF) which branched out from the Episcopal Church. Founded in the mid-fifties, by a group of clergymen including the Reverend Arthur Ford (famed for his TV performance during which he apparently contacted the spirit of Bishop Pike's son), the Fellowship aims frankly at restoring the miraculous aspects of the Church. It is equally frankly opposed to the clergy's growing preoccupation with social and material issues.

With its national headquarters in Evanston, Illinois, the movement now has over five thousand ardent members; a considerable force in Episcopal politics.

"We try to foster three main functions: spiritual healing, mystical prayer, and evidence of survival after death," Rev. Alan MacKillop explained to me. "These fields have been—er—somewhat neglected by the Church." He cleared his throat and proceeded carefully: "We also wish to explore and interpret the increasing interest in psychic phenomena."

"Does that include spirits?" I asked.

"It includes anything that comes under the heading of psychic phenomena."

MacKillop is the Fellowship's New York area chairman, but appears far more professional than spiritualist. A fair, youngish man with an outdoor complexion and a soft, meticulous college debater's voice, he added that the movement was by no means confined to church members. "We're really an interfaith body, open to anyone who is interested in what we are trying to achieve. But, of course—well—we do reflect the congregations we would get at services. Which means about two-thirds are women."

The Reverend's studious and rather cautious approach, however, does not reflect the sentiments of some of his more fervently mystical fellow members. At the time of writing, in fact, these were busily forming highly vocal pressure groups in favor of a much more free-swinging, less scholarly attitude. Led by several vociferously dedicated ladies, they are working hard at transforming the SFF into an uncritically occult outfit.

But regardless of such internal ruptures, the Fellowship is building real bridges between the religious establishment and the spiritualist fringe. The late Bishop Pike had to separate himself from his church in order to expound his metaphysical beliefs. If the SFF and kindred bodies get their way this will no longer be necessary in future.

The main links between the two factions are the mediums, who now lecture impartially to both church and secular audiences. These are not, however, the physical mediums described earlier, but somewhat more cerebral practitioners. While equally involved with the spirit world, they don't—as a rule—deal in ghost materializations. Their contacts are made on the mental plane only, their spirit guides and celestial messengers reveal themselves only through their *voices;* occasionally through feats of clairvoyance and other forms of ESP.

The distinction is subtle but vital. For whereas physical mediums are dying out rapidly because of too frequent exposure, the mentalists are increasing at a fabulous rate. New York City alone now has more than six hundred of them— mostly part-timers, but with a large core of professionals.

The lesser fry among them are available for the innumerable private séances currently adding ethereal flavor to the afternoons of housewives in Westchester County and its equivalents throughout the nation. People like Phil Begalsky, who divides his working time between a Manhattan antique shop and various suburban spirit seekers. He is a languidly handsome young man of twenty-six, and speaks with low-keyed but unassailable authority on metaphysical matters.

"Women are much more psychic than men, you know," he confided in me. "Why? Because they think less and *feel* more. That's what I keep telling the ladies at my séances. Don't try and think this out, I tell them, just *feel* it. And most of them respond—oh, wonderfully."

He placed a pale hand on his forehead. "Let me give you an example—no, please don't interrupt—let me give you an example. I have an aura, you see. No, of course, *you* don't see it. That's because you obviously have no psychic talents at all. But— and I don't care if you *don't* believe me—six out of ten ladies notice it the moment we dim the lights. I always make a point of asking whether those present can see my aura in the candlelight. And six out of ten do. That," he added slowly, "is a *fantastic* proportion."

He turned out to be quite correct. At the séance I attended with him, no fewer than four out of the seven housewives noticed his aura the moment he mentioned it.

The rest of the sitting was spent listening to Mr. Begalsky's

monologues and trying some elementary spiritualist exercises.
One of them entailed closing our eyes and imagining we were
walking through a pitch-black tunnel. "Now," Begalsky whispered
throatily, "there is a lantern coming toward you from the other
end. You can't make out the figure yet—just that unsteady amber
light approaching. Closer . . . closer . . . quite close now . . ."
His voice was barely audible. "Now the light is in front of you—it
rises . . ." He suddenly screamed, "Now you see the face!"

The ladies jumped at his roar. He asked them, singly, whose
face they had seen. In one case it was Frankenstein's monster.
Two of the sitters had seen deceased relatives; one uncle and one
stepsister.

"And those," said Mr. Begalsky firmly, "were spirits."

Higher up on the occult scale are full-time mediums like
William Daut; an ordained spiritualist minister, doctor of metaphysics, Yogi, psychic, and several other things. Mr. Daut has
his own circle of disciples, who meet at his home in Paterson,
New Jersey, but also lectures before general audiences.

He is a burly man, hair and beard shot through with gray,
given to wearing turtleneck sweaters under formal business suits.
He takes an astonishingly jovial view of the "other side," sprinkling his observations with mild witticisms which are sometimes
hard to follow, because he has (or had) several front teeth missing.

His communication with those who have "passed over" is
almost instant. Someone gives him the name of a departed person, Daut covers his eyes for a moment, concentrates, then comes
right out with the message: "Yes, Mabel Bristow, that's right.
Was there any trouble with her hair? No? Well, she says there
were three people who had hurt her very much in life. No, I can't
say who these people were—she won't say—but there were three.
Definitely. She is very happy and fulfilled now. She sends her love
and blessings."

He cocks an ear for the next name. "Charles O'Malley?"
Again the eye-covering gesture. A few seconds of concentration.
Then: "Yes, here he is. Did he drown, by any chance? Did
he have trouble with his lungs—breathing? I feel he had. He is
happy now. He sends greetings."

In this rapid-fire fashion, Mr. Daut can deal with a remarkable number of loved ones in half an hour. Without exception they are all blissful and serene, regardless of their former lives. "I have never yet," he summarizes, "heard from an unhappy spirit."

Daut's happy end formula extends to the picture he paints of the "other side." According to his information it's never a letdown.

"If you imagine that Heaven is a mansion with colonial furniture, then that's just how it will be. And if"—he gives a prolonged chuckle—"you imagine it as a place filled with beautiful blondes, then that is what it will have. The other side—remember this—is always just what you expect it to be." He beams.

His audience—reassured, comforted, and vastly entertained—beams back.

There is, however, still another class of mediums; unfortunately by far the smallest. You could call them the "introspectives," for want of a more specific term. They are the handful of men and women more concerned with fathoming the nature and meaning of their phenomena than in providing snappy travelogues of the celestial regions.

The greatest of them, perhaps, was the late Eileen J. Garrett. An Irishwoman, born in County Meath just before the turn of the century, she had a quality I found in very few psychics: a genuine awe of and a burning curiosity about the forces whose touch she felt all her life.

She was thrown back upon her inner resources by a traumatic youth. Both her parents committed suicide when she was a baby, her three sons died in infancy, her first marriage ended in divorce, her second husband was killed at Ypres in World War I.

These tragedies seemed to heighten and sharpen the psychic perception Eileen Garrett had possessed since her childhood. On several occasions she "saw" events which took place hundreds of miles away—the battlefield death of her officer husband among them.

In her trances she spoke with the voices of her four "controls," often in foreign languages she didn't know, frequently in technical terms she couldn't even pronounce in her waking state. But she never reached the stage of glib familiarity with her "spirits" that makes other mediums sound as if they were tourist guides through ghostland.

"I don't know who they are," she said, "I don't know where they come from. And I don't know why they come. They may be split-offs of my own personality, fragments of myself. I've left this question open in my own mind. All I know is that through them I am—sometimes—able to gain helpful information."

Mrs. Garrett never claimed that pragmatic researchers either hampered or persecuted her. She cooperated with them—the more questioning and skeptical the better. It corresponded with her own constantly probing and questioning attitude. She worked with both Jungian and Freudian psychologists, and of the two she much preferred the less mystically oriented Freudians. "Why? Because I knew the precise level of their inquiry. Also they had some fascinating things to say about subconscious sexual motivation."

She always retained ambivalent feelings about the independent reality of her controls, as she had about the entire spirit realm. "We have no way of telling how much of these phenomena is a projection of ourselves and how much—if any—exists as an outside entity."

Her entire life was a search for some sort of certainty about the quality of her own gift—or affliction. It sent her shuttling between Europe and America and into the test laboratories of Oxford, Johns Hopkins and Duke universities, investigating herself with the aid of topflight scientists like Dr. Alexis Carrel and Dr. J. B. Rhine.

Her books, largely autobiographical, made most others on the subject read like the primitive PR blurbs they are. And interviewing her, after talking to a couple of dozen lesser psychics, gave me the feeling of having met my first literate adult in months. Even in her seventies she was a striking woman, equipped with a truly Celtic sense of the absurd, an ironic streak of humor that accounted for her detachment and her inability to puff herself up into a "messenger from the beyond."

"Always be on guard against cult leaders and psychic celebrities who talk grandly of 'God in me,' " she said with a slightly grim half-smile. "That is what I call the Fascist Impulse—and an awful lot of people are prone to it these days."

In 1951 Eileen Garrett formed the American Parapsychology Foundation in New York. Its function is to provide the means for research projects in the metaphysical field. The Foundation grinds no axes and conducts no experiments of its own. It merely lays frequent golden eggs on behalf of investigators, publishes an excellent newsletter, sponsors conferences, and places its superb 6,400-volume library at the gratis disposal of anyone interested. Among other ventures it helped to fund the Brooklyn Dream Laboratory and recent tests by polygraph on the reaction of plants to human thought waves (both of which we'll meet in later chapters).

Mrs. Garrett's approach was far too tentative and fallible to satisfy the millions who crave reassurance that the horizonless region of shadows is, after all, just an unfurnished extension of their living rooms. But in her own modest way she may have been edging considerably closer to the truth than all our hunters after packaged, labeled, classified and indexed assembly line spirits.

XI

GURUS, COMMUNES, AND MESSIAHS

My FRIEND Zia Haduri, who is an Indian from Nagpur, was standing at a Manhattan street corner glowering at members of the Hare Krishna movement chanting their ancient mantra:

> Hare Krishna, Hare Krishna,
> Krishna Krishna, Hare Hare
> Hare Rama, Hare Rama,
> Rama Rama, Hare Hare.

The shaven-headed boys and sari-garbed girls looked radiant as they gyrated to the tinkling of their little cymbals. Spectators smiled strained New Yorker smiles.

Zia turned to me, his face a mixture of bafflement and wrath. "This I cannot understand," he said in his clipped melodious voice that always sounds vaguely like Peter Sellers's. "In India we are struggling to break free of this—this—pathetic comedy. And here these children are trying to spread it. Why?"

"Maybe they think you have something that we need," I ventured.

"Certainly we have," he said acidly. "Illiteracy, mass starvation, a hundred endemic diseases and the highest birthrate in the world. All as a result of meditating on Karma when we should have been studying scientific agriculture." He gave a backward glance at the swaying figures and added, "It is because of our plague of swamis and gurus that we now rate as an underdeveloped nation. So perhaps it is good that so many of them are coming over here. I wish you luck with them. The same luck *we* have had."

"Well, those kids seem pretty happy," I suggested.

"Because they have full bellies. They wouldn't have them if *their* ancestors had joined in that Krishna chanting instead of harnessing machinery and inventing good chemical fertilizers."

He raised his little finger; invariably a sign of agitation with him. "Look, I know about this Bhaktivedanta Swami Prabhupada who founded this Krishna movement. He is an idiot. He came over to America in 1969, and he went around saying that everybody should live on a little plot of land with a cow to give him milk. That way everyone would be happy. Hah!"

Zia snorted contemptuously. "We have 400 million people in India. How can they all have a plot of land? And do you know the quality of our milk? It's terrible—like water; and do you know why?" His finger stabbed the air. "Because our sadhus —men like him—insist that cows are sacred animals and cannot be used for cross-breeding. That is why we have the worst dairy cattle on earth!"

I tried to put in a good word for the maligned swami: "I heard him speak once. He seemed a pleasantly gentle soul."

"Oh, yes, gentle. They are all gentle until they meet another sadhu who is in competition. Then you should hear them—they spit like hags in the market." Zia broke into an imitation of high-pitched rage: "Do not follow this false rascal—he will mislead you. Only follow me! I have the only truth! Do not give contributions to him—give them only to me!"

He took a deep breath. "And another thing. All these gurus

teach universal love, right? But not such love to abolish our caste system in India—which makes millions of pariahs untouchable, like dogs—lower than dogs. Oh, no—that must stay. It is holy."

Zia's viewpoint, surprisingly, is quite common among Indians, Pakistanis and Persians in this country. Especially the younger ones tend to share his bewildered irritation at America's starry-eyed welcome for what they regard as the worst features of Eastern occultism. The idea of strong, prosperous Westerners looking toward the feeble, undernourished Orient for "serenity" strikes them as the height of black humor.

As the Iranian novelist F. M. Esfandiary wrote in the New York *Times:* "It is appalling to see bright, educated city-dwellers swallow the nonsense that these soothsayers, clairvoyants, spiritualists, prophets, dish out. There is something pathetic about this hunger for fairy tales."

The Hare Krishna movement, the most conspicuous Indian cult in the United States today, is their special bête noir. Formed as recently as 1966, this organization now has sixteen offices in twelve states, and several thousand saffron-robed youngsters collecting alms for its benefit by chanting and dancing at metropolitan street corners. The aim of the Movement is simply to achieve a state of "Samadhi"—a permanent condition of ecstatic God-consciousness. Also to establish more offices. It attracts attention through "Sankirtan"—congregational chanting—reciting the name of Lord Krishna, the supreme Godhead, over and over in various combinations.

Its founder and teacher, however, can do more than chant; and occasionally his ecstatic God-consciousness has been known to evaporate. In June 1969, for instance, he forcefully interrupted the service of a rival cult in the Waikiki Shell, Honolulu, by shouting that the competing guru was "old and wrinkled and ugly, ready for death to take him. . . ."

His International Society for Krishna Consciousness (ISKCON) is only one of around a dozen similar organizations attracting hundreds of thousands of followers from coast to coast. Their similarities are far more striking than their differences. All of them are based on some form of Hindu mysticism. All center around the personality of one guru (teacher). And all espouse simplicity as a cardinal virtue.

The simplicity part does not always thrive in the American climate. It is difficult to discover traces of it in the thirteen-acre Lake Shrine of the Self-Realization Fellowship in Los Angeles. The Shrine sports gold-leafed lotus towers, imported Dutch and Australian swans, life-sized statues of Jesus Christ and Buddha, birds of paradise, wishing wells, an artificial lake beside an equally artificial windmill, and a gilded brass chest allegedly housing some of Gandhi's ashes. The Shrine does a roaring trade with books and records, mushroomburgers and ice cream, while Muzak fills the air with, alternatively, Hindu chants, Baptist hymns, light opera and the *Ave Maria.*

The SRF was the creation of an Indian banker's son named Lal Ghosh, who became Yogi Master Paramahansa Yogananda before he entered the United States. He died here in 1952, and was interred in one of the swankest graves of Forest Lawn. His bronze casket has a glass see-through lid. This offered the Forest Lawn mortuary management an opportunity to observe the revered "Highest Swan" after his demise. As they subsequently testified to the SRF (in writing):

"No physical disintegration was visible even 20 days after his death. This state of perfect preservation of a body is unparalleled in mortuary annals. Yogananda's body was apparently in a phenomenal state of immutability. No odor of decay emanated from his body at any time."

The greatest boost for the simplicity cults, however, was accomplished by a laughing little man who calls himself Maharishi Mahesh Yogi and looks like an undersized Hairy Ainu. Known as Mahashi for short, he had been traveling the circuit of Western capitals for years before the Beatles discovered him and made him their group guru. In their footsteps followed a string of celebrities like the Rolling Stones, Mia Farrow and Shirley MacLaine, plus an estimated 150,000 lesser mortals who could afford to contribute one week's salary a year for the cause.

Mahashi's message, delivered in a piping singsong voice, interspersed with giggles, is "transcendental meditation." This novel form of meditation is performed by concentrating not on a thought but on one word. Or rather the sound of one word, because you are supposed to forget its meaning, lose yourself in the tone alone. By meditating twice daily for half an hour on the ring of a word like "Rah," you can—according to Mahashi—achieve cosmic consciousness. There is not much more to it. No strictures, no dogma, no really strenuous exercises. Just "Rah" for thirty minutes, twice a day. The trick lies in totally forgetting its meaning, which can be difficult.

The word you receive is supposed to be yours alone, shared by no other living soul. But as the number of his disciples snowballed, Mahashi seems to have exhausted his vocabulary. Three graduates of transcendentalism in New York recently compared notes and discovered that they had all been given the same word to meditate on.

The Beatles quickly grew disillusioned with their guru and departed, taking most of their galaxy along. But by then the little man was comfortably ensconced in his own academy near the foothills of the Himalayas.

I was startled to discover how humiliated some Indian intellectuals feel about having their nation identified with these simplistic saints. "It is as if we were to judge Western philosophy by the mouthings of some hillbilly revivalist preachers," a Bombay newspaperman fumed to me.

"Yes, I admit some of them have a following at home, but these are ignorant villagers—what you call the yokels. It is only in the West that they can rope in men and women of culture. Most of them are simply charlatans. They are constantly bickering with each other, taking each other to court. And before elections they often sell their political influence to the party that offers them the most money."

"But this wouldn't apply to all?" I asked.

"No, it doesn't," he said. "But it applies to all you are liable to meet. The genuine sadhus—the real religious philosophers—are not interested in gathering followers or touring America. They stay out of crowds, they think and write by themselves, and they cannot be interviewed."

It is not necessary to hail from India to set up shop as an Indian guru in the United States. In 1970 a young denizen of New York's Greenwich Village tried a private experiment. He donned an off-white dhoti, painted some haphazard stripes on his forehead, and announced that he was Namilti Musdra Swami

Halagensi, about to launch his creed of Transverse Soul Duality in a local church hall.

He got the place half-full, and proceeded to lecture his audience as follows (I quote verbatim):

"I am here, my beloved, to reveal the great Rama's eternal concept of Soul Duality. What is meant by this duality? It means a oneness—a pairing—of our spirits, our fibers, our atoms, our very molecules in the Nine Ways of the Lord Vishnu which bring bliss. Oh, yes, you too can—if you *will it*—attain Mokhsha, beyond which there is no infinity, but only the Transversing Oneness that is promised to those who have the longing to gain the Seventeen Purities mentioned in the *Book of the Alkori*. What is this book? My beloved, it is the all-encompassing testament of immortal erudition gathered by the illustrious pilgrim Swami Ohib Missumil Ahandra during the last ninety-seven years of his earthly existence and handed down to us through eleven centuries. It reveals the folly of all desire or even *thoughts* of desire or even thoughts that lead to thoughts of desire. . . ."

He kept this up for a solid hour. Nobody walked out on him, although one or two people were seen to doze off. Afterwards he asked for donations to aid him in spreading his creed. He collected $31.26. Five people approached him to ask where they could buy that wonderful *Book of the Alkori*. Three asked if they could visit him for private lessons in Soul Duality. One lady social worker assured him that he had revealed to her the true meaning of the term "spiritual fiber."

He had made up every word of his lecture as he went along, including the *Book of the Alkori*.

But his joke still runs a poor second to reality. Nobody could *invent* a figure like Francis Heindswater Pencovic, alias Ben Covic, alias Krishna Venta.

A Californian by birth, Mr. Pencovic had been arrested in five states on charges including burglary, petty theft, larceny, vagrancy, nonpayment of alimony, contravening the Mann Act, and writing threatening letters to the President.

After much wandering, Mr. Pencovic settled in Los Angeles, where he donned flowing robes and sandals and henceforth called himself Krishna Venta. He started a movement he named

the Foundation of the World Fellowship, which taught the
virtues of communal living, the pooling of all material possessions
and unswerving obedience to the Messiah. The Messiah was
Krishna Venta.

He was not, as his name might have indicated, an Eastern
sage, but the modern reincarnation of both Jesus Christ and Adam.
The first he proved by assuring his disciples, "I cannot tell a lie to
please you. I must tell you the truth in the sight of God. I *am* the
son of God!" The second he documented by assuring the faithful
that he had no navel.

Venta-Pencovic ran his Fellowship on autocratic lines. The
rank and file were forbidden to smoke, drink, gamble, curse or
fornicate outside wedlock. For the Messiah the rules were relaxed
to permit him to visit nightclubs, bars, and Las Vegas casinos "in
order to reveal himself to the sinners foregathered there."

It must not be said that Venta was a complete con artist.
He was at least partially a genuine lunatic who had been under
psychiatric observation in Sweden, England and Italy as well as
in the United States.

His community flourished until 1958, when two of his
followers suspected him of sleeping with their wives. Whereupon
they planted a dynamite bomb in his headquarters and blew the
Messiah, themselves and seven other members to smithereens.
Mr. Pencovic was so scattered that he had to be identified by
his dentures.

In cold print many of these eccentric cults may appear exclusive gatherings of mental defectives. But the written word
is one-dimensional and can't really convey the dynamics that give
them velocity.

To start with, most of them center around the magnetism of a
particular leader or teacher, depending not so much on what he
says but on what he *is*. Mere quotations rarely do them justice.
Mahashi, for instance, is an immensely attractive little man and
a complete spellbinder who could probably keep a party en-
chanted by just reciting the alphabet. The late Krishna Venta was
nearly seven feet tall, had blazing blue eyes and the thunder of
such consummate conviction in his voice that he seemed to be
expounding gospel when he ordered a dry martini. Shorn of the

overwhelming personal presence of their messiahs, these movements come through like sunsets with the technicolor left out.

If you take the trouble to read the sermons of Aimee Semple McPherson you will very likely be struck by the sheer banality of what she preached. Missing is the wonderfully throaty richness of her delivery, the sensuous sway of her hips, the dramatic mimicry with which she acted out her parables, the exultant shouts of her massed choirs, the stage tableaux, lighting effects, and the whole irresistible *joie de vivre* that made her services gala events in the otherwise drab lives of her congregation. And not having experienced this we find it hard to appreciate the quality of excitement she generated, which made her adherents worship her as an idol long after she was shown to have shapely legs of clay.

Leadership personalities, however, don't create a tendency toward cultism; they merely utilize it. And the United States has been a cultist haven ever since its creation.

The reasons for this are partly economical. Since religious corporations are tax exempt and no criterion exists as to what, exactly, constitutes a religion, the road lies open for anyone with two friends and twenty dollars to found a new faith and start rattling the collection box. The resultant benefits go far beyond the cash value of the donations. Cults can ordain ministers entitled to marry, baptize and bury, apart from having access to prisons and hospitals. On top of the handy prefix "Rev." they can also award themselves doctorates in their particular bracket. While such a degree may lack academic standing, it will impress thousands of potential followers who have no idea of its worthlessness. I once interviewed a learned D.D. who had written his own (handsomely framed) diploma and misspelled five of the forty words in it.

America's singular passion for wayout cults undoubtedly began as an assertion of individualism vis-à-vis the orthodoxy of the Old World churches. Today this passion runs higher than ever, but the motivation has changed. Most contemporary cultists are not withdrawing from established religions but from a social pattern. And they are not seeking salvation so much as the company of others who feel equally out of step. The spiritual aspect has become secondary—it is the "differentness" that counts. Thus Madelyn

Murray, the militant atheist lady from Texas, is currently attracting a fair following for her incorporated church that is actually an antichurch, known as the Pagan School of Mindcraft.

Two other outstanding trends mark the present cult scene. The first is a tremendous swing from age to youth. The second a less noticeable but persistent drift *away* from California.

Until about a decade ago the prototype of an American cultist was a senior citizen, politically arch-conservative, living on a small nest egg in southern California and following some more or less bizarre theology, which nevertheless had its basic roots in Christianity. He had not really abandoned his former outlook and religion, but merely pushed them to an extreme, as it were. Instead of, for example, regarding the Second Coming as a nebulously distant prophecy he had been persuaded that it was either imminent or had already occurred. He still clung to his lifelong ideals regarding sexual morality, patriotism, and the capitalist system of free enterprise, except that here, too, he had become more drastic in his convictions. He was, in other words, his former self *in extremis*.

There are still millions like him (or her). But the typical cult follower today is more likely to be in his late teens or early twenties and to have broken completely with whatever creed he was brought up in. The various Eastern sects, unconnected with our Judeo-Christian heritage, draw the vast majority of their members from the 100 million or so Americans now under the age of twenty-seven. Together with his religious groundings the new prototype will also have scuttled his social and political heritage in favor of a pacifist, noncompetitive, antiproperty ideal. He will probably—though by no means invariably—be experimenting with hallucinogenic drugs.

The contemporary cultist, therefore, represents a much more radical departure from the American norm than his predecessor.

The gradual shift of sectarians now under way into the wilder regions of Arizona, New Mexico and Colorado also stems from their heightened degree of extremism. The new cultists no longer care much about proselytizing society—they want to quit it.

But at present California remains the Valhalla of the way-outs. For nearly a century, America's oddbodies have descended on the Golden State, causing an accumulation too huge to be depleted in less than a generation. California was as far west as these folks could go, and since they could push no further they stayed.

The unaccustomed climate seems to have altered even many of those who arrived with perfectly rational attitudes. As John Gunther remarked in his *Inside U.S.A.*:

"My friend Walter Duranty suggests a point here. It is the effect of excessive sunlight on northerners. 'Iowa gets here,' he put it, 'and goes crazy.' Something of the same characteristic may be observed in the south of France. The Provençal natives don't become eccentric, but the invading British do. Even Aldous Huxley became a mystic when exposed to the California sun long enough."

To bolster this theory there is the undeniable fact that the sunnier—southern—portion of the state also boasts the lion's share of eccentrics.

As the sectarians acquired property (for some organizations it runs into seven-figure brackets) they gained influence and could elect state politicians who were—if not *of* them—at least very amiably disposed toward them. In due course cultism was woven into the Californian mystique and became part of the local backdrop an much as film studios, oil wells and freeways. The state specialized in spectaculars, and so did the cults.

It must be pointed out, however, that none of them ever quite matched the grotesqueries of their European forerunners.

In the 1750s, for instance, the Moravian "Herrnhuters" were led by one Count Zinzendorf, a pathological specimen of rare dimensions. He preached the doctrine that salvation was to be found exclusively in the wound inflicted on Jesus Christ's body by the spear of a Roman soldier during the Crucifixion. Zinzendorf equated this gash with the female vagina and the spear thrust that had caused it with the sexual act. Ergo, he reasoned, the faithful must constantly reenact the wounding incident by copulation before, after, and sometimes during, religious services.

This ritualistic intercourse was governed by strict rules, each rank within the sect being allowed only a certain number of movements during a regulated time span. It was performed either en masse on narrow church benches or in an enclosed four-poster known as the Blue Cabinet, which had a special window reserved as a peephole for the "Most Excellent Papa"—Zinzendorf. The Count also composed hymns, describing the action in minute detail, which were sung by mixed choirs while the couples "worshiped."

If the Herrnhuters exalted sex, the Skoptsi regarded it as a devilish aberration. In the second half of the nineteenth century they were a sect numbering close to a million members, spread over western Russia, Romania and parts of Poland. The Skoptsi's chief act of piety was castration—slicing off the sex organs of male members and the clitoris of females. The more fanatical among them did not confine themselves to their own kind. They roamed the countryside in bands, forcibly castrating men, women and even children who fell into their hands— to preserve them from future sins.

These lunatic outbursts were usually the result of a manic obsession with one particular point of doctrine which—in the minds of the obsessed—became more important than all the rest of the creed. The transatlantic cults avoided this danger by keeping their dogma stretchable in all directions. Their flexibility was such, in fact, that they could embrace innovations ranging from flying saucers to rock music without cracking their original structure.

In consequence most American sects today are patchwork quilts of so many colors that it's often difficult to find the pattern. Some appear to have picked the raisins and spices out of a dozen or more occult recipes, stewing them together into one glorious goulash whose basic ingredient is known only to the chef.

A classic example of this is the so-called ESP Laboratory, whose resemblance to a laboratory is not even passing. You could call it a universalist-mystical movement, but even that doesn't do justice to its multiplicity. It employs methods and rituals gleaned from Christian Science, Zen Buddhism, Soka Gakkai, Sufism, theosophy, Subud, Synanon and anthroposophy, to mention just a few, combined with old-fashioned faith healing, spiritualism, a dash of Positive Thought, and the assistance of a mysterious and appealing tribe of invisible ghost-pixies known as Gronkydoddles.

All of which is exactly how its creator and director intended it to be. "We have one Lab Motto," he told me, "and that's Results! I'm no dogmatist. I don't follow any standard religion.

I'll adopt anything from any creed as long as it's legal and looks promising. My mission is to help people, and I'll use any tool that comes to hand."

Alcie Gwyn Manning looks and talks more like a college athletics coach than a cult leader. A slim, brown-haired Texan, with just a trace of a Southern accent, he exudes a stimulating mixture of vitality, good humor and unquenchable enthusiasm. He chortled when I asked him whether the ESP Lab was his full-time occupation.

"I'd starve to death pretty fast if it were," he grinned. "This place"—he swept an arm around his cluttered office—"doesn't even cover expenses. I'm a C.P.A. and I keep up my practice on top of running the Lab. Have to."

The ESP Laboratory, marked by a neon sign, occupies a small corner building in a sleazier stretch of Los Angeles's Santa Monica Boulevard, competing with skin flicks, Adults Only bookshops and photographic studios advertising "live naked models."

Members meet thrice weekly under glaring fluorescent lights to perform the astonishing range of functions their movement sponsors. The majority are middle-aged or older, but there are usually one or two kids from the neighborhood who just dropped in to "watch Al do his thing."

Manning, in shirt sleeves, starts off by giving a casual, rambling lecture that is partly a prayer and covers fifteen kinds of occult experiences in as many minutes. Informality is the keynote —members smoke, walk in and out, jockey for chairs while he talks. Then the lights are dimmed and the action starts.

The program is varied. It may begin with "experimental psychometry" in which people exchange objects, try to "tune in with the vibrations" and report what they have felt. Tensions . . . fears . . . hopes . . . in the person whose object they held. A lot of laughter, occasionally surprise—"Could you *really* feel that?"

This may be followed by service at the Altar of Divine Companionship. For a fee of a dollar a month, members can put up their names for this. The entire congregation then joins in impromptu but powerful prayer chants designed to attract a perfect mate for the donor or improve his/her marital relationship.

Sometimes the proceedings are interrupted by ghosts. A

cheerfully psychic lady calls out in the dark, "Al, did you know a
sergeant whose name began with a B? Well, he just walked
through the door and stood in front of you and smiled. You
didn't? He was definitely a sergeant—I saw his stripes. Oh, yes,
he's dead all right, but he seemed happy—far as I could tell."

Light treatment plays a large role in the movement and comes
in three distinct shades. There's the Green Light of Prosperity,
the Blue Light of Healing, and the White Light of Protection
and Spiritual Growth (two weeks for twenty-five dollars or one
month for fifty). These lights, however, are not the mundane
electrical kind, but thought energy beamed out by the congregation. Receivers tune in on them upon rising and at bedtime by
the simple act of mentally picturing themselves surrounded by
whatever shade of light they require. They bask in the invisible
rays for a few minutes, then offer a prayer of affirmation, con-
cluding the treatment.

Manning also provides personal treatment for an infinite
variety of ailments. The patient sits in a chair while Manning
goes to work on his or her aura, gently soothing and stroking at
first, then directing what looks like rapid karate chops at the
invisible emanation a few inches from the patient's head. Manning talks in encouraging undertones all the while. The patient
smiles blissfully.

Most Lab members swear to the efficacy of Al's aura manipulations. A Dutchman told me that they had cured his migraine
headaches. His pretty American wife found that they relieved her
congenital spinal ailment. Two other women testified that they
eliminated sinusitis and head colds.

But the chief beneficiary seems to have been Manning himself. Smiling his twinkle-eyed collegiate grin he related, "Let me
tell you, I used to be a wreck. I had stomach ulcers, migraine,
and such godawful astigmatism that I needed *two* pair of glasses.
That was before I took up my study of the occult sciences." He
pointed inward with two expressive forefingers: "*Now* look at
me."

As Californian cults go, the ESP Laboratory is a midget. The
Aetherius Society, on the other hand, lays claim to being "the
largest Metaphysical Society of its kind now on Earth." Of its kind
it is also the only one.

The Society was distilled rather than created by Dr. (of Divinity) George King, an erstwhile English cabdriver whose mother once met Jesus Christ (thinly disguised as a Venusian), who obligingly pronounced one of her son's books "now and forever—Holy."

The above is merely a facet of Mr. King's self-revealed background. It has no direct bearing on his organization, except to indicate the esteem in which he is being held by the Higher Powers. This esteem was manifested on a Saturday morning, early in May 1954, when a voice of "deep penetrating quality, not possessed by any ordinary earthly voice," commanded him to: "Prepare yourself, you are to become the Voice of Interplanetary Parliament."

The chief spokesman of this assembly turned out to be a great Cosmic Master calling himself Aetherius and dwelling on the planet Venus. He has been talking to—or rather through—Mr. King ever since. Hence the title Aetherius Society. The procedure is for King to go into a Yoga trance, whereupon Aetherius delivers a message via *his* vocal chords (in English, with a North Country accent). Each message is recorded on three tapes—one to be played to the faithful, the other two stored in vaults for posterity.

The Society was launched in London in 1956. In due course King collected a flock of disciples with whom he climbed various Holy Mountains in the British Isles, charging them as "New Age Power Centers" by means of "Cosmic Batteries." On one of these expeditions it was King's turn to encounter Jesus Christ, who is another of the Cosmic Masters. Most of his orders, however, continued to come from Master Aetherius.

In 1959 King brought his mission to the United States. Despite some initial prejudice (comedian Jackie Gleason called him a phoney on the "Long John" Nebel radio show), the Society flourished mightily in the fertile soil of California. Its headquarters, a cluster of bright pink buildings, now occupies a twenty-thousand-square-foot plot in the heart of Hollywood. Apart from sumptuous living accommodations for the President and staff, a chapel garlanded with plastic flowers, offices and conference rooms, it also houses an air-conditioned trance chamber into which King retires when he feels an interplanetary message coming on. Everyone entering this sacred chamber must remove their shoes.

After perusing the Society's literature I had imagined Mr. King as an ascetic visionary. He appeared, however, to have a distinctly epicurean streak. He greeted me in an impeccably tailored English suit (suspenders instead of belt), with a cigarette in one hand and a Scotch in the other.

"After many years of Yogic discipline," he informed me, "I want to disengage. I think that by now I deserve some of the good things of life."

The good things include, among sundry other items, a sleek thirty-one-foot cabin cruiser and a very attractive Belgian assistant, who doubles as a gourmet cook.

King looks like the cinematic image of a British diplomat —tall, gray-haired and distinguished, with bushy eyebrows twirled up at the ends and a conversational style that seems to be delivering memoranda even when he is discussing the weather.

His background was such that pronouncements from the cosmic realm occasion him no surprise. "I come from a very psychic family," he stated. "My mother was a really great medium —people used to be scared of her. And when I was a small kid I used to go out and play with the fairies."

The President's ponderous calm makes it hard to realize that he and his Society are engaged in a life and death struggle on behalf of humanity. Most of his trance messages, in fact, come as appeals for help in the titanic combat waged by cosmic forces somewhere in the lower astral realm.

The exact nature of this struggle is difficult to convey, since King takes the precaution of having his Society newsletters copyrighted, which prevents me from quoting them verbatim.

He is also considerably more subdued in his claims when talking to an interviewer than when addressing his flock. What I'm giving here, therefore, is a very watery version of the phantasmagoric saga of Aetherius.

Lost, for instance, is the wonderful military flavor of some of his bulletins, which often read like communiqués from the Western front: commando raids into the lower astral realm, action in Jupiter Sector 92, destruction of an enemy computer complex; all described in brisk war correspondent's style.

The various battles, referred to as Phase 17, Phase 24, and so on, are mostly touch-and-go affairs, results teetering in the balance from one newsletter to the next. To further heighten suspense, certain actions are marked "strictly classified"—which means that details cannot be released until a later date. One encounter actually changed "the future history of the world."

The enemy units are "alien" or "Satanic" forces, given to operating centers of black magic where ritualistic human sacrifices are performed "with helpless and terrified female victims." Their ultimate war aim, however, is the complete physical and mental enslavement of mankind.

In this they are opposed by the Five Adepts, supercharged fighters and nimble tacticians who bear a striking similarity to the Fantastic Four of comic book fame. The Adepts frequently score smashing victories, but they face a frustrating task. No matter how often the armies of darkness are ambushed, outflanked and decimated, they always live to fight another day.

The Adepts also suffer from the distinctly erratic behavior of the Cosmic Masters (Aetherius, Jesus, etc.). For reasons not fully explained, the Masters may suddenly deny them the use of an absolutely essential "Line of Force" which runs between two "Psychic Centers."

Which is where President King's Society comes in.

Members can actually help the Adepts in the "greatest conflict between good and evil ever seen on this Earth." They can do this by helping to improve mankind's "Karmic pattern," thus qualifying us for "additional Divine Intervention." The help may take the form of either prayer or cash donations—preferably both.

The donations pay for the technical equipment needed for the Society's various operations benefiting our Karmic pattern. These operations are frequently of mind-boggling complexity, owing to the fact that Dr. King uses an even mixture of metaphysical, electronic, and self-coined terms to explain them. But although their precise nature often defies comprehension, they share one relatively simple common denominator: they cost lots of money.

Operation Karmalight, for example, entailed the purchase of a new motor launch for $7,500. The reason given was that

King's own cruiser had to be used for an equally urgent con-
current undertaking (Operation Sunbeam) and was therefore
unavailable.

The Society's mightiest weapon is known as the "Spiritual
energy radiator"—Dr. King's personal invention. From the outside it looks like a series of boxes and tubes. But this wondrous
apparatus can accomplish feats undreamed of in any scientific
textbook extant.

For Operation Sunbeam (Phase II) a special task force of
pilgrims set up a pyramid-shaped "collector" on the top of a
Holy Mountain in England. During the night two Masters
from the Planetary System of Gotha manipulated Spiritual energy
into it. This power then flowed into the Spiritual energy radiator
in Los Angeles, charging its Spiritual power battery. The battery
was loaded on board a motor cruiser and taken to a designated
Psychic Center, sixteen miles out at sea from Santa Barbara.
There the battery was discharged into the ocean by means of
a heavy cable linked to a floating "transducer" (see Figure 29).

All this may strike some readers as an exercise in perfect
futility. For the followers of Aetherius, however, it meant restoring
vital energies to Mother Earth and thereby raising humanity's
badly damaged Karmic pattern. They considered it well worth
the cost.

Dr. King stroked the smooth flanks of his miracle machine
and asked if I had any questions.

"Yes. Where did you get your training in electronics?"

He gave me a thin diplomatic smile. "Ah, well, let me
illustrate this for you. I knew a civil servant once, in England,
and this man would occasionally paint. Beautiful little flowers.
Somebody suggested he should take art lessons, because if he
could paint like that without art lessons, what could he do with
training! He started to take lessons, and his painting went down
like this." King snapped his fingers. "And this is one reason why
I myself have not—er—cluttered up my mind with too much of
what you might call—uh—college education."

But George King can design more than machines that collect
energy from air.

He showed me the drawing of a projected "Temple with

Shape Power." In this case the title means exactly what it implies: power arising from shape! By its mere shape and measurements, he explained, the Temple would have "strong magical properties." The Master Aetherius had described it as a "dynamic, tremendously powerful machine, capable of the reception and transmission of mighty, uplifting, transmuting, dynamic energies."

The sketch showed an edifice consisting of three cones, one dome and a sphere, put together in an architectural style best described as Buck Rogers Baroque. Built in Washington, D.C., it could pass for the Martian Embassy.

"It might take us a while to erect this Temple," King said in parting. "It means a very large investment. But I'm sure we will accomplish it."

He has my fullest confidence.

If the Aetherius Society thrives on combat, the Institute of Mentalphysics breathes tranquillity. Compared to the shrill clamor of most cult organizations, the Institute's message is beamed in a blissfully moderate key.

This may have something to do with the fact that its founder had already made his fortune before launching it.

The Science of Mentalphysics (actually a corporate church) was brought to this country by a remarkable Englishman named Edwin John Dingle. The difference between him and other Eastern-oriented mysticists is that he had not only crossed China on foot, but actually lived in a Tibetan monastery for nine months. You can, furthermore, verify his biographical details in international press records; which makes him practically unique in cultist circles.

Dingle was not the only Westerner to have resided in a lamasery, but he was certainly the only one to emerge and become a millionaire afterwards. Shortly after World War I he published a series of commercial manuals and business gazettes covering the new Chinese Republic. They made him a rich man within a few years.

When he went to the United States it was therefore not to earn money, but to retire—very comfortably—on what he had made.

He didn't stay retired for long. The knowledge he had acquired in the Far East was germinating within him, clamoring for expression. As one of his Tibetan mentors had predicted years earlier, "You will never be happy, my son, unless you teach."

Dingle adopted the name bestowed on him in China—Ding Le Mei—and began to teach. What he taught was essentially a blending of Christian and Buddhist mysticism with a leavening of physical health practices he had learned from the Tibetan Lamaists. He called it the science of Mentalphysics.

In 1927 he founded the Institute of Mentalphysics, which was incorporated as a religion seven years later. But religion is altogether the wrong label for it. Mentalphysics is not a creed but a method. It doesn't expound a dogma, but a life style (see Figure 30).

At the core it is pantheistic—teaching that there is only God, and God is all there is. The major religions, of course, teach that too, but they insist on qualifying this by bringing in prophets, saints or a Holy Trinity. Mentalphysics sticks to the original concept—all manifestation is a manifestation of God. There are no go-betweens, and everything in the universe is God's spiritual essence.

Based on this abstraction, however, is an eminently practical health cult with the motto "Breath Is Life." Students learn to adapt their breathing to their body actions, to preserve, replenish and increase their supply of "prana"—the Eastern concept of the life essence that permeates all space. What they are learning are essentially the kind of breathing practices that enabled Houdini to perform his legendary feats of breath control.

Ding Le Mei is now very old and retired from active leadership. His cult, though operating with a minimum of noise and publicity, has spread from America to England, Australia, France, Germany and India, with a current membership of 213,000 students. The study courses are fairly arduous but inexpensive. Members pay eight dollars at their initiation, then four dollars a month for their lessons.

The Institute of Mentalphysics is a cool Spanish mission-styled building in Los Angeles and forms the administrative headquarters. But the core of the movement lies in the Yucca valley, 125 miles southeast. There, blending with the mountain and desert scenery, stands a so-called "caravansary"—actually an entire village devoted to Mentalphysics in all its forms, spiritual, social and physical. It is certainly the most tasteful sanctuary created by any American cult movement: a spread of low, unostentatious stone buildings, kept in consistently modern tone, wreathed by plants and shrubs and exuding an atmosphere of light, quiet and serenity.

As mentioned earlier in this chapter, the tide of esoteric cults is now flooding over the entire country, producing rococo growths in the unlikeliest places.

Upstate New York, for instance, harbors the self-styled Gheez Nation, a group liable to drive future theological researchers to despair. Its members claim kinship with the Falasha—the primitive African Jews of Ethiopia. The Falasha, who inhabit the wild mountain ranges in the province of Gondar, stuck to their Hebrew faith when the rest of the people turned to Christianity during the fourth century. Although they shared the Semitic background of most Ethiopians (whose emperor is still known as the Lion of Judah) they effectively isolated themselves from the mainstream, clinging to an archaic form of worship unaltered since biblical times.

New York's Gheez people, however, are neither Semitic nor Ethiopian nor even technically Jewish. Their kinship rests entirely on color—they are American Negroes.

Maintaining a highly disciplined matriarchy at Mount Helion Sanctuary, the Gheez are led by Her Majesty Mysikiitta Fa Senntao, Imperial Ruler of the Gheez Temple. Her Majesty claims to have come to earth from the sun in order to redeem her people.

"Life on the sun is very comfortable," she related. "The sun has a mean temperature of seventy-eight degrees all year round— only when its rays enter the earth's atmosphere do they become unbearably hot. Many, many of the spaceships we keep sighting come from the sun. My own particular husband drives a cigar-shaped ship."

Her Majesty is a plump, elderly lady of formidable dignity, wearing dark glasses, masses of beads and a gold mesh hairnet. I was quite unable to discover whether she had an English name as well.

Gheez ceremonies include religious dancing in ecstatic, yet

superbly controlled groups that aroused unqualified admiration from the great Katherine Dunham when she saw them. After the dance ritual I witnessed, Her Majesty received numbers of her subjects who greeted her with deep bows and a disturbingly Fascist-style salute with outstretched right hand. Men demonstrated karate exercises in her honor, white-robed girls recited poetry expressing their joy at being Gheez.

In conclusion, Her Majesty delivered a speech that culminated in a series of oratorial questions:

"How many people have I brought back from the dead?"

"Hundreds!" responded her followers.

"Have I ever charged a dime for it?"

"No—never!" came the hundred-throated roar. "Amen!"

It was an exciting gathering. But I never did find out just where the connection with the Falasha came in.

Whereas the majority of cult movements tend to be rather vague about their aims, the Individualist Society make theirs unmistakably clear: it is getting rich. As the Society's International Director phrased it, "I am an Evangelist for only one thing in this world; I preach prosperity!"

The Society is based in Tahlequah, Oklahoma, though its head spends part of each winter on his rancho in Mexico. He is a handsomely mustached man named Jack L. Felts, who claims to have turned a capital of fifty dollars into forty thousand (after taxes) within one year. His avowed ambition is to teach a select group of citizens (his followers) to do the same.

His international record puts this country's Foreign Aid program to shame. To quote from his own testimony: "In 1957 I counseled a group of German industrialists and financiers, teaching them this system. Germany is now rich. In 1959 a group of French psychologists, remotely connected to the government, were counseled by myself and staff in this system. France is now rich. Last year representatives from Israel, South Africa, Italy, Spain, and a number of Latin American nations were given intensive counseling in this system. They now grow prosperous. . . ."

Mr. Felts claims to have learned his recipe from one Yogi Ram Bashida and several other psychics. It was, he recalls, "incredibly simple, effective, and effortless." It consists of mastering a "money magnetizing" process, a knack allegedly already known to those 10 percent of the people of the United States of America who are rich. In the Director's words: "Money comes to you in proportion to your legitimate needs. Thus, by creating within yourself and within your sphere of influence a legitimate need for the money energy, you attract natural flows of this basic social energy."

Members of the Individualist Society receive an intensive twelve-lesson course in this process. While studying it, the Yogi Ram Bashida and others assist in setting up the proper magnetism to enable them to assimilate what they are learning. The course, Mr. Felts assures his readers, is easily assimilable, despite the fact that it involves the use of psychometry, focal hypnosis, transference of higher mind energies, and other components developed by the IS.

The whole process costs just twenty-five dollars. If you haven't that sum, Mr. Felts advises you to beg or borrow it, "—after you have completed the course, you should have plenty of reserve to repay the loan."

The current trend of cultism, however, runs in a diametrically opposite direction. Its entire rationale is antimaterialistic, non-acquisitive, contrary to the principles of a production-directed, competitive consumer society and at least partially inspired by the rustic idyllicism of Henry David Thoreau.

Newspapers have dubbed its adherents "hippies," but this term—derived from the old jitterbug adjective "hep" (to be "with it")—is generically about as descriptive as the label "Italian" for assorted Milanese, Romans and Sicilians. "Psychedelics" comes closer to the mark, except that it can indicate a brand of narcotics as well as a philosophy. Psychedelic means literally "consciousness-expanding" and methods of achieving such expansion may range from LSD to sun worship, from group orgasms to backbreaking physical toil.

The original "flower children" who poured into San Francisco's Haight-Ashbury district in the summer of 1967 have given way to a diversified and widely scattered throng, often with little in common but long hair. The flower stage was over almost before it had begun, crushed by the chilling realization that unprotected gentleness is an open invitation to robbery, rape and sometimes murder. The wide-eyed "love generation" quickly came to resemble shoals of frolicsome flounders with sharks cruising around the fringes.

Since then the sharks have gained much of the limelight. The Charlie Manson "family" of Death Valley demonstrated that beads and beards do not exclude violence in its starkest form, and they were by no means the only group of that stripe. The hills around Taos, New Mexico, contain an ominous sprinkling of gun-toting, knife-strapping hippie clans, quite paranoid enough for latter-day Hatfields and McCoys.

But they are no more typical of the movement than Count Zinzendorf's Herrnhuters were of eighteenth-century Christianity.

What *is* typical is a pervasive urge to escape from the "bad vibes" of city life into some form of communal existence close to nature. An estimated fifteen thousand psychedelics have already settled in the more or less wide-open spaces of New England, the southwestern states and California, and the trickle is continuing month after month.

But having once cut loose from the nation's urban and suburban strata, their behavior follows no sharply defined guidelines. Some establish genuine communes and become closely knit, exclusive social microcosms sharing all means of production and aiming at complete economic independence. Others retain fluidity, with new arrivals drifting in and out and each "family" looking after its own shelter and food supply aided, perhaps, by a communal vegetable patch. Others still remain largely parasitical, with the majority of members panhandling in the neighborhood or depending on funds supplied by their "square" relatives.

Some communes discourage or ban the use of all drugs, some permit grass (marijuana) but draw the line at acid (LSD). A third category keeps open house for everything, limited only by the difficulties of obtaining the stuff. Sexual morality varies just as widely. A few—very few—communes practice free love in the totally promiscuous meaning of the phrase, but these rarely seem to survive much longer than six months. The majority become surprisingly pristine, with couples paired off in unofficial but clearly established monogamy and transgressions rarer than among the legally wedded bourgeoisie.

These units—variously termed communes, cooperatives, colonies, affinity groups or families—follow no distinctive religious line. There is a Buddhist commune in Louisiana, several Black Muslim communal farms in Alabama, conservative Christian communes operated by the "Children of God" in Texas, Kentucky and California, and at least one colony of animists in New Mexico. (New Mexico, incidentally, has become so packed with rural communes that early comers recently advertised in several underground publications asking the throng to stay away, "there's no more room here.")

The majority of psychedelics have not accepted any codified creed, at least not yet. Nearly all of them profess belief in various mystical forces, and a large proportion hold vague romanticized views on reincarnation; though not in accordance with any particular theological dogma. What they practice is mostly a home-brewed medley of Zen Buddhism, primitive Christianity, Hinduism and Zoroastrianism, permeated with the nature worship of the Hopi Indians, Gandhi's philosophical pacifism and some of the Arcadian gospel of innocence as preached by Rousseau.

But their spiritual beliefs have little influence on their pattern of existence, which ranges from the hand-to-mouth to the scientifically blueprinted. Large numbers (though not as large as some newspapers would have us believe) rely on welfare payments or federal food stamps. A fair proportion live on handicrafts, which they sell in nearby stores with the profits going into a community chest. And there are a growing number of enterprises like Raintree Investments, Indiana, which has turned five hundred acres into organic farmland, raising crops without the aid of either chemical fertilizers or pest controls.

What mainly distinguishes the psychedelics from the older forms of cultism is the absence among them of fire-breathing dogmatists, of the nit-picking, blinkered, antiintellectual Yahoo patriarchs or matriarchs who have turned scores of esoteric movements into mental concentration camps for their adherents. The psychedelics have avoided this trap—chiefly because they possess no dogma to dogmatize.

But those of them who have actually accomplished the break away from the mainstream share at least one fervent conviction: that their deviation represents an entirely new trend in American history. All but a few of them believe that their social experiment is the first of its kind since the arrival of the

Pilgrim Fathers. Actually, of course, they are following the path trodden before them by the Oneida Christian Communists, the Jemimakins, the Millerites, the Mormons, the shaking Quakers, the Harrisites, the Brook Farmers, the Glory Foresters, the Universologists, the Apostolic Enlightened, the Medmanites, and the hundred or so other American sects who once determined to opt out of society and form their own.

Whether their ultimate destiny will be any different remains to be seen.

XII

SATAN IN THE SUBURBS

No OFFICIAL census has yet been taken of this country's devil worshipers. But according to the meager statistics available, they must number somewhere between ten and fifteen thousand.

This is a puny figure as occult followings go, though apparently quite large enough to fill a great many people with shocked and incredulous dismay.

In the words of one lady, who has so far worked her way through spiritualism, scientology and Rosicrucianism: "I can't believe it—it's horrible. How can anyone worship evil?"

The answer to this must be that evil—like beauty—frequently lies in the eyes of the beholder. And this is not meant as a mere conversational gambit. For the devil's origin and genealogy are so enigmatic that his identification with the Evil One should not be taken for granted. His name, for instance, need have no malevolent connotations at all. It derives from the Indian word *devi* —which happens to mean "god."

In most of mankind's religions he is exactly that; a divinity in his own right, an essential negative force equal and supplementary to the positive godhead. He usually had a fifty-fifty share in the creation of the universe and man. Some creeds took the dividing process so far that they declared God responsible only for the upper half of our bodies; the devil had fashioned—and was in control of—the lower.

On the other hand he plays only a minute role in the Jewish Old Testament, and not a spectacularly wicked one at that. He argues with Yahweh and plagues Job, and thereby earns the best-known of his many names: Satan—adversary.

Not until the apocryphal writings and later the New Testament does he emerge as full-fledged Prince of Darkness and "foul fiend." Only then is he definitely identified with the (originally anonymous) serpent who tempts Eve in Paradise, and proclaimed responsible for sin and sickness as well as lust.

The theological reason for making a scapegoat of the devil was to preserve the total goodness of God. But in turning over fleshly desires to Satan's preserve, the Church fathers took a step that was to produce an unimaginable amount of misery, terror and cruelty in the Christian world.

For during the early Middle Ages the Church authorities gained the secular powers to enforce what had hitherto been a largely theoretical code. And since lust—meaning sex—was a weapon in Satan's armory, it seemed logical to try and reduce it to its purely procreative function. Consequently, the medieval ecclesiasts compiled a series of "penitential books" aimed at limiting human intercourse to the mere act of coitus—and even that only during severely circumscribed periods.

By gradually adding days of abstinence to the Christian calendar, the Church finally curtailed legitimate lovemaking between married couples to the equivalent of about four months of the year. The positions of the act were likewise regulated— and only one was wholly permissible.

There were penalties for intercourse outside holy wedlock, sharply increased if the girl was a virgin. Some twenty paragraphs dealt with every conceivable form of masturbation (all outlawed under severe penalties) and several more with such involuntary acts as erotic dreams and nocturnal emissions. It was also an offense to harbor "lewd and unchaste thoughts" and yet another to experience "unclean desires" at any time of the day or night.

These strictures, of course, were as unenforceable as Prohibition and they had a similar result of stimulating exactly what they were meant to suppress. The more powerfully Holy Church strove against the "Satanic" manifestations of the flesh, the more they seemed to multiply . . . even among the clergy.

The Church scholars could find only one explanation for this deplorable process—that Satan's minions were larger and more versatile than had been supposed. They set out to number and classify them in much the same spirit as medical researchers grade microbes, and in due course came up with a demonology that staggers the imagination.

The most famous such inventory was compiled by the learned Johann Weier in 1568. Master Weier based his calculations on the biblical passage in which a devil (through the mouth of the Gadarene madman) tells Jesus, "My name is Legion: for we are many." Taking the ration strength of a Roman legion at four thousand men, Weier then multiplied this figure by what he assumed to be the total of Satanically afflicted people in Christendom. Thus he arrived at an army of 7,405,926 devils and demons, organized in 1,111 divisions of 6,666 imps each.

But this—Roman Catholic—total was considered ridiculously low by the Reformation. The Lutherans produced their own revised *Theatrum Diabolorum* in which the number of existing devils was raised to 2,665,866,746,664. The more radical Calvinists condemned this as still a gross understatement and put the figure at nothing less than 10 thousand billion!

This astronomical horde of hell was divided into specialized units, all under the supreme command of Satan, who only occasionally took the field in person. His deputy (according to some scholars his alter ego) was Beelzebub, Lord of the Flies. Directly below them came Astaroth and Asmodeus, the respective demons of love and lust, assisted by a large group of superior officers whose names, ranks and functions varied considerably according to which demonological dictionary you consulted.

The rank and file were listed in three main branches. There

were the *striga* or flying spirits, who murdered and ate children. The *malefica*, who came in animal or human shapes, raised thunderstorms, created unexplained noises, and caused disease and death. But the main force consisted of the *concubitus daemonum* and came in two sexes: the male incubus, who seduced women in their sleep and fathered demon infants on them, and the female succubus, who lay with men and robbed them of their potency. The succubi had a special commander of their own. She was Lilith, according to Hebrew legendry the first wife of Adam before the creation of Eve, a truly devastating creature whose role was a combination of Lucrezia Borgia and Mata Hari (her forte was worming top-secret ecclesiastical information from cardinals, bishops and inquisitors).

The primary aim of these myriads was to lure Christians away from the Church and into the clutches of Satan. They accomplished this either through more or less subtle seductions (frequently in their victims' sleep) or by a forcible takeover that culminated in complete "demonic possession." It was the latter alternative that resulted in some of history's most spine-chilling episodes.

For the clerical scholars held that for demons to gain possession of a baptized person's body they needed the aid of a third party. They could be "injected" by means of magic spells—and thousands of alleged sorcerers and witches were burned at the stake for doing that. But they could also achieve entry through sexual intercourse, providing one of the partners assisted them.

During the first quarter of the seventeenth century, the whole of France was shaken by a series of such cases occurring—to the stark horror of the populace—within the confines of the Church. To the benighted spectators of the time it seemed as if Satan were launching a concerted mass attack at the very heart of Holy Church.

The chain began in a small Ursuline convent in Aix-en-Provence in the fall of 1609. The cloister held only six nuns, all of them with aristocratic family background, which made the affair doubly outrageous. The youngest of the nuns was Madeleine de Demandolx de la Palud, a thin, pale, highly strung girl of sixteen, who had a history of emotional instability which had forced two other nunneries to get rid of her. Now she began to display unmistakable symptoms of "demonic possession." She swore and spat during services, threw herself on the tiles in hideous convulsions and screamed that demons were plucking at her breasts and belly.

The elderly Jesuit Father Romillon hurried from nearby Marseilles to cure the girl by exorcism. He failed completely, but in between strings of curses and obscenities the afflicted girl gasped out some very grave charges against her former confessor, Father Louis Gaufridi. She claimed that he had been making love to her ever since she turned thirteen, that he had given her powders to procure abortions, and that he had assured her that though he could not marry her in the eyes of God he could do so in the eyes of the devil.

Gaufridi was a type of priest then very common in France, and ironically celebrated in a thousand tavern ballads and couplets. A tall, handsome, ruddy-cheeked Provençal on whom the tonsure sat lightly, he had charmed a score of noble ladies in his Marseilles parish—among them Madeleine's mother. He had, in fact, been warned to pay less attention to the young daughter and had subsequently held himself aloof from her. What he had done earlier, nobody knows for certain. Whatever it might have been, the experienced Father Romillon could see that Madeleine was insanely in love with Gaufridi, desperate to meet him again, and yet obsessed with hatred for him.

It was a dangerous situation, and apparently old Father Romillon did his level best to hush up the matter. But then— one by one—the other nuns in the little convent started to rave! Soon the whole place was echoing with moans and shrieks and the crash of splintering crosses, and people were stopping in the street to listen to the din.

Something had to be done. Reluctantly, Father Romillon called in Sebastian Michaelis, the Grand Inquisitor and scourge of all demons in southern France.

By then another nun was far outconvulsing Madeleine. She was Sister Louise Capeau, aged twenty-five, who had always been jealous of the blue-blooded youngest and the attentions she received. Now she seemed determined to capture the limelight.

Before the Grand Inquisitor, Louise howled, bellowed,

neighed like a horse, tore open her habit and raised her skirts, finally producing the hoarse voices of three famous devils: Grésil, Vérin and Sonnillon. It was Vérin who informed the Inquisitor that Father Gaufridi was a devil worshiper and "grand magician," that—by breaking Madeleine's hymen—he had introduced into her belly 6,666 of the most evil spirits, including Leviathan and the mighty Beelzebub himself.

This was quite enough for the Inquisitor. He had Gaufridi summoned and ordered *him* to conduct the exorcism. The result was as damning as expected. The very sight of the priest drove the women into demented frenzy. They—or rather the devils within them—took turns in accusing Gaufridi of literally unprintable sex perversions (although the court scribes took them down in painstaking detail). They also added charges of cannibalism. "Louis Gaufridi feigns to abstain from flesh; nevertheless he makes himself drunk with the flesh of little children. Some he has eaten, others he has suffocated and afterwards dug up, all cry before God for vengeance upon crimes so execrable . . ."

Again and again Madeleine would break off her tirades and drop on the floor, moaning with lust, her legs flaying wildly, her arms outstretched toward Gaufridi, panting, "Come to me—now —come my fair prince, my delight—now—*now* . . ."

Gaufridi seemed totally stunned by this double assault. He mumbled denials, but in a feeble, almost absent-minded fashion. To the Grand Inquisitor this showed definite signs of guilt, but it is much more likely that the priest simply couldn't bring himself to grasp the enormity of the accusations hurled at him.

The Inquisition could not arrest him immediately. Gaufridi had powerful backing from his parish in Marseilles, where he remained popular. But Michaelis was a wise hand at this game and took his time. He merely ordered that records be kept of the ravings of Madeleine and Louise. In due course he collected a mountain of "evidence"—enough to bring the priest to trial.

Proceedings opened in Aix in February 1611, with the whole country following them avidly. The possessed nuns put on a skin-crawling performance, convulsing their bodies so hideously that their necks seemed disjointed, Madeleine going through what was obviously an orgasm before the aghast assembly. The devils within them shrilled and bellowed, spraying spittle and endless strings of blasphemies.

The Inquisitor also produced a parchment, written by Satan himself and signed by Gaufridi in his own blood, in which he swore allegiance to the devil in return for "making all women subject to my pleasure and will." (The document is still on display in the Avignon museum, though unrecognizably faded.)

Normally this would have been quite sufficient for a conviction, but because the accused was a priest, Michaelis insisted on a confession. Gaufridi was put to the torture, confessed, retracted the following day, was tortured again, confessed once more, but again retracted.

After five weeks of exquisitely graduated agonies he underwent "Squassation." He was hoisted to the ceiling by his twisted arms, with heavy weights dangling from his legs. By means of sudden sharp drops his limbs were wrenched from their sockets. When the torturers let him down slivers of broken bones were protruding through his skin.

Gaufridi was broken. In his third and final confession he admitted eating the "fine smoked flesh" of unbaptized babies, celebrating Black Mass in his priestly raiments, and introducing demons into the bodies of hundreds of women and several young boys. "More than a thousand persons have been poisoned by the attraction of my breath, which filled them with passion . . ."

A twitching drooling wreck, Gaufridi was dragged on a hurdle through the streets before being taken to the place of execution. There—"by the mercy of his holy judges"—he was strangled before the flames reached his body.

The Aix case was closed, but it was merely the first of a long line of similar ones—all involving possessed nuns—that drove the Church to near desperation. At Limoges and Bordeaux, in Paris, Tours, Loudon, Louviers and other places, highly esteemed clerics seemed to revel in doing Satan's work and infecting those around them with their hellish plague.

It would be too glib to ascribe all "demonic possession" to outbreaks of hysteria stemming from the sexual frustration of cloistered women. Some of them, at least, were produced by sheer terror often mingled with overpowering guilt feelings. For the fact is that a surprising number of the clergy *did* dabble in Satanism.

The cult involved not merely portions of the lower clergy, but large segments of the populace. It had almost reached the proportions of an underground movement. Its peculiar attraction can be understood only in the light of prevailing social conditions.

The France of Louis XIV—the richest and strongest country in Europe—was an autocracy comparable only to Stalinist Russia. The entire nation had been reduced to puppets, with the beringed fingers of the *Roi Soleil* manipulating the strings. The aristocracy might live in splendor and the lower orders in reeking misery, but all were subject to the same royal whim that could promote or beggar, enrich or destroy them with one casual squiggle of the quill. The king's will extended even into the spiritual realm, for Louis had emasculated the Church just as effectively as the nobility. By using leading prelates like Cardinal Mazarin as his ministers, this extraordinarily intelligent tyrant had turned the Church into nothing more than an uncommonly corrupt government department.

The feeling of complete helplessness that permeated society from top to bottom had macabre side effects. It gave rise to a rash of "black" cults and practices, all designed to snatch at least a snippet of personal power for the practitioners. Literally millions of men and women tried alchemy, necromancy, sorcery and divination as a means of gaining control over something or someone instead of being the eternally controlled.

Satanism offered a double inducement. It was not only a method of achieving power, but also a way of hitting back at the dehumanizingly oppressive combination of Church and State.

If the hierarchy proclaimed Lucifer as their mortal enemy, well, then it followed that he was the natural ally of all those who detested the venal, luxuriating princes of the Church—and they included thousands of the miserably paid and bullied lower clergy. And if he demanded certain unpleasant rituals in return for the aid he rendered, it was no more than his due. Nobody did anything for nothing.

The curious feature about devil worship was that the worshipers had to rely on Church chronicles for their entire liturgical knowledge; sources, that is, more prone to anti-Satanic propaganda than historical research. The Black Mass, for instance, the traditional high ceremony of Satanism, was taken *in toto* from ecclesiastical literature and would probably never have been performed if the authors hadn't described it in such painstaking detail. All the psychotically obscene and blasphemous minutiae of the ritual came from the scholarly tomes put out by Church inquisitioners. It consists of an unappetizing mélange of pagan sacrificial rites and mock-Christian ceremonial and has no anthropological basis whatever.

One of its supposed rules (faithfully adhered to by the Satanists) was that an ordained priest had to officiate. According to a list captured by the police, there were no fewer than 50 priests available for this purpose in Paris alone. Since the city then had a population of under 200,000, this figure is truly staggering and conveys a very graphic idea of the proportions of the cult.

Neither the civil nor the clerical authorities, however, realized the extent of the growth until the so-called "Chambre Ardente" investigations blew the lid off in the late 1670s. The resultant stench made even the case-hardened King Louis hold his nose.

The Chambre Ardente commission—named after the chamber in the Paris Arsenal where it sat—was instituted by the king to check into a crop of rumors concerning mass poisonings which were buzzing around the capital. It was headed by the police prefect of Paris, a shrewd, tenacious, utterly incorruptible official named Nicholas de la Reynie.

By using both male and female detectives as decoys, the prefect unearthed a nationwide ring of poison dealers operating under the guise of fortune-tellers. They were mostly women who also acted as abortionists, but their main income derived from selling "potions"—sometimes aphrodisiacs, more often belladonna and arsenic, together with detailed instructions on how to make their results look like natural deaths. Between them they had accounted for a fabulous number of victims—the contemporary Archives de la Bastille calculate them as "upwards of 3,000," not including those merely rendered blind, lame or insane by their dosing.

The first shock came when Reynie zeroed in on the chief of the ring. He turned out to be the noble Francois de Chasteuil, prior of the Carmelite Order in Paris, who used his poison profits to maintain two mistresses in elegant apartments *inside* his monastery. The good prior escaped to Spain before he could be arrested, but Reynie's agents nabbed most of the underlings.

This was in January 1679, and over the next four years the commission pieced together a nightmare mosaic of murder and perversion, so widespread and high-ranking that Louis had to suspend further investigations to prevent a goodly percentage of his courtiers from being arrested.

At the center of the web, like a venomous spider, sat a woman whose real name was Catherine Deshayes, but who called herself La Voisin. A guttersnipe of unknown origins, she could neither read nor write and spoke the juicy argot of Parisian prostitutes. Yet she had built a reputation as the capital's foremost astrologer and crystal gazer and was famous for her "lucky candles"—made from the fat of hanged murderers, which was supplied to her by the two executioners of Paris, both of whom were her lovers.

But this was merely a cover. La Voisin's real stock in trade was preparing and dispensing poisons in expertly measured doses, and the arranging of Black Masses on request. The clients merely came and paid, she supplied all the necessary requisites, including officiating priest and sacrificial victims.

Her Satanic high priest was a creature straight out of Edgar Allan Poe; the hunchbacked, bloated, pox-ridden, sixty-year-old Abbé Guibourg, who constantly needed money because he kept four female mistresses and an exceptionally handsome young Italian boy named Simoni. The Abbé occasionally earned a bonus by selling one of his own illegitimate infants to La Voisin to be used as a sacrifice.

Most of her supply of babies, however, came from slum mothers, street girls, and unwed ladies of good families, many of whom thought that their offspring was being adopted. La Voisin's only stipulation was that the child be unbaptized—so that Satan could take immediate possession of its soul. At her trial witnesses stated that she must have used around 2,400 infants in her ceremonies "and that she had never paid more than three livres for any of them."

To La Voisin's large thick-walled house in the Rue Beauregard in the Villeneuve district came an endless string of highly placed personalities with special requests. They came in coaches and litters and they always came at night.

There was a swarm of high-ranking army officers, including the Duc de Luxembourg, Captain of the Royal Foot Guard, who desired to "converse with the devil." There was a bevy of court beauties, including the Princess de Tingry, who came for poisons, love philters, abortions, and to acquire certain powers through communion with Satan. There were—and this was the crowning shock—Mmes. de Polignac and de Montespan, past and current mistresses of His Majesty, who ordered Black Masses in the hope of either regaining or holding the king's favor.

For obvious reasons the commission was particularly interested in the activities of the royal mistresses, and therefore left an unusually detailed account of them. According to their records, Madame de Montespan attended five masses, accompanied by her lady-in-waiting, Madame de la Desoeillets. On another occasion the two ladies made a love charm "intended to be used on the Royal person of His Majesty," consisting of flour, bat's blood, male sperm (supplied by a cavalry lieutenant who happened to be on the premises) and a few drops of Montespan's menstrual blood, mixed to a paste in an altar chalice.

During the actual mass, Madame served as a "living altar" by lying naked on a black-draped stone slab. Seven candles, made from human fat, burned around her. The incense, which stank abominably, was a mixture of sulfur, alum, human excrement and asafoetida. Beneath the crucifix, which stood upside down, lay a criminal's skull and a urine-soaked Bible.

The Abbé Guibourg acted as high priest. His two acolytes were Madame de la Desoeillets and a fifteen-year-old prostitute named Jeanneton, who was the niece of the city hangman.

We have the record of Guibourg's own confession for what happened then. The Abbé held a squalling infant over Montespan's nude body and—with one swift strike of the knife—cut its throat so that the blood splashed over the "altar." He then offered, on her behalf, the following conjuration:

"O Astaroth, O Asmodeus, princes of friendship and love, I invoke thee to accept graciously my sacrifice, this child I offer up to thee for the things I ask of thee. They are that the friendship and love of the King and the Dauphin may be assured me, that I may

be honored by all the princes and princesses of the Court, that
the King may deny me nothing I ask, whether it be for my person, my relatives or for any of my household and friends."

I could fill the rest of this chapter with these lavatorial ba-
nalities (the original transcripts covered more than four hundred
handwritten pages) but for the monotony this would involve.
From the sociological angle it is of interest that the commissioners
seemed far more perturbed about the lady's intention to slip a
love charm to the king than over the confessed infanticide. France,
after all, had only one *Roi Soleil,* while the country was crawling
with unwanted babies.

The end results of the investigations developed in the same
spirit. A total of forty-one poison dispensers were executed—La
Voisin was burned at the stake, screaming curses until the smoke
got into her throat. But there was only one aristocrat in the lot,
and none among the sixteen sent to the galleys or branded. Most
of the nobles involved were either banished or quietly allowed to
escape.

Historically, these trials are said to mark the apex of devil
worship in the Western world. But who was the devil the participants meant to worship? He was an image handed to them in its
entirety by his proclaimed arch-enemies, the Church scholars. Not
an independent deity at all, but merely a kind of anti-God who
could be wooed by staging a savage and obscene parody of the
Christian mass. Which—as modern Satanists point out—is a totally
false picture.

Even within the framework of Christian legendry it is possible
to establish a case for Lucifer as a much-wronged creature. Tradi-
tionally he is always approaching man with offers of wealth, fame,
love or strength in exchange for his immortal soul. In the most
celebrated of these compacts—that of Dr. Faustus—the offer was
wisdom. In none of the hundreds of stories and poems concerning
such deals was Mephistopheles ever accused of welching; of delivering less than promised or collecting before the stipulated
time.

He, on the other hand, is continually cheated out of his
rights by the interference of various saints who—at the crucial
moment—deprive him of his prey. In Stephen Vincent Benét's

classic "The Devil and Daniel Webster" it isn't even a saint, but merely a cunning New England politician who stymies the devil by turning an airtight legal contract into an emotional jury trial.

Medieval theologians credited Satan with building Hadrian's Wall on the Scottish border, with the construction of the beautiful bridge at Avignon and—strange as it may seem—the architectural plans of the Cologne cathedral. After each of these feats he was swindled of his promised reward by divine intervention and forced to retreat empty-handed. The Christian reader was meant to delight in these examples of "pious fraud." Seen from another viewpoint, however, they can also arouse sympathy for the defraudee.

It is from this reverse viewpoint that we must regard the current revival of Satanism in America. The devil involved here is not the malevolent caricature drawn by his clerical foes, epitomized by Goethe as *"die Spottgeburt aus Dreck und Feuer"* —the mock creation of filth and fire. Rather than the Hebrew adversary—Yaweh's opponent—he is the Roman god Lucifer who, though by now unrecognizably distorted, began his career as the bearer of light. A little of his original role had stuck to him through all the centuries of playing Public Enemy No. 1. For among the baits with which he tempted man was always wisdom—meaning enlightenment.

He is also the Greek god Pan, from whom the Christian theologians had borrowed the horns and cloven hoof of their devil image (in a few tales he was even given a reed pipe). Far from being an evil sprite, Pan symbolized fertility—of the earth as well as the womb—the carnal as much as the creative side of nature. He was a decidedly joyful god thousands of years before his physical characteristics were foisted upon the demon of negativity with whom he had nothing in common except erotic prowess.

This, roughly, is the composite deity envisioned by our contemporary Satanists. Their form of worship bears only a faint and rigorously dry-cleaned resemblance to the rites of their European predecessors. And they have the added distinction of being undisputedly legal.

All you have to do is ring a certain San Francisco telephone number and wait until a chirpy secretarial voice at the other end says, "Good morning, Church of Satan." It is, let's face it, a wee bit anticlimactic.

The Church was founded in 1966 by Chicago-born Anton Szandor LaVey, whose exotic names derive from Romanian, Alsatian and Georgian ancestry. He got off to a rather creaky start when—in order to raise support for his movement—he staged some embarrassingly näive nightclub rituals involving topless witches and a bikini-clad "inquisitioner"; allegedly a former counselor for Billy Graham (see Figure 31).

But two years later came the film release of *Rosemary's Baby* and with it a tremendous upsurge of popular interest in matters demoniacal. The Catholic Legion of Decency helped by bestowing a "C" (condemned) rating on the movie. This positively convinced vast segments of the public that they were getting inside dope on witchcraft and/or Satanism, despite the fact that director Roman Polanski's knowledge of—and interest in—either subject amounted to zero. (There was, incidentally, more concentrated evil in one pallid smile of Cocteau's *Infants Terrible* than in Rosemary's entire pregnancy.)

Millions of moviegoers saw LaVey in action, although his name didn't appear on the credit list. He was the curiously reptilian Satan who raped Rosemary. The film's box office success resulted in a blaze of publicity for America's only registered Satanic Church and enabled its High Priest to drop his nightclub routine. At the moment you have to shoehorn your way into his presence through throngs of newspaper reporters, magazine interviewers, occultist researchers, and would-be adherents.

Before meeting LaVey, I was inclined to regard him as an American version of Aleister Crowley, the gentleman from Leamington, England, who called himself The Great Beast, imbibed ten grains of heroin per day and never got much beyond being a grubby little boy thinly disguised as a monster.

I once met a Reuters correspondent who had known Crowley well before his death in 1947. And I recalled his comment on the self-styled "Wickedest Man in the World": "Crowley was a fine mountaineer and a pretty good chess player, but as a Satanist he was a crashing bore. You see, everything about him

37. "Witch's Cradle" at the Foundation for Mind Research. Device is set into slight swinging motion, produces state of semitrance in subject (PHOTO:ARTEMIS SMITH).

38. "Electric Circus"—correctl
known as Audio-Visual Environment—a computerized
blending of moving slides and
sound effects ranging from
mystical to macabre.

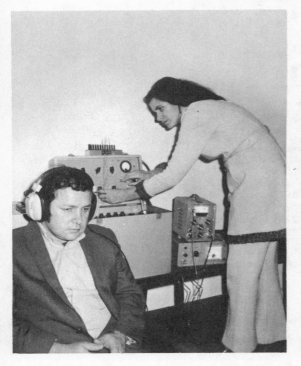

39. Jean Houston monitoring
husband Robert Masters' alpha
brain waves at Foundation of
Mind Research laboratory.

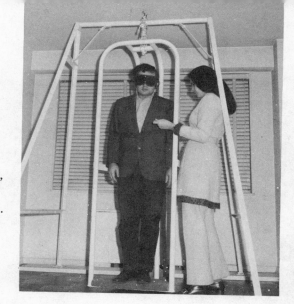

40. Jean Houston strapping Masters into "Witch's Cradle." Couple are co-directors of Foundation for Mind Research.

41. Sleep volunteer wired for dreaming at the Dream Laboratory at Brooklyn, N.Y., Medical Center. Subject's rapid eye movements will indicate dreaming process has started (PHOTO: JOHN LARSEN).

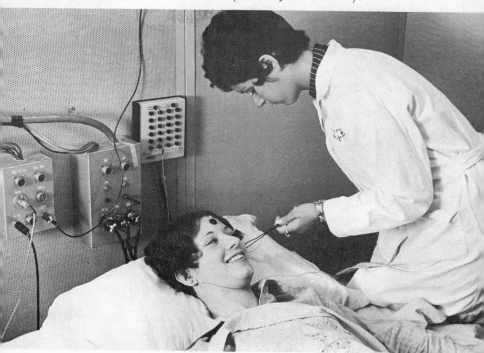

42. Ouija board has replaced Monopoly as America's favorite board game. Couple sits, legs touching, so-called "ideomotor movements" guiding their fingertips on pointer.

43. U.S. toy industry is introducing youngsters to occultism. Here children play game Astrology.

44. Another occult product of America's toy industry. Children playing Prediction game.

45. Witch Valerie, member of a New Jersey coven and partner in a supply firm of metaphysical products appropriately called The Witches' Cauldron.

46. The Reverend Benjamin Anthony Harris who runs the Timeless
Occult Shop above Hollywood's Sunset Boulevard.

47. Ann Caston lighting skull candle. These candles symbolize enemies—you can watch them melt before your eyes.

was secondhand. Even his motto, 'Do what thou wilt shall be the whole of the Law.' He had lifted that from Rabelais."

LaVey, as it turned out, did not resemble Crowley. He is no bore.

The Church of Satan is a black-painted Victorian structure of memorable ugliness. The type of house rampant in London's Bayswater district, but rare in San Francisco. A plate on the door said, "Do Not Ring Unless You Have An Appointment," but there was a very welcoming black Manx cat sitting underneath. Anyway, I had an appointment.

I was greeted by Mrs. LaVey, a smiling, outgoing, hospitable little blonde, with long hair and stylish spectacles. "Please sit down," she said. "Anton will be here in a few minutes." She kept me company, but refused to be interviewed. "That's Anton's department."

The front parlor smelled like the inside of an antique mattress; either the walls were damp or the windows were never opened. I sat down beside a tombstone serving as coffee table and admired the fittings. There was a regular dentist's chair, an operating table, a hanging skeleton, a lumpily stuffed possum, and a large bookcase with the warning: "Whoever removes books from this shelf will have his hands chopped off." The telephone, decorated with a Satanic seal, bore the notice: "Do not make outside calls from this phone." The Church, it appeared, was big on notices.

LaVey made a good entrance. He is a massive six-footer in his early forties, dressed completely in black, wearing a clerical collar and a silver pentagram medallion around his neck. His skull is clean-shaven, Tartar fashion, and he sports a black chin beard à la Ivan the Terrible.

He has a forceful, calm voice, a surprisingly amiable laugh, and a patiently cautious way of answering questions he must have heard several hundred times before.

"How do we visualize Satan? Purely symbolically, as the all-pervasive force. The only true God, in fact."

"Well, then whose adversary is he?"

LaVey smiled. "The adversary of all man-made spiritual religion. To all that we consider the contemptible crutches man has had to invent. We totally reject the concept of there being an antithesis to God. He *is* God."

"In other words," I said, "you consider Satan the personification of life—good and evil. Do you think that evil outweighs the good?"

"Well, we consider that what the theologians regard as man's predilection for evil will always outweigh the good. So—from the theological point of view—we are evil individuals."

He did not, however, go along with the dramatization of evil as performed in the original Black Mass. "Those," he explained, "were psychodramas at a time when people really needed them. They had to express their opposition, their rebellion against an established church. Our rituals are suitably modified to express the needs of *our* particular era."

The rituals are outlined in LaVey's *Satanic Bible*, a piquant mixture of liturgy, history, and magical recipes, such as how "to Cause the Destruction of an Enemy" or "to Summon One for Lustful Purpose or Establish a Sexually Gratifying Situation." It's an intriguing book, although chunks of it are written in a mysterious tongue called Enochian, rendering certain parts—literally—unspeakable.

For a time LaVey also played the role of a sulphurous Ann Landers by running a weekly tabloid column, "Letters from the Devil." Among the do-it-yourself tips he passed out were the correct specifications for a voodoo doll, and the brewing of love potions, using ginseng root as a substitute for the hard to get (in fact unobtainable) Mandrake.

"Our religion," he said gravely, "is the only one, I think, in complete accordance with human nature. It is based on indulgence. Instead of commanding our members to repress their natural urges, we teach that they should follow them. This includes physical lusts, the desire for revenge, the drive for material possessions."

LaVey gave a slow rumbling laugh that seemed to come from his solar plexus. "That's how most of them live already, in any case. Only hitherto they've been following the devil's creed without giving the devil his due. And suffering from guilt complexes because their hypocritical faiths kept telling them they ought to live differently. This religious dichotomy is a breeding ground for neuroses. We free them of such conflicts by making it clear that Satan—or God—*meant* them to live according to their inborn tendencies."

"Does that mean," I asked, "that you encourage drug habits or alcoholism?"

He fielded that one easily. "We certainly don't. Both are self-destructive, typical of losers. And we don't want losers. Satanism is a winner's creed. Now"—a sweep of his black-sleeved arm—"would you care to see the rest of the house?"

The Church is a veritable Fu Manchu castle, bristling with hidden doors and secret panels. Wildly sinister or high camp, depending on your attitude. The parlor fireplace and sections of the bookcase swing inward on silent hinges, revealing dark passages into the bowels of the place. The smell gets mustier the deeper you penetrate.

Downstairs is the Ritual Chamber, draped in black and scarlet. The centerpiece consists of the altar, next to it a large Hammond organ, which LaVey plays with magnificent flourish. (He used to play a calliope in a circus.) "No, we don't have any special Satanic music." He ran a finger over the keys. "We use Wagner for some ceremonies, Berlioz, Liszt, even church tunes."

Everywhere you look there are artfully gruesome masks, a titanic papier-mâché spider, an arms collector's dream of carbines, pistols, swords, daggers, maces, clubs; some ceremonial, others businesslike. Also skulls, phallic symbols, the inevitable black candles, a bell, and a very handsome chalice. The whole sanctum is rather like a cross between a chapel, an arsenal, and the clubhouse of a juvenile gang.

By opening a case containing a mummy you step into the Red Room next door. Most of it is occupied by a towering bed, hung with black drapes, contemplated from the ceiling by ceremonial masks that look as if they remembered everything that went on below.

Upstairs we were joined by seven-year-old Zeena LaVey, just back from school. Zeena was the cause of a minor scandal some years ago when her father baptized her into his Church.

Although, as a minister, he was entitled to do so, he created considerable indignation by performing the ceremony before the live, nude and female diabolical altar, sprinkling his daughter with earth and water while intoning, "Welcome, Zeena, new mistress, creature of magic light, child of joy. . . ."

When we arrived back in the parlor, the child of joy was being hauled off the hinged fireplace by her mother. "How many times have we told you not to step on the fireplace! We've already had it fixed twice."

She abandoned the fireplace and agreed to show me her art class work. Her drawings were lively, imaginative and mostly of ponies. I asked her if she intended to become an artist when she grew up.

She thought for a moment, then shook her head. "No. I'm going to be a ballet dancer."

LaVey said, "I'm sorry we can't show you our lion. He used to live in the back. We had to present him to the zoo, unfortunately. The neighbors complained about his roaring at night."

The Satanic Church has less trouble with hostile elements than might be expected. "Occasionally some nut comes to the door, but I can handle that," grinned the devil's High Priest. "And we have very good burglar alarms in the house."

He grew rather laconic when I asked about membership figures.

"We stopped divulging them after we reached seven thousand. That was—er—some time ago. But I can tell you that the Church is nationwide. We have grottoes—that's what we call them—all over the country. And then there are large numbers of crypto-Satanists. People who are not Church members, but like what we're doing. We get quite a lot of donations from them."

LaVey began his career by dropping out of high school and joining the Clyde Beatty Circus as a cage boy—which meant feeding lions, tigers and leopards. He also had a decided musical bent, taught himself piano and organ and played the oboe in the San Francisco Ballet Symphony Orchestra.

From the circus he graduated to a carnival, learning hypnotism, stage magic, and the elements of carny spieling. Then— oddly enough—he enrolled in college as a criminology major, which—even odder—led to a job as forensic photographer with the San Francisco Police Department. He made—and maintained

—some handy contacts during his three years with the force. In consequence the Church of Satan is one of the best protected establishments in town.

Before shaving his skull and emerging as "Black Pope," LaVey was one of the thousands of rather shadowy figures operating in America's metaphysical twilight world; an occult all-rounder with his powerful fingers in half a dozen esoteric pies. He dabbled in astrology and ESP, lectured on hypnosis and black magic, conducted a bit of psychical research.

"I went ghost hunting long before Hans Holzer thought of it," he told me. "But instead of taking along a medium— the way he does it—I went at it with electronic alarms and infrared cameras. Maybe that's the reason why I never came to believe in ghosts."

His Church evolved from his private clientele who came to hear him lecture. "One night I had something like a break-through into the gray area between religion and psychiatry," he remembered. "I found I could help people by bringing the devil into the open, so to speak. By proclaiming *his* creed as a legitimate, active faith."

LaVey's main concern is to keep out the "losers"—his pet expletive for the varieties of kooks inevitably drawn to a cult that allegedly conducts weekly orgies.

Candidates must fill in a lengthy questionnaire containing points like, "What do you expect to gain from Satanism?" and "If you are a woman, would you consider being an altar?" They also have to pass muster at a confrontation, which is frequently arranged by subterfuge. If accepted they pay a forty dollar registration fee, then an annual ten dollars, which is not expensive by cultist standards.

The Satanic congregation tends to be on the young side of thirty, and composed of very much the same types you would find in, say, scientology or Golden Circle meetings. Good-looking, rather tense, and slightly vague men and women who indicate that they know what everything is about, but can't quite express it. The High Priest—or another appropriate guru—does it for them.

Friday night is the big night for Satanists, the night of the High (not Black) Mass. It opens with a lengthy ceremony in the Ritual Chamber, conducted by LaVey in full regalia, complete with a silken horned cap. Organ music and chanting, which has Gregorian overtones, punctuated by the exclamations "Shemhamforash!" and "Hail Satan!" repeated by the entire congregation.

The naked altar girl lies fairly comfortably on a fur rug. After LaVey has emptied the chalice (contents optional) he places the vessel on her belly or pubic region, where it stays for the remainder of the ritual.

Then follows the business part of the evening, but it's a fair way removed from the orgiastic.

Members come forward to lay their requests before Satan. Often in the form of almost classical maledictions directed at unseen enemies: "Let his rotting dungheap brain writhe in unending agony as hordes of phantom rats gnaw at his diseased spirit for the rest of his life . . ." Others, in a gentler vein, ask for love, sensual pleasures, business triumphs.

LaVey touches them with his sword, rather as if dubbing them knights, while the congregation joins in a united "willing" of fulfillment, their voices rising in a thunderous "Hail Satan!" to drive their message home.

Occasionally there is an elaborate psychodrama, in which one member impersonates someone he or she detests. It can be a boss, a rival in love or—frequently—a father or mother. The actor hams up the role gleefully; ranting, lecturing or whining to bring out the ugliest, most ludicrous feature of the subject. LaVey plays judge, the congregation the jury, as they sit in trial over the hate object. If their verdict is "guilty" (depending on the virulence of the impersonation), they can bring down any of a score of horrific punishments on the (absent) offender.

At the end of the evening the participants are emotionally replete, warmed with a sense of accomplishment, and pleasantly relaxed. Their curses are cursed, their hatreds spilled, their enemies smitten hip and thigh. They are—temporarily—at peace. And their peace may quite possibly endure until the next High Mass, come Friday.

At the moment LaVey heads the only officially recognized Satanist movement in the United States; the only one, that is, entitled to baptize, marry and bury its members, and enjoying the tax-exempt status of a church.

But there are others, more feral and less efficiently organized, but growing and scattering their offshoots over the land.

There is the Brotherhood of the Ram in Los Angeles, whose members greet each other with "Ave Satan," worship beneath a crucified skeleton and claim private communion with demons. There are the Luciferians of New Orleans, consisting exclusively of former Roman Catholics who call their deity Pope Satan I, grant him infallibility in matters of faith and doctrine, and expound a complex theological creed based on the "True Holy Trinity" comprising God, Satan, and the Serpent—"who are three and yet are *one.*"

And there is the Asmodeus Society, whose followers make a point of never pronouncing Satan's "sacred name" but always refer to him by alternative titles such as the Persian Ahriman, the Greek Apollyon, the Arabic Shaitan or the Syrian Rimmon. The Society functions in at least four states, although each group operates in strict independence and none recognizes a formal head.

The particular unit I was privileged to observe meets in the best manicured portion of New York's Westchester County and seems to have sprung from the pages of a John Cheever story. Their meeting place was the luxury home of a dental surgeon, their High Priestess (for that night only) a twenty-one-year-old commercial artist named Judy, whose recent engagement had made the society columns of the New York *Times.*

The group gathered in the large indoor gym of their host. Parallel bars, vaulting horse and rowing machine had been pushed aside and replaced by an impromptu altar draped—for some unfathomable reason—in a tattered Brazilian flag.

There were eleven people present, three of them black. As far as I could tell, all participants were high on something, possibly hashish, more probably DMT, certainly not liquor. They were the only Satanists I have seen using drugs *during* an actual ceremony. It gave the entire procedure a curiously jerky, absent-minded air, some of the worshipers wandering around with their private visions, others laughing uncontrollably.

One of the Negro girls emerged naked and lay down on the flag of Brazil. She had an Afro hairdo and magnificent breasts and seemed to fall asleep immediately. Later I learned that she belonged to the cast of a current Broadway musical. The High Priestess began reading from a book—reciting the endless list of names by which Satan is known. She read monotonously and badly, stumbling over the more difficult words like Demogorgon and Tezcatlipoca. Each name was echoed by the congregation, at least by most of them. Several were totally engrossed in staring into the light of the arm-thick black candles grouped around the altar and didn't respond to anything.

Now a blast of shrill, throbbing Haitian music came from the tape recorder, an ancient voodoo chant repeating the same lines over and over.

L'Appé vini, le Grand Zombi,
L'Appé vini, pou fe gris-gris!

The chant went on and on until all heads were turned toward the door as if expecting the Grand Zombi to appear. An aura of nervous excitement seemed to be building up beneath the dope haze.

Then the door opened and a figure walked in, like a leftover from a bad dream. It was a naked man wearing a goat's head with horns. He was so hairy that his body almost matched the mask. He carried a white coffin in his arms, just large enough for a baby.

Without looking right or left the man slowly walked—or rather swayed in rhythm with the music—to the altar, his large belly swaying separately. He put the coffin down, removed the lid and took out a gleaming razor. Then he produced a live, white chicken, its legs and wings tied with twine. Still swaying he chanted something in a high, ridiculously cracked voice, the words drowned out by the voodoo rattles from the tape. He gripped the razor and, clumsily, cut the chicken's head off, the blood spurting all over the sleeping girl.

She sat up and said audibly, "Shee-it!" Nobody laughed.

This was the climax of the ceremony. From then on the proceedings disintegrated into a haphazard milling around by everybody. Several people crowded around the black altar girl, smearing the blood into her skin and over each other. After a while she appeared to get tired of this and walked out. The party broke up.

There are only faint traces of formalized Satanism discernible in the rituals of the Asmodeans. They represent a hotchpotch of devil worship, voodoo, and the antics performed by the late Aleister Crowley on his off nights. Some of them are undoubtedly innovations suggested by acid trips and incorporated as they went along.

But the basic theme remains unmistakable. It is a reaching out for some dark and potent power vaguely connected with blood, nakedness and violence; all the elements otherwise banished from suburban life.

Satanism plays only an infinitesimal role in America's occult upsurge. The puzzling feature is why—at this time and in our society—it should exist at all.

The sole clue we are offered lies in the fact that the beginnings of devil worship in America coincided with the surmise by certain theologians that God was dead.

XIII
THE SCIENTIFIC SCENE

OVER THE PAST four years an increasing number of academic institutions throughout the country have cautiously begun to add classes on psychic and occult subjects to their curricula.

At present, universities in New York, Connecticut and California offer courses on parapsychology, the University of Colorado has one on Altered States of Consciousness; Long Island's Hofstra features Dreams, Religion and ESP; the University of Minnesota teaches on Psi Phenomena; and Cedar Crest College, Pennsylvania, runs an Introduction to Psychical Research.

The above are merely a few of the courses now available, and the response to them has been tremendous. Some classes which were expected to draw under a hundred students enrolled four or five times that many. Others still have long waiting lists.

On the surface it seems as if America's occult explosion has thus been accompanied by a parallel surge of interest on part of the academic establishment. That impression, however, is misleading. For most of the lecture series involved are given by the extension divisions of the institutions, frequently at night classes, and rarely on a credit basis. Students are lucky if they receive half the credit normally given to a full-time course.

In August 1970 there was a blistering row at UC Berkeley, when Dean Willis Shotwell unceremoniously evicted a Mrs. Sakoian and her astrology class from the campus. The reason was a leaflet handed to students, implying that special course credit could be obtained for the lectures.

"I wanted to make it perfectly clear," declared the dean, "that the university is not sponsoring an astrology course for credit."

With a few notable exceptions, academicians don't share the occultist enthusiasm of their students. Most of them retain a profound aversion for any subject starting with the prefix "para." And the very term "occult science" strikes them as a semantic contradiction.

This is by no means entirely due to prejudice. "Para," according to the dictionary, means "beside" or "beyond." Set before an appropriate noun it can be utilized to transform every branch of knowledge into something so abstruse and indeterminate that any charlatan can set himself up as an expert in it. We have hundreds of spiritualist primitives passing as parapsychologists and equal numbers of blatant medical quacks posing as paraphysicists. That magic prefix saves them from the necessity of having to know anything concrete about the noun.

There is also a world of difference between "occult science" and science as applied to the occult. In order to function, science must necessarily exclude faith and demand proof. But occultism requires faith in a given premise before it can furnish proof. That premise may simply be faith in the veracity of a certain person. Once this is given, the sequence of proofs may follow in a logical fashion. But science, by its very nature, cannot provide this initial acceptance by faith and therefore must disregard the subsequent proofs.

It is on precisely this ground that science clashed with theology which, after all, also demands an initial act of faith. The two achieved their current state of academic coexistence primarily because of a tacit agreement not to prod into each other's territories, and secondly because both accepted certain scholastic disciplines within their own ranks.

Neither of these prerequisites apply to occultism. Unlike the established theologians, occultists keep poking into any and every sphere, including medicine, psychiatry, astronomy, physics, philosophy, archeology and even metallurgy. They won't—or can't—set up educational qualifications that would insure that their assorted "doctors" of divinity, metaphysics, cosmology, and what-have-you at least possess the scholarship to compose a grammatical sentence before being let loose on juvenile pupils.

Worst of all, they will not accept standardized methods of research and refuse to adhere to the progression of thesis—antithesis—synthesis that might render their conclusions to some degree verifiable. The antithesis portion is almost invariably missing. Their line of reasoning is apt to run: so-and-so testifies that he witnessed such-and-such. Ergo such-and-such has occurred. The possibility that so-and-so may be (a) suffering from delusions or (b) lying, is rarely if ever taken into consideration. It is, in fact, regarded as being in extremely poor taste.

This, of course, does not mean that the scientifically correct deductive process necessarily leads to correct conclusions. A scientist could, for instance, watch a man get drunk on scotch and soda the first night, on bourbon and soda the second night, and on rye and soda the third night, and then deduct—logically—that the factor causing his inebriation was soda.

But no matter how erroneous the result, if it was arrived at by an established thinking procedure it can be understood, repeated and rectified by another scientist. Which would not be the case if the first observer had used a deductive formula known only to himself and from it concluded that his subject's high was produced by—say—the influence of gamma rays from the planet Venus.

This is the perfectly reasonable basis of academia's distrust for unqualified outsiders. Unfortunately it doesn't end there. For the scientific fraternity shows even greater hostility toward those of its own members who tend to harbor "odd" views. Any scholar whose concepts seriously challenge the status quo is quite liable to have his research funds cut off, his appointments vetoed, his lectures canceled, and his professional career wrecked. He may even be socially ostracized by his conservative peers.

It is therefore hardly surprising that very few trained scientists have had the courage to embark on the "oddest" of all scholastic pursuits—psychical research. Compared to the thousands of occultist movements in America, the number of organizations conducting serious, disciplined studies of psychic phenomena is ridiculously small.

By this I don't mean the kind of "research" undertaken by bodies like the Astara Foundation or the Rosicrucians, which is little more than high-powered commercialized mysticism couched in pseudo-religious terms. What we are dealing with in this chapter are the handful of trained men and women who are applying controlled laboratory techniques to a field most of their colleagues shun like the plague. There are probably no more than about 150 of them in the entire country.

Their oldest—and for a long time only—vehicle is the American Society for Psychical Research (ASPR), founded in 1884 as the transatlantic branch of the British SPR. The Society's stated purpose is "to advance man's understanding of phenomena called parapsychological or psychic or paranormal." Its approach is both rational and neutral, trying neither to prove nor to debunk, but solely to explain.

The Society was born during the heyday of mediumism and most of its early investigations dealt with allegedly psychic personalities who produced spirit knocks and levitations. Since then, however, both its aims and its methods have become vastly more sophisticated. Rather than concentrating on individuals, the ASPR now deals with three basic manifestations which together make up what is generally called the supernatural. They are Paranormal Cognition (telepathy, clairvoyance, etc.), Paranormal Physical Phenomena (including poltergeists and psychokinesis), and Subconscious Processes (automatic writing, trance speech, etc.).

The entire image of the Society is reflected in its New York headquarters. An exceptionally handsome turn-of-the-century mansion near Central Park, it looks like an elegant and dignified club somewhere in London's West End. Inside, the mahogany paneling encloses the finest psychical research laboratory in the world, complete with soundproofed, electrically isolated experimental rooms, polygraphs, closed-circuit television, a small computer and first-class filing system.

The most striking apparatus resembles a telephone switchboard bristling with coils of multicolored wires. This is the recently invented ESPateacher, which doesn't teach ESP but tests it. The machine has a panel of five different colored lights flicking on and off in random order. The person being tested goes into another room with a console equipped with five buttons in the same colorings, attached to the robot by a cable. The testee presses the color button he guesses (or feels) is lit up on the machine. If the choice was correct, a chime sounds, thus providing an instant feedback of results. The machine automatically tabulates the number of hits and misses, indicating the testee's ESP quotient (see Figure 32).

Another, more complex, ESP experiment involves a closed-circuit TV setup. One member, the receiver, sits in a curtained booth before a table containing twenty-five white tiles. Another person, the sender, sits in a soundproofed chamber some distance away, watching a TV screen on which he can see the receiver's hand moving over the tiles. The sender concentrates mentally on one particular tile, trying to "push" his partner's hand to it by his thought waves. The order of the tiles has been chosen before the start of the experiment, and neutral observers keep score how often the Sender succeeds in "guiding" the Receiver's fingers to the selected square (see Figures 33 and 34).

The largest scale experiment recently undertaken was conducted by Dr. Karlis Osis, the Society's director of research. The idea was to discover whether "psi"—the mysterious factor underlying ESP—is dependent on physical variables, such as distance (see Figure 35).

Dr. Osis's experiment—in which participants had to try and sense the order in which one hundred picture postcards were laid down—ranged from very near (one-third mile) to very far (over ten thousand miles). Three participants were stationed in New York, Los Angeles, and Tasmania, Australia. The results indicated that "psi" does indeed decrease over long distances— but only by a mere 4.4 percent for every additional thousand miles of distance, as measured by ESP scores (see Figure 36).

The above are examples of the coolly mathematical attitude that guides the Society's research methods. It is an attitude that produces respect in academic circles and profound irritation among mysticists. As one lady spiritualist phrased it: "They're taking all the *magic* out of the field."

Which, of course, is precisely what the Society is trying to do. By applying laboratory yardsticks and electronic controls to their subject, people like Dr. Osis are slowly shifting parapsychology from the medium's parlor into the scientist's lab. Whether this process is bringing us closer to the core of the mystery is another story. For occasionally you get the feeling that the ASPR may be ignoring the woods for the trees.

In the April 1969 issue of the Society's excellently produced and compiled journal, was an account of a poltergeist manifestation in Newark, given by researcher William Roll. It may rank as perhaps the most minutely detailed such report ever printed —but certainly not as the most illuminating.

Mr. Roll painstakingly tabulated all the objects thrown, moved or dropped during the disturbances, listing the directions of their travels, their chemical composition, their distance from members of the household, the curvature of their flight, and frequency of their displacements. He furnished charts, tables and sketches graphically illustrating this information, and even analyzed the electrical properties of every moved item, from mirrors to a can of paint. But the entire effort somehow resembles a man watching a shooting and becoming so engrossed in the technical details of the gun that he forgets that a murder has been committed. The dark, unnerving riddle of the manifestation per se remains just as arcane as before.

Nevertheless, the principle of tackling the supranormal by means of statistical charts may be our only means of getting the entire phenomenon into some sort of focus, rendering it predictable and thereby manageable. The man who first adopted it today ranks as the Sigmund Freud of the parapsychological world.

He is Dr. (later Professor) Joseph Banks Rhine of Duke University, North Carolina. A plant physiologist by training, Rhine more than forty years ago developed the idea of using the test procedures of the trained naturalist to explore the supernatural. The terms he coined in the process have become standard dictionary words. One he applied to the entire field of telepathy, clairvoyance, precognition and related phenomena, which he called "extrasensory perception" or ESP. The other he used for the unknown, maddeningly unstable activating factor behind it —the "psi" (for psychic) trait.

Rhine also invented the ESP cards, marked with five different symbols, which are still being used as basic testing equipment throughout the world.

It was these cards that enabled Rhine to present the first statistical proof for the existence of ESP to the scientific community. His subject was a former divinity student named Hubert Pearce who worked with a psychology graduate, J. G. Pratt, under Rhine's supervision.

Pratt, in one building, shuffled and drew the cards at a certain pace while Pearce—sitting in a library one hundred yards away—recorded his guesses as to which symbol card Pratt had drawn. After 1,850 cards had been drawn, Rhine tallied the score. According to mathematical probability—that is if only chance were operative—Pearce should have guessed about one-fifth of the symbols correctly. Instead of the expected 370 right guesses, he scored 558 hits. The odds against *that* happening by sheer chance are astronomical.

It is difficult for a layman to appreciate the significance of this in scientific terms, but when Rhine published the results of his tests in 1934 he caused one of the greatest furors in academic history. There were professors who wouldn't—couldn't—bring themselves to believe in the validity of Rhine's findings, which shook the very basis of their rationalist philosophy. After R. A. Fisher, the country's leading specialist in probability calculus, found Rhine's statistics accurate, attacks were launched against his system of precautions. Additional safeguards were implemented, but still the test results continued high above chance levels.

When the smoke of battle had cleared, both sides were richer by a discovery. The rationalists had learned that ESP was not a parlor pastime, but a fact of life. Rhine had become aware of the unreliability of the "psi" factor—a ghostly will-o'-the-wisp that grows and shrinks, comes and vanishes in people gifted with ESP, following no known rules and capable of spoiling the most promising experiment.

He could never tighten his laboratory controls sufficiently to satisfy all his critics. And the sharp fluctuations of the "psi" trait—which seems to vary with the physical as well as mental state of the subject—gave his test results a very uneven quality over the years.

The Parapsychology Laboratory at Duke is now closed. Rhine and his wife have established a private institution with less specific aims: the Foundation for Research on the Nature of Man. But regardless of what emerges from the later venture, his old testing ground in Durham, North Carolina, will remain a pioneering monument akin to Freud's modest consulting office in Vienna's Berggasse.

Today other pioneers are probing deeper than Rhine dreamed of doing. Their target is the probable seat of the "psi" factor— man's subconscious. An entirely new world had to be created to describe the combination of hypnotic and mechanical techniques that form their tools of operation. The term is "psychenautics."

America's pioneer psychenauts are a husband-and-wife team, Robert E. L. Masters and Jean Houston, Ph.D., who together run the Foundation for Mind Research. Their laboratory lies on the top floor of the Manhattan apartment building in which they live, and it is difficult to decide which of the two premises is the more fascinating.

Their large apartment is sprinkled with museum pieces: a mummy case dating from 400 B.C., a statue of Egypt's lion-headed goddess Sekhmet, three thousand years old and with "living" eyes, a drinking cup that once belonged to King James of England, a painting of the Indian Peyote God from South America, a bowl from ancient Troy. . . .

A notice on the door warns you to "Beware of the Cat," and refers to their Siamese called Psyche.

"We had to put it up," said Jean Houston apologetically. "She bites. An Indian swami was here the other day, and Psyche bit him right in the middle of a dissertation on spiritual tranquillity."

A tall long-legged brunette with an enchanting stage voice, Jean is a great-great-great-granddaughter of Sam Houston, born in Brooklyn "by mistake." After starting her career as an award-winning actress and director, she decided that she hated actors and took a Ph.D. instead. Today she holds a professorship in psychology at Marymount College on top of her work at the Foundation.

Her partnership with her husband sprang partly from their shared research background with psychedelic drugs; Jean worked with LSD, Bob Masters with LSD and peyote. Although their present project doesn't involve narcotics, they owe some of their most valuable insights to their years of experiments with (clinically controlled) hallucinogenics.

Missouri-born Bob Masters, who bears a slight resemblance to Dylan Thomas, is an erstwhile poet and sexologist who authored fourteen books and achieved literary fame with two of them: *Eros and Evil* and *The Cradle of Erotica*.

Together they form a unique team; two trained scientists with an artistic past, a rare mixture of academic discipline and imaginative creativity. Both are also highly skilled hypnotists, and in some ways hypnotic trance has replaced the consciousness-expanding qualities of the drugs they formerly used.

Their target area is the gray borderline between the mental and the physical world, the shadow region where inner experiences overlap with actual events, and which may be the birthland for *all* of man's religious, mystical and occult cognition.

One of their most significant experiments dealt with trance-induced time distortion, a method by which a subject is hypnotized and told that a few minutes of actual time (clock time) will become the equivalent of hours or even days.

"We had an art student with a year's training, whose work was not very good," Jean Houston related. "I put her in a deep trance and told her that I would give her five minutes of clock time, and that would be the equivalent of eight or nine hours of working with Mr. L, her favorite arts teacher. It will be intensive work and you will be permanently imprinted with whatever you learn during that period.

"Five minutes later I brought her back to consciousness, and the first thing she said was, 'My goodness, it's still light.' She was firmly convinced that about eight and a half hours had passed. And she had spent those hours learning shading and composition under Mr. L. I then asked her to draw me a tree. And here," she added, "are two of her sketches, both of trees. One drawn before and one after her trance lesson."

Even to my layman's eyes the difference between the two pictures was unmistakable.

"We repeated this trance process in five sessions," Jean went on. "I instructed her to concentrate on heads the next time, on landscapes after that, and so on. Then, at the fifth session, I gave her thirty minutes of clock time—this was equivalent to her entire next term in arts class, three and a half months. After I woke her she did an enormously elaborate 'Tree of Life' painting that took her five days of solid work to complete. And—well, here it is."

She showed me the picture. This was no longer a student's work but a graduate's. And the difference lay in a total of fifty-five minutes of hypnotic suggestion.

"I never put the girl in a trance again because I wanted to see whether she would regress," said Jean. "She hasn't. The skills she has acquired have stayed with her for—well, it's over a year now."

This is merely one instance of the potentials of our subconscious. Bob Masters told me another:

"This subject was a songwriter. Again using time distortion I put her in a trance that I told her would last one minute. During that time I suggested that she would go to a cabaret, where a singer would sing several songs. She would linger there for as long as she liked, have a drink perhaps, and commit those songs to her memory so that she could sing them back to us.

"After a minute I brought her out. Then she sang to us one complete song and two others that were fragments. One of them she liked enough to publish later on. And she'd heard them in a 'cabaret' that existed only in her own mind."

These examples are startling but, on their own terms, entirely logical. In both cases the subject was already involved in the experiences suggested. Hypnotic trance had merely telescoped and concentrated their essence and apparently focused concentration in a manner unattainable in a waking state.

The same logic seems to apply to the experiences of those people who went back beyond the memory of their own lives under trance, describing sights and sounds of events that must have taken place thousands of years ago. To the mysticists this is "soul travel"—the remembrance of former incarnations. To Jean Houston it has a strictly rational explanation:

"Most of this material is based on self-acquired information," she said. "By that I mean films they had seen or books and magazines they'd read."

We went upstairs to the laboratory—an enthralling and faintly terrifying hybrid between a playground and a torture chamber. Contributing to the playground impression is the "Witch's Cradle" (correctly an "Altered States of Consciousness Induction Device" or ASCID) which resembles an iron children's swing. The subject is strapped into the thing in an upright position, blindfolded, with arms fastened to the sides. Slight muscular movements cause the cradle to swing gently, producing a state of semitrance, a totally removed aloneness with his or her thoughts. The experience is disorienting, but oddly pleasant, almost euphoric. Physical sensations are removed, and you become completely wrapped in mental processes usually obscured by outside stimuli (see Figure 37).

Bob Masters demonstrated the "Electric Circus" (actually an Audio-Visual Environment). You sit behind a semicircular screen on which a projector flashes a computer-programmed series of polarized slides, which move and shift fantastically before your eyes. Simultaneously two stereo speakers produce appropriately matched music and sound effects, blending the show into a single unit. The impact is overwhelming, and it can vary from the erotic or mystical to the starkly horrifying, depending on the selection of pictures and sounds (see Figure 38).

"Our experiments show that when the subject reaches a certain point of sensory overload, the brain reacts by throwing on the screen of the subject's mind its own counterimages," Masters explained.

"And what would be the significance of that?" I asked.

"The significance?" His voice became one degree slower and more cautious. "If such a sensory overload should build up naturally—in the outside world—and the brain reacts in that fashion, the person concerned may think he's in contact with some divine entity. This may explain how certain mystical hallucinations come about. How, for instance, the Book of Mormon was dictated—or any number of similar experiences."

The laboratory has other devices to elicit visual imagery. A machine that sends (painless) electrical impulses into the brain via electrodes. Industrial stroboscopic lights which can penetrate closed eyelids. A cork-lined "Sensory Deprivation Chamber" that totally blocks out sound and light, producing something close to a conscious and fairly comfortable state of death.

The main purpose of these machines—and the techniques the psychenauts have developed with them—is to shift, to deepen, our states of consciousness. Masters and Houston maintain that they are not so much inducing experiences, as making it possible for them to occur. By forcing the mind inward, so to speak, it can explore and utilize portions of our psyche most of us never use or even know exist within us (see Figures 39 and 40).

Some of the results they achieve are practical. They have helped a writer overcome his "creativity blocks," eliminated fear from the nightmares of a small girl (by having her contact and befriend the phantoms recurring in them), and enabled a former Jesuit priest to accomplish the spiritual exercises which had proved beyond him during his prescribed retreats.

These, however, are only subsidiary achievements. The scope of their work extends much further. One of their aims is to attain some measure of control over the enigmatic state of mind known variously as "samadhi," "satori," or cosmic consciousness—the retort in which, presumably, man's mystic experiences are distilled.

They have also delved into straight parapsychology, mostly in the area best suited to laboratory investigation: telepathy. In one series of experiments the Foundation for Mind Research cooperated with another remarkable pioneering enterprise; the Sleep and Dream Laboratory of the Maimonides Hospital of Brooklyn. The joint venture produced a unique linking of technical resources that—hopefully—may indicate the shape of things to come in the parapsychological world.

The purpose of these all-night experiments was to discover whether the impressions of the Foundation's Electric Circus could be transmitted to a sleeper at the Brooklyn Dream Lab, fourteen miles away.

In Brooklyn a subject, or receiver, was put to bed wired with electrodes from an electroencephalograph (EEG). At the Foundation an agent, or sender, was placed behind the screen of the

Audio-Visual Environment. When the subject began to dream
(a state indicated by rapid eye movements) Masters and Houston received a telephone call and began their slide projection. At
the end of the program they rang the hospital and the sleeper
was awakened.

The sleeper then recounted his or her dream images. It was
left to a panel of independent judges to decide whether those
dreams had any connection with the slide projections. The judges
were not told which one of six selected slide programs had
actually been screened. They had to choose one on the basis of
the subject's dream account alone.

In eight successive experiments the judges picked the correct
series, entirely by the sleeper's description of his dreams. One
related that he had seen "a rather beautiful face. Squarish, with
slanted eyes. Eastern, I would think. Clean-shaven . . ."

The program screened during his dream had been a sequence
of Buddha paintings and figures from various Eastern countries.

The pilot experiments were—scientifically speaking—incon-
clusive. But they represented a controlled step in the exploration
of one of man's most familiar yet least known mental states—
dreams. The entire study of sleep is only in its beginning stages, its
connection with dreaming barely scratched. It seems almost ridic-
ulous that after a couple of centuries of scientific research we only
quite recently discovered that there are several variations of sleep,
including one that enables you to register what's going on around
you while remaining, technically, asleep. Hardly anything has
been done to gauge the fantastic time warp that occurs in some
dreams. How, for instance, a drop of water splashed on a sleeper's
face for a second before awakening can induce an impression of
hours of walking in the rain.

Prophetic dreams, of course, have haunted us since prebibli-
cal times, but the modern world relegated them into the realm of
Gypsy Mary's Dream Book or its equivalents. Even Freud, who
discovered their symbolic connotations, remained uninterested in
their precognitive possibilities.

But in 1970 a Soviet psychiatrist, Dr. Vasily Kasatkin, came
out with a startling report based on a twenty-eight-year study involving eight thousand dreams.

Kasatkin concluded that a person's dreams can warn him

about the approach of a serious illness, sometimes several months before it strikes. Someone due for an attack of gastritis, for instance, may dream about unappetizing food and experience sensations of vomiting. If he dreams of being breathless after running, he may be about to come down with TB or pleurisy.

According to the Russian, this has nothing to do with prophecy in the clairvoyant sense. Kasatkin held that the human brain is so sensitive that it notes the most imperceptible symptoms in the body before its owner becomes consciously aware of them. The brain signals a dream warning—it is up to us to recognize the message.

If the brain can presage illness via dream images, what else may be happening during those inert sleep periods? Some of the answers—or rather the preludes to the answers—are emerging from the experiments conducted by the William C. Menninger Dream Laboratory. The Lab was founded in 1962, as part of the Maimonides Medical Center in Brooklyn, New York. Its purpose is to study dreams in general and their parapsychological implications in particular.

Founder of the Dream Lab is Dr. Montague Ullman, a professor of psychiatry at the State University of New York. Dr. Stanley Krippner, a psychologist, acts as director. And a fascinatingly variegated group of volunteers—from housewives to professional mediums—act as guinea pigs.

The work of the Laboratory was given its present impetus by the discovery during the mid-1950s that dreaming is invariably accompanied by rapid eye movements back and forth, rather as if the sleeper were watching a film or reading the dream from the pages of a book.

These movements—known as REM—can be detected by the aforementioned EEG or electroencephalograph. The EEG was originally developed to pick up brain waves, which it does via tiny electrodes glued to the scalp, amplifying the impulses up to a million times and recording them on a graph. (In this fashion the machine can actually measure a patient's headache.) It also indicates to the observer exactly when a subject starts and stops dreaming.

Once these control conditions were established—which meant that a sleeper could be awakened before a particular dream had faded from memory or been overshadowed by others—the scene was set for a statistical study of the hypothesis that telepathic dreams can be produced experimentally.

These experiments began in 1964, and are still proceeding. The setup has a macabre 1984 flavor—but only in appearance. None of the participants suffer any discomfort.

The subjects—one or several—are bedded down in a sound-deadened "sleep room," wired for dreaming with electrodes glued to their skin. In another room sits the agent or sender, and a third room contains the EEG apparatus and an experimenter who monitors the brain-wave pattern of the sleeper (see Figure 41).

When the REM indicate that the subject has begun to dream, the experimenter buzzes the agent, who then concentrates on a target, usually a postcard-sized art print. The moment the dream stops, the experimenter wakes the subject via intercom and asks him or her to relate the dream, which is tape-recorded. Only the agent knows which of twelve possible target pictures he had concentrated on. First the subject and later three judges have to decide on a target, their choice governed entirely by the content of the dream.

In a total of 134 sessions the overall results were 97 hits and 37 misses, but very unevenly distributed. After some sessions the judges correctly matched seven out of ten dreams and targets, in others only one or none. Dr. Krippner found that the scores followed a discernible pattern, dependent on the agent-subject combination. The most successful duo were always two men, second best a female agent with a male subject, worst scorers were two females.

Although statistically not conclusive—so far—some of the results were so striking as to virtually rule out coincidence. On one occasion a subject reported dreaming that he went to a prize fight at Madison Square Garden. The agent had been focusing on a picture showing the famous Dempsey-Firpo battle. Another subject had dreamed of his black-haired, deeply tanned girlfriend and remembered admiring her exotic features. The agent's target had been the painting of a nude Tahitian girl by Gauguin.

Whatever else the Dream Lab may discover, it has already proved one thing: the effect—we don't know to what extent—of one person's waking mental processes on another's dreams. This is perhaps the most vital clue yet unearthed about the validity of paranormal cognition—the factor behind those countless reports of wives dreaming about their husbands' car accidents at the very moment they occur miles away. Those and thousands of similar accounts undoubtedly involve the same mysterious dynamics created artificially in the Brooklyn establishment.

The Backster School of Lie Detection in midtown Manhattan is not exactly a laboratory, but it was the cradle of an experiment that opened the door to a means of communication between man and nature not heard of outside the realms of mysticism.

I first met Cleve Backster in 1968, when we both appeared on the same Art Linkletter TV show. He was there to demonstrate a discovery so fabulous that it made my own purpose—publicizing my latest book—seem somewhat puny.

Backster, a tall hawk-featured man with prominent cheekbones and penetrating eyes, is one of America's top polygraph specialists. He was, in fact, trained by the late Leonarde Keeler, the inventor of the lie detector that bears his name. He worked as an interrogator for the CIA, was appointed director of the Keeler Polygraph Institute in Chicago, and later established his own lie detector school in New York.

The polygraph is a machine that tests a subject's emotional reactions, not necessarily connected with lying. It uses electrodes which measure—among other things—galvanic skin responses and transfers them to a graph record. If an emotional reaction occurs, the graph goes up—the degree of the upstroke governed by the volume of emotion registered. This emotional response to questioning is strongest when the subject feels threatened by an inquiry—which is usually when he is lying.

Backster is a ceaseless experimenter, who has at one time or another attached his electrodes to every living thing within reach. Early in 1966 this happened to be a potted plant in his office. He was curious to discover whether the plant would give out a noticeable graph reaction after having two galvanic skin-response electrodes fastened to its leaves. In order to provide a stimulus he thought of burning its stem.

But before he could take out his matches, the pen on the graph record jerked upward!

It took Backster a while to grasp—or rather to believe—what he had witnessed. The plant had responded to a *thought* in his mind. As he later reported the event: "I had not moved, or touched the plant, so the timing of the pen activity suggested that it might have been triggered by the mere thought of the harm I intended to inflict upon the plant."

The implications of this were almost beyond belief—including Backster's belief. He spent the next two years devising more and more intricate and conclusive experiments to prove—mainly to himself—that his eyesight hadn't been playing tricks. That there was such a thing as floral ESP.

He found that a vast variety of pot plants he tested showed precisely the same fear response to his thoughts of damaging them . . . the same unmistakable upstroke of the graph pen. But beyond that, he discovered that plants react to the destruction of other living things, vegetable or animal.

In order to demonstrate this, Backster developed the so-called "brine shrimp test," which became a classic of its kind. In his office he set up a mechanical contraption which—at various intervals—dumped tiny live brine shrimp into a bowl of boiling water, causing their instant deaths. In a far part of the office he had three different plants wired with electrodes. Invariably at the precise moment the shrimps died, the graph patterns of the plants leaped upward.

For his television appearance, Backster kept his demonstration confined to the ESP portion of his discovery. He first showed the normal plant rhythms on the chart, then the dramatic change that occurred when he contemplated its destruction.

And not only he. Four people, picked at random, approached the plants one by one. Three of them could think anything they wanted, a fourth was asked to harbor "dangerous thoughts" as he went near the philodendron. Again the needle registered alarm.

After the show I asked Backster whether his discovery had affected his outlook on life. He nodded. "In a way it has," he said quietly. "I've become very considerate of my house plants. You might say I've established a rapport with them. And they with me."

A video show is not an ideal platform for a demonstration of this kind. The miracle tube has a knack of reducing everything to entertainment size. Backster's act aroused about the same volume of comment as might have been engendered by an unusual juggling feat.

Fortunately he released several reports that year which became the subject of articles in the *International Journal of Parapsychology*. They attracted widespread academic attention, and as a result several American and one British university went through similar series of experiments. The mills of science grind slowly, and the final data have not yet been compiled.

But meanwhile Backster is forging ahead on his own track, applying tests on fresh fruit and vegetables, various yeasts, amoebae, and even mold cultures. He came to the conclusion that every living cell is gifted with "primary perception"—meaning some form of consciousness capable of reacting, marking them as beings rather than mere shapes of existence.

Together with a group of associates he has established the Backster Research Foundation, which is now probing into what has turned out to be an entirely new—and as yet unnamed—branch of parapsychology. Even that general term may be a misnomer. It is by no means certain that the responses Backster discovered have nonphysical causes. Rather than plant ESP, they may be activated by, say, an electromagnetic field which has so far escaped human perception. The same set of vibrations may also account for the puzzling affinity certain people have with plant life of every description—the proverbial green thumb.

By and large, suspicion against the "parapeople" still permeates our academic scene. But on the second to last day of 1969, one of the barriers came down with a crash that echoed around the nation's campuses. On that day the Parapsychological Association was solemnly admitted as an affiliate of the American Association for the Advancement of Science.

The PA is the professional organization of university personnel engaged in the psychic field. It had been hammering at the gate of the august AAAS for six years, getting little but snubs for its efforts. During 1969, however, world-famous anthropologist Dr. Margaret Mead reminded her fellow scientists of what their predecessors had once said of Galileo (or herself, for that matter). Her remarks were merely an echo of the chorus of public opinion whose clamor is just beginning to penetrate the strongholds of orthodox science.

The PA was allowed entry—at last. And, as Professor Douglas Dean summarized: "This event represents a significant milestone in the progress of parapsychology toward recognition as an established branch of science."

XIV

THE OCCULT GOLDMINE

THE YEAR 1967 was a historic milestone for the United States toy industry. In that year Americans ditched their longest-standing favorite among board games, Monopoly, and elevated Ouija boards to its place.

Since then approximately ten million of these boards have been sold, making them a $50,000,000 business and assuring that a basic minimum of 20 million Americans have played with them.

I picked out a fairly random lot of thirty dedicated Ouija players and asked them if they could tell me where the game originated and what the name meant. Most of them, as it turned out, believed that it was a Far Eastern device, its origins lost in antiquity, its title meaning something or other in either Chinese, Hindi or Korean. One lone individualist held out for Hebrew, another had it on the authority of her card-reading girlfriend that Ouija meant "spirit" in either Sanskrit or Persian.

The fact is that the Ouija board was invented and patented

in 1892 by one William Fuld of Baltimore, Maryland. At first he and his brother called the contraption Mystifying Oracle, but found the label too long and hit on the combination of the French and German word for "yes" as an alternative.

Until 1966 the boards were made exclusively by the Fuld family's Southern Toy Company. Then Parker Brothers—who also manufacture Monopoly—bought the rights. To their astonishment the new acquisition outsold their No. 1 hit from the word go!

There was, of course, a certain amount of sales push behind it. Ads—"Give One to a Friend"—in magazines, and a crescendo ditty, "Hey, Ouija, we needja . . ." blasted over various rock-oriented radio stations. There was also the war in Vietnam, confirming the pattern noted during both World Wars and Korea that Ouija boards always sell well in wartime.

But their current dizzying surge is the result of a totally unexpected market combination. The usual wives, mothers and sweethearts of servicemen were joined by millions of teenagers, right down to the thirteen-year-old level, who had never previously shown much interest in these gadgets. And while the involvement of servicemen's relatives had obvious reasons, the sudden enthusiasm of the teeners remains a mystery—even to Parker Brothers.

A Ouija board is a wooden square on which the alphabet, numbers, and words like "yes" and "no" are printed. On top of it rests a small pointer which can move across the surface. Two people sit close together, legs touching, the board resting on their knees. They place their fingers lightly on the pointer and wait. Within a few minutes the pointer begins to slide over the board, indicating letters, numbers, words. The idea is to ask questions—preferably simple ones—and let the board answer.

What makes the pointer move? The manufacturers are intriguingly coy about that, merely hinting that mysterious forces *might* be at work, but leaving no doubt that they are selling the board as just another parlor game. Mysticists are convinced that spirits or psychic powers speak through the board. Most of the players evince a kind of giggling half-belief . . . you never know, there *may* be something to it (see Figure 42).

There is, indeed, something to it; a genuine phenomenon

psychologists call "automatism." In its most familiar form this is demonstrated by women knitting while watching television or a pianist idly playing while chatting to a friend. On the Ouija board it manifests itself through "ideomotor movements"—meaning physiological responses in the fingertips under conditions of expectant attention.

These movements are involuntary, dictated by our subconscious, and the results—when transformed into spelled words—can therefore come as surprises to the players. Particularly to those blissfully unaware of what their subconscious mind may harbor.

Some of the thousands of letters board-owners sent to Parker Brothers are pretty indicative of this. One woman wrote that her particular Ouija gave very good answers early in the day, but very dirty ones at night. Was there something wrong with it? Another young lady complained: "The Ouija board told me some very bad news, and I don't believe it, because I'm not that kind of girl (if you know what I mean). I would never do anything like that in my life. Will you please tell me the truth about the Ouija board, as I am quite worried."

Unfortunately nobody as yet knows the "truth" about the board, since the entire spectrum of automatism remains largely unexplored. And consulting Mr. Fuld's brainchild on matters like "Will I marry Joe?" or "Who'll win the World Series?" is at least as efficacious as gazing into tea leaves. The story is told that the Fuld brothers once asked their invention how they could improve their sales figures. The gadget answered: "Make more Ouija boards." No business counselor could have done better.

But Ouija boards are merely a ripple in the flood of psychic paraphernalia now inundating the country. For America's occult revolution has been accompanied by a gargantuan boom of what might be called "consumer mysticism." So much so that cynical observers have accused business interests of creating the entire metaphysical renaissance in the first place.

Similar feats have been accomplished before. England's Victorian shopkeepers—aided by Charles Dickens and Prince Albert—virtually invented our modern version of Christmas. But America's magical metamorphosis began quite genuinely from below. Commercialism merely kept a sharp ear on the underground, jumped in with both feet, and has been keeping the movement under a full head of steam ever since.

Department stores throughout the nation periodically go occult for entire weeks at a time. Abraham & Straus of New York hired "travel astrologer" Rita St. John to map out zodiacal holiday trips for patrons on the eighth floor, while an occult team of one palmist, one numerologist and three specialists in Tarot, I Ching and Ouija gave gratis demonstrations in the basement.

The $3-billion United States toy industry is marketing astrological, palm-reading and witchcraft games, plus ghost costumes, monster puppets, mechanical UFOs, plastic apparitions and skulls, walking zombis, magic wands, and a Barnaby Collins game, based on the vampire character who haunts the TV soap opera "Dark Shadows" (see Figures 43 and 44).

In June 1970 Brentano's bookstores launched a permanent Boutique of the Occult in their largest New York shop. The department is devoted exclusively to mystic merchandise, ranging from books, cards and posters to zodiacal stationery, acrylic desk accessories, contemplation lights and birthstones.

In the same month a young, cool and exceedingly with-it lady named Gail Kuhn inaugurated a unique enterprise, The Witches' Cauldron. Located in the plush portion of Manhattan's East Thirties, this is basically a wholesale supplier of metaphysical products, except that some of the products come live. For Miss Kuhn has contracted a large assortment of attractive witches (male and female), mini-witches (meaning junior apprentices), palmists, card readers, psychics and astrologers. These can be rented for endorsements, "product identification" or as consulting experts in the occult field.

Gail herself claims no esoteric wisdom, in fact she admits to a certain amount of skepticism. But her business partner is a full-fledged witch called Valerie; a very pretty and rather fey blonde who belongs to a New Jersey coven and once worked as an interior designer (see Figure 45).

The debut of the Cauldron made PR history, even in blasé New York. Drinks were served by white-robed mini-witches under Valerie's supervision. At intervals selected batches of guests were taken to a separate room where—screened behind transparent gauze—a girl and boy witch went through an abbreviated "initiation ceremony." Both were strikingly good looking and stark naked.

"What we want to do," said Gail, "is to help educate the people who are really interested in obtaining more knowledge about the craft. We don't," she added firmly, "intend to become another botanica with hokey items."

Printed on her brochures is the caution: ". . . while we make no supernatural claims about our products—one never really knows regarding matters of the Occult."

Most of the wholesale catalogs display similar safeguards, labeling the listed goods as "curios only." But this is not the spirit in which they are sold. It would be hard to imagine a more grimly earnest breed of customers than those who patronize the hundreds of occult stores that have mushroomed across the country.

These shops fall into two distinct categories. One are the botanicas which sell items related to Espiritsmo, a magical faith rooted in African beliefs and Caribbean voodooism. The majority of botanicas are run on strict traditional lines, their clients are overwhelmingly West Indian, Latino, black and underprivileged. The others bear an endless variety of titles, have no tradition to speak of and a clientele that is mainly white, middle class and under thirty. Whereas the botanicas tend to be solemn places; their white counterparts have a decidedly free-swinging air.

Above Hollywood's Sunset Boulevard stands a little pink house with a sign saying "Timeless Occult Shop." This is the realm of Rev. Benjamin Anthony Harris, twenty-nine, who wears a headband to keep his mane out of his black glasses, hails from Chicago, and claims to have studied psychology, depth analysis, narco-pharmacology and Yoga (see Figure 46).

"Yeah, man, I opened this place in 1968, because the vibes were right then," said the Rev. "Yeah, business is great. Lotsa tourists and some of the local cats buy stuff here. You writing a book, huh? Yeah, the vibes are good for that. What's your sign?"

His shop is small and not exactly overstocked, but some of the merchandise could run into real money. Decks of hand-painted Tarot cards for $200 (though he has others for $3), crystal balls starting at $25 going up to $100.

He also has a line of mod clothes, body scents, occult books and incense, plus varieties of offbeat oils in tiny bottles. Master Oil for magic rituals and Concentration Oil for successful meditation, both at $1.25.

"That one?" Harris looked up from the astrological calculations he does between customers. "That's essence of Bendover, for voodoo rituals. Gives you power, man. Like it's for voodoo. Were you born in 1938, by any chance?"

I told him that I was born a fair distance earlier.

"Yeah? Oh, well, that's too bad," said the Rev. and went back to his calculations.

Mrs. Yvonne Purtell, who runs the Solunar Gift Shop in San Francisco, was not concerned over my birth year. "Most of my customers here are professional people," she said with quiet pride. "Doctors and stockbrokers who use astrology in their daily lives. One doctor does sun charts on every baby he delivers."

Her shop, devoted mainly to astrology and Tarot, is booming. A tiny back room doubles as consulting office for several mediums and psychics. Usually there are people waiting for readings.

"When I first opened up about four years ago, I had to plead with the wholesalers to make up some of the more unusual items," she remembered. "Now I can order anything I want. It's wonderful the way the world is coming around to the New Thought—to change things, to try to live right . . ." She moved off to attend to a trio of unisexers who wanted astrological perfumes, "Two Libras and one Moon Child, and have you any Capricorn . . . ?"

There is little demand for astrology at The House of Candles and Talismans in New York's Lower East Side.

The customers are black, Puerto Rican and South American, with here and there a self-conscious hippie. Ann Caston, the resident expert behind the counter, has Jamaican-Haitian ancestry. "Where did I learn about these things?" Ann smiled like a searchlight. "I just picked it up, I guess. This is like ham and eggs to us."

The shop is large, spotless, impeccably neat, and smells like a cross between a church and an opium den. The merchandise stands in parade-ground rows; voodoo and macumba segregated from crucifixes, Holy Bibles and multicolored prints depicting saints. Blue incense spirals permanently to the ceiling.

The candles come in four basic shades: white for inspiration, green for new beginnings, orange for sex, black for evil. Before they leave the shop, Ann "dresses" them—cuts them with pentagram designs and sprinkles them with silver powder to increase their potency. Then there are candles in the shapes of naked men and women, black or white. To draw people together you place them belly to belly, light them up and let them melt into each other. Still other candles are shaped like skulls, with a wick on top. These symbolize enemies. Light the wick and watch your enemy's skull melt slowly before your eyes. You can scratch his or her name on the forehead first (see Figure 47).

The shop also sells other means of dealing with enemies. There are baskets full of little clothed dolls, male or female at seventy-five cents each. "Stomp on them, burn 'em, push pins through them," Ann explained. "They can be just anyone you don't like." As a defense measure you can buy small brown roots for a quarter. Cut into pieces and chewed they keep you safe in fights. They taste terrible.

In the back stand shelves with aerosol sprays. All cost $1.25, but they have different purposes. Some remove jinxes, others attract money, still others squirt house blessings or call the Seven Saints to the assistance of the sprayer. The can doesn't say the names of the saints, but a free prayer comes with the package. Next to them stand the oils. Master Gambling Oil for anointing the armpits to win games of chance. Commanding Oil to make others obey you. High-John the Conqueror oils and bathwater that bring good luck into your home. You can also wash floors with it.

A man comes to the counter with an armload of candles, sprays and oils. As an afterthought he also picks a jar of Fast Luck Powder. He pays nine dollars for the lot. He wears no overcoat in February and his face is almost blue with cold. Ann looks after him as he walks out into the freezing drizzle. She gives a very faint shrug. "Well . . . it's cheaper than psychiatry."

The truly awesome miracles, however, are not sold over the counter. They come by mail order. The occult mail-order business is supposed to be the boomingest of all, but you can't get figures on it. And you can rarely meet the people who handle it. Most of them seem to live in P.O. boxes and speak only through their ads. But they speak mightily.

A Mr. (Mrs.? Miss?) Reese P. Dubin will send you a Mental Earphone with which to hear the thoughts of others, a Hypno-Phone to broadcast "silent commands," a Tele-Photo Transmitter to "teleport the object of your desire to you, from an invisible world," providing you send him (her?) an order for any of those marvels, costing $7.20.

For $9.95 you can get authentic Aura Goggles from a company in Evanston, Illinois. They come in adjustable leather frames and supposedly enable you to behold what has hitherto been visible only to selected psychics—the human aura. This is a colored emanation surrounding our bodies, said to be caused by physical and mental magnetic forces. The goggles make you see— well, something. Whether it is an aura depends on your attitude as much as your eyesight.

Even more exciting is the offer announced by one Michael Korns of Pittsburg, Kansas. Nothing less than invisibility. "You can learn to make yourself invisible at will," writes Mr. Korns. "This is not a trick or novelty. It is done entirely by the hypnotic effects of the mind . . . I am breaking an ancient code by offering it. This secret is priceless!" However, he's willing to let you in on it for a mere fifteen dollars ppd.

Then there is money, and it's virtually being hurled at you. In a single issue of a recent occultist periodical I found four mail-order ads promising to render me middling rich. The College of Mental Science (another P.O. box) proclaims "$1,000 Through the Subconscious." But I preferred the statement, "Ten Dollars Can Bring You Unlimited Money Supply" issued by the Scientific Prayer Ministry of La Jolla, California.

The headline was plain enough, but the rest took a bit of figuring. It was, apparently, a course of instructions enabling me to achieve "Prosperity Consciousness." I had to take it in order to fix in my mind an awareness of my Unlimited Money Supply . . . "so that you may bring prosperity into your life through Subconsciousness attraction of increased money in your experience." Whatever that was supposed to mean, it required the dispatch of ten dollars "Seed Money"(?) to the above Ministry.

Considerably more straightforward are the offers of divinity status. One issued by the Church of Universal Brotherhood runs:

Be Doctor & Reverend—World's Most Useful Titles. Career enrichment, best treatment from the establishment. Counsel, Collect Fees, Donations. Start your own church. Marry, military tranquility. Print name desired on honorary Doctor of Divinity Degree. Ordination Certificate and I.D. Card. All for $10.00.

Another outfit, the Universal Free Life Church, will ordain you as one of its clergymen (sight unseen) for a bargain one dollar. A Doctor of Divinity tag, accompanied by "Missionary" status, is twenty dollars. The N.Y. Attorney General has declared that the degrees and certificates issued by this church are worthless. But, with all due respect, the Attorney General was wrong. Hardly anyone ever checks on the validity of a given D.D. Even the three states which insist on licensing marriage counselors—California, Michigan and New Jersey—automatically exempt "ministers offering counsel in conjunction with their work" from licensing requirements. *All* ministers.

The publishing industry approached the occult in a gingerly fashion. For years the reputable hardcover houses refused to admit to publishing occult material at all. They called it "Religion and Philosophy" instead. By now most of them have dropped the disguise and accepted their role as one of the chief beneficiaries of the esoteric tidal wave. Over the past three years occult book sales (a rose by any other name) have more than doubled generally and tripled in the paperback field.

Doubleday, America's hardcover giant, entered the fray in 1956, and scored a bull's-eye with the first shot. It was *The Search for Bridey Murphy*, written by a Pueblo businessman-hypnotist named Morey Bernstein, which topped the national best-seller list for weeks and sold over 157,000 copies. Almost in the same league was *The Sleeping Prophet* (on Edgar Cayce), with sales above 123,000.

Nevertheless, Doubleday has retained a certain amount of caution concerning the genre and makes a point of steering clear of the "wayouts." These are usually left to the paperback houses, though the distinguishing line may be open to argument. What, after all, is "way-out" when it comes to mysticism?

In the paperback field Dell Publishing had a head start. They produce thirty horoscope magazines annually, and sold 8 million of them in 1968. Remarkably enough their biggest winner in book form was also an Edgar Cayce volume. *There Is a River*, which went into thirteen printings, totaling 1,050,000 copies.

The big-timer in occult paperback production is a comparative latecomer, Ace Publishing. Although they only took the plunge in 1962 (with a soft-cover reprint of Charles Fort's *Book Of The Damned*) they now have approximately 6,850,000 books of this kind in print and are turning them out at a rate of two per month.

Their star seller so far was *Strange Worlds* by the late Frank Edwards, of which some 220,000 went into print. The book is a good illustration of what wows the occult paperback market. Edwards, who ran his own radio program, collected hundreds of "unexplained and unexplainable" experiences and stuck them into half a dozen or so books. He never bothered with either analysis or investigation, but simply put the incidents down as they were told to him by "credible witnesses."

Book clubs have always provided an infallible gauge of American reading tastes. The fastest growing among them is the Universe Book Club, which started in 1968 and reached a membership of 150,000 two years later. Its selections are entirely occult, and they cover the whole spectrum of contemporary mysticism: from comfortable parlor ESP to the flesh-crawling Black Arts.

The woman responsible for the selections is young and brisk Elaine Landis Geiger, who seems gifted with a special knack for hitting popularity jackpots. Her top sellers so far have been *Heaven Knows What*, a kind of do-it-yourself horoscope guide by the late Grant Lewi; Jeane Dixon's autobiographical *My Life and Prophecies*; and Daniel Logan's *The Reluctant Prophet* (see Chapter II).

"One thing that struck me is that most of our members seem to be in the older age bracket," Mrs. Geiger told me.

"All those occult-minded kids we hear about apparently prefer to pick out their own books."

If you walk into any of the metaphysical bookshops throughout the country, you will see that she is probably right. At least three-quarters of the browsers and buyers will be around draft age. Most of them looking as if they were vaguely related to each other.

These specialized reading stores are perhaps the most perfect symbols of America's Age of Magic you can find. Ten years ago hardly any of them existed in their present form. Now every large city has at least one, and they are springing up in the smaller towns as well. Their chief characteristic is that they deal *only*—or almost only—in occult literature. But what differentiates them completely from ordinary shops is that the staff not only sells but participates. It's one of the unwritten rules of the game.

Few customers would expect delicatessen clerks to be gourmets or flower sellers horticulturalists. But the mystical-minded demand kindred souls and get them, sometimes fanatically so. Hazel Emerson, who operates the Metaphysical Book Shop in Chicago's Loop, deals with everything esoteric but will not tolerate books about magic on her premises. "They upset the vibrations of the whole place," she insisted. "I won't stand for it."

There are no such restrictions at Samuel Weiser, Inc., on New York's lower Broadway. With fifty thousand volumes on the shelves and in the basement, this is the leading occult book center in America—quite possibly in the world. Weiser is a second-generation establishment (founded in 1926), and began as a general bookstore. Over the years more and more space was devoted to matters metaphysical until—after its last move in 1969—the entire shop turned occult, staff included.

The employees tend to specialize in one particular branch, but Don Weiser, son of the founder, is a veritable encyclopedia on the whole field. Wearing a well-groomed graying beard and conservative clothes, Weiser looks like a philosophy professor *should* look (but rarely does). His knowledge of what has been written—or is in the process of being written—on the occult is breathtaking. He is the only man in the business I've met who could—without much pondering—name me three books about the obscure sixteenth-century German healer and alchemist Paracelsus. His stock is almost as extensive as his cognizance. It ranges from ninety-five-cent paperbacks to leatherbound tomes on witchcraft, astrology and spiritualism dating back to 1525 and costing anything up to four hundred dollars.

Weiser's equivalent on the West Coast is the Metaphysical Book Shop in San Francisco. Owned by a former antique dealer named Harold G. White, it began in one small room in 1965 and has now expanded to five large ones. Over the same period the volume of business shot up from an annual $4,000 to about $110,000—which accurately reflects the occult boom.

Although White's establishment can't match Weiser's magnificent stock (nobody in the United States can), it fulfills an additional function. At night some of the floorspace is given over to metaphysical lectures and meetings, catering to a demand that has become almost frantic. White's rooms are booked out months in advance.

Alongside the occultist literature you will find rows of esoteric magazines of every size and format. Until recently hardly any of them ever penetrated into the general trade. Now a few— a tiny fraction—has edged in beside the nonarcane periodicals, but nowhere near enough to give ordinary newsstand browsers an inkling of their multiplicity.

One day somebody will write a plump and learned treatise on the sociological and psychological significance of these publications. It has already been done for comic strips and boys' weeklies, and nothing less will render them justice.

Reading them is like stepping through Alice's Looking Glass into a private world that follows its own clocks, lays down its own rules of evidence, decides its own scale of values and shivers before its very own terrors. The effect resembles an off-station transistor radio hitting you with several sets of voices at once.

This is caused by the random selection of actual and mystical news sources, bestowing on both the same level of credibility. Spirit messages, visitations by angels and fairies, encounters with interplanetary aliens, and attacks by space monsters or "men in black" are featured side by side with perfectly straight reports culled from the daily press.

A medical article may tell you that diseases are not caused by bacteria but—contrariwise—bacteria are caused by diseases.

The writer, to your consternation, will be a "doctor"—but nobody bothers to inform you that the title implies a D.D. instead of an M.D.

For within these pages the educational or technical qualifications of the outside world simply don't count. Nor do most of the scientific verities you've ever heard about. This is an egalitarian wonderland in which a barely literate paperback produced by a Californian road worker represents just as valid a source as a university textbook.

A George Adamski becomes an "internationally recognized authority on space travel," Atlantis and Lemuria become geographical entities, the Bible a historical reference work, Cayce's prophecies integral parts of tomorrow's calendar, the Loch Ness monster a zoological reality, out-of-body movement a widespread means of transportation, the human aura an established physical fact, and the Golden City on Mount Shasta a popular tourist attraction.

One of my favorite sample pieces is a feature written by one Kurt Glemser in a recent issue of *Search* magazine. In it Mr. Glemser warns us that the earth's axis is in more or less imminent danger of flipping over, with disastrous consequences for mankind. The authorities he quotes for this prediction are the *advertisements* of two occultist books on the subject. Not the actual book contents, mind you, but the ad blurbs! With Mr. Glemser, I feel, human trust has scaled its ultimate peak.

Luckily there are several occult magazines operating on a higher journalistic level. I only have space to mention two of them, but they provide an intriguing study in contrast: one is the sturdiest veteran in the field, the other the most promising newcomer.

Fate, a pocket-sized monthly, is run by an exceptionally well-coordinated husband-and-wife team; Curtis and Mary Fuller. Their publication is twenty-three years old, a near-record in this ephemeral territory. It began as a moonlighting partnership between Curtis Fuller and Ray Palmer; the gentleman with the hole-in-the-pole theory. In 1955 Fuller bought Palmer out, and in due course turned the single magazine into a unit of a thriving publishing firm.

The company's headquarters in suburban Fort Sheridan,

Illinois, looks more like a villa than a business office and is
furnished with equal degrees of lavishness and good taste. Fuller,
who has a white-haired senatorial presence, smiled a trifle un-
easily when I asked him about his attitude toward the occult.

"Well, I'll tell you honestly, when I started this magazine I
didn't even believe there was any such thing as a poltergeist.
Since then," he added, "I have become—hm—tentative."

The tall and vivacious Mrs. Fuller takes a rather more
positive view. Together they form a perfectly balanced editorial
duo, which manifests itself in the circulation figures. *Fate* sold
around 50,000 copies in its early years, and has since climbed to
120,000, making it the heavyweight of its class.

It flourishes in a state of happy schizophrenia, changing
style and approach so drastically from one page to the next
that you occasionally wonder whether you're still reading the same
book.

Coexisting cheek by jowl may be a crisply written, thoroughly
researched article on modern British witchcraft and a grade school
level piece of purple gush on a bunch of hallucinating Californian cult preachers passing for Old Testament prophetesses.
Another issue may contain an expert dissertation on the aero-
dynamics of UFO flight almost next door to a dangerously
ecstatic propaganda blurb on behalf of a hillbilly reverend performing "bloodless etheric surgery" in rural Georgia.

Curtis Fuller's own editorials, titled "I See by the Papers,"
are among the most urbanely levelheaded and consistently intelligent products of esoteric journalism. But he gets sat on
ferociously by his less urbane readers whenever he dares nudge
one of their innumerable sacred cows.

One of them happens to be Noah's Ark. On the occasion
of yet another rumored search expedition for its mystical remains
on Mount Ararat, Fuller had the temerity to suggest that the
concept of a vessel housing two of each animal species (plus a
large human family) need not be taken too literally. The reply
was a high-pitched shriek of fury in the form of letters intimating
that he had libeled God, Christianity and Mom's apple pie.
The general message was that only True Believers had the right
to comment on such matters at all. When I mentioned this to

him he answered with a gently tolerant shoulder shrug that showed considerably more Christian forbearance than his attackers had demonstrated.

The magazine's oddly split personality extends to the book review section. *Fate* has, in the shape of its staff reviewer David Techter, a singularly knowledgeable, concise and erudite specialist. Techter is one of the few men in this bracket who actually *reviews* books instead of listing their contents.

Unfortunately he only handles the important volumes. The rest are dealt with by assorted free-lancers, some of them recruited from the ranks of the little-green-men devotees and their spiritual brethren. And this is where the quality yardsticks go overboard again, where expertise, style and plausibility count for nothing as long as the book provides more grist for the miracle mill. The most dismal fantasy concoctions, chock-a-block with orgasmic Venusians, are presented on the same factuality level as a reportage of Apollo 11.

Fuller's house rules on advertising matter are more evident by what *isn't* there than by what is. "We definitely won't accept ads that call for personal visits," he told me. "That's to prevent our readers being exploited by glib and charming con men. We've turned down quite a big proportion of revenue because of this rule."

But that still leaves considerable scope, and *Fate*'s advertising sections frequently offer more insight into the occult scene than the editorial contents.

There are correspondence courses in applied witchcraft and magic (black or white according to choice), instructions in astral travel, invitations to participate in "Divine Cybernetics," cut-price, secondhand crystal balls (only slightly used), equipment for alchemists' laboratories, spirit guide portraits painted to order (send in impression of guide), long-distance analyses of auras, Karma, and psychic potential, and recipes for mystic face creams, Eskimo slimming diets, chemical UFO detectors, and parapsychological rejuvenation potions. Not to mention self-defense methods for warding off "Psychic Attacks," and at least one way of achieving "Instant Evolution."

In appearance *Fate* is rather sparrowlike compared to its

spectacular new rival, the West Coast publication *Psychic*. This represents one of the most ambitious ventures ever undertaken in the occult field, and at this time its success still hangs very much in the balance.

Psychic is the creation of a dedicated former PR executive, James Grayson Bolen, who abandoned a considerably more lucrative post in order to put all his eggs into one very handsome basket. Launched in June 1969 (the first issue is already a collector's item), this bimonthly boasts a rare combination of adult reading matter and superb artwork—some of the covers could be framed and hung in a living room.

Bolen works out of a charmingly rustic-looking office on San Francisco's bay front. He and his wife, a practicing psychiatrist, were co-founders and she joins him after work to lend a hand with the magazine. Otherwise it's just Bolen, a secretary, and a small select stable of free-lance contributors, plus one of the finest photographic editors in the business.

An intense, youngish and vibrantly energetic man with long dark sideburns, Bolen came to California from Iowa and projects a degree of enthusiasm that seems to electrify the air in his office.

"Yes, I suppose you could call me a 'believer'—otherwise I wouldn't have taken such a cut in income to start this outfit." He grinned a little ruefully. "But I try to take a—well, cerebral attitude to the occult."

"And to your magazine?" I asked.

He nodded. "I won't run any of the 'Believe-it-or-Not' type of article. If I don't believe it, I don't print it."

As a result *Psychic* avoids the crudely naïve daydream material most occultist periodicals consider their staff of life. Instead it leans toward scientific themes, but without falling into the statistical sandpaper dryness that makes the ASPR journals, for example, barely readable.

If one word could summarize the magazine's character it is inquisitiveness. Its writers—from the editor down—are obviously fascinated by the world of the paranormal, but not hypnotized by it. They possess *real* curiosity—as distinct from the fake kind whose questions are merely so much rhetoric designed to produce an already agreed upon answer. *Psychic*'s question marks are more than journalistic ploys, they signify genuine probing. They are never so dazzled by a phenomenon that they forget to ask "How?"

This is particularly apparent in the astonishingly three-dimensional interviews conducted by Bolen himself. In every issue he tackles a different celebrity of the metaphysical scene and usually manages to reveal more about their personalities than volumes of sycophantic hack work. (His one conversation with Jeane Dixon gave a clearer picture of the woman than her entire autobiography.) The technique he uses is perfectly courteous and never resembles a grilling. He merely persuades his subjects to display their thought processes, rather than taping endless recitals of their occult feats.

Bolen imposes some strict, idealistic rules on his publication. He will not accept ads for the kind of mystical-commercial gadgetry and literature that form a large chunk of other periodicals' incomes. And he has refused several offers to adapt his contents to the taste of a certain large spiritualist organization, even though it would have meant tripling his present circulation of around thirty-five thousand.

Whether *Psychic* can survive in a landscape littered with the bleached bones of quality journals remains a moot point. Particularly as the cosmic current seems to be flowing in a different direction.

Over the past few years the solemn face of mysticism has acquired distinctly frivolous features. Extraneous influences began to change its former otherworldliness to a kind of ubiquitous pop culture. The rock groups may have started it when they incorporated the supernatural into their musical offerings. (One album called "Witchcraft"—said to have been inspired by Black Mass themes—claims on the jacket that it "destroys minds and reaps souls.")

The department stores helped the process along by introducing astrological services into their fashion sales ("Beige is *the* celestial color for Virgos, madam"). In the upper social stratas it was "Come As You Were" parties. You had your guru or swami check the Akashic Records and give you a selection of your previous incarnations. Then you picked out a fetching one— say High Priestess of Ram or temple dancer—and went costumed as her. To a house possibly decorated with luminous pentagrams and protected by a plastic "moaning cross" (gives off melodious sighs at intervals as warning signals to "malign influences, demons, and hostile aliens").

The shape of the future may be embodied in the Occult Festivals now spluttering throughout the country. Their prototype was launched by a New York psychic named Marc Reymont, who began his career by giving ESP demonstrations in Greenwich Village coffeehouses. From there, Reymont graduated to nightclubs and television, and earned himself headlines by predicting the headlines of Chicago and Baltimore newspapers. In April 1970 he inaugurated the first Festival of the Occult Arts at New York's Fillmore East auditorium.

He described it as a "multimedia entertainment and information program," which about sums it up. It had something for everybody, including the retail trade. The package contained a "rock-cosmic music" group, a psychedelic light show, a screen appearance by witch Sybil Leek, "psychic humor" delivered by a comedienne, a film on Edgar Cayce sponsored by the ARE, folk ballads sung by their composer, audience participation ESP acts, a talk on reincarnation and a spot of meditation.

In the lobby you could buy esoteric literature, join an occult book club, have your palm read, order a computerized horoscope or stock up on magic cosmetics. Some 2,554 people attended the affair. With tickets averaging $4.50 each, it was indeed a festive occasion for the entrepeneurs.

This mélange has since become standard fare at such festivals. Their success is allegedly due to the fact that they contain the basic formula of American mysticism. All the ingredients thrown into one pot, mixed thoroughly, sprinkled with inspiration, and served on small plates.

But a basic formula is not necessarily an end product. It can just as well be the topsoil—the manure, if you like—from which something else is growing. The question is—what?

Attempting to answer it is like working on a jigsaw puzzle with a dozen pieces still missing. You can assemble those you have, but until all the missing ones drop into place you only get a surmise of the picture. The clues are here, though, and they are beginning to add up.

Zodiac signs, for instance, have acquired meaning beyond

their astrological significance. Those believers grouped under one particular symbol are transcending the customary barriers of sex, age, race, class and religion and forming entirely new units oblivious of the categories into which society once divided them. The stock inquiry, "What's your sign?" has become akin to asking for a password. The right answer may signify entry into a brotherhood that demands no qualifications other than the right birthdate.

Even more significant is the melting process of religious symbols and figures. Believers now tend to wear crosses, stars of David, rosary beads, Egyptian ankhs, pentagrams, seals of Solomon, Aku-Aku charms, Buddha figures, Jesus medals and eyes of Isis with total disregard of their original religious status. To them these objects symbolize spirituality that is general, all-embracing, unconfined to any one doctrine. Their protective or inspirational powers apply to all wearers. They are the badges of a new fraternity, a benign order of antirationalists, of magic devotees unconcerned about the origins or doctrinal differences of their amulets.

The same applies to religious personalities. The figure of Jesus has been taken out of its New Testament context and transformed into an international, multiracial guru. One of the "masters"—but only one of them. The hippie cry, "I'm on a Jesus trip!" does not imply a statement for Christ in its old evangelistic sense. It means devotion to a nonmaterialistic figure of love, a kindred spirit who was once just as much at odds with the establishment as the crier himself. As theologian Harvey Cox pointed out: "The figure of Christ is ubiquitous. He is now beginning to appear as Christ the Harlequin: the personification of celebration and fantasy in an age that has lost both."

The occult firmament has other deities as well—Buddha, Krishna, Ra, and the elemental gods of red Indian, African and Polynesian beliefs are all accorded more or less equal divinity status. While below them the Old Testament prophets, Lao-tse, Zoroaster and a score more rank as equally enlightened sages and bearers of truth.

The eventual result of this fusion may be a new and amazingly unified form of religious expression. A truly ecumenical miracle creed, less institutionalized than any existing church.

A faith not divided into Protestant, Catholic and Jewish boxes, but embracing the mystical aspects of all of them, plus relevant portions of Buddhism, Hinduism and the nature worship of the original Americans.

If this is the outcome—and there are signs that it may very well be—then America's occult revolution will have achieved something it never consciously intended: a step forward on the road leading to the brotherhood of man.

GLOSSARY OF TERMS

AKASHIC RECORD Imperishable records of every thought and deed contained in the spiritual spheres.

ALCHEMY The art of transforming matter from one thing to another, e.g. turning base metals into gold.

ARCANUM A mystery.

ASPR American Society for Psychical Research.

ASTRAL BODY The nonphysical facsimile of the human form which may separate itself from the actual body.

ASTROMANCY Prophecy by the stars. (Not Astrology.)

AUGURY Generic term for all forms of prophecy.

AURA An emanation from bodies, both animal and inanimate, said to be caused by mental and physical magnetic forces.

AUTOMATIC WRITING Writing while under the control of a supernatural intelligence (or the subconscious).

BASILISK Legendary beast, half-cock, half-reptile.

BEELZEBUB Lord of the Flies, one of the higher demons.

CLAIRAUDIENCE To hear beyond the ordinary physical sense.

CLAIRVOYANCE To see beyond ordinary time and space limits, also known as Second Sight.

DÉJÀ VU   The illusion of having previously experienced something actually being encountered for the first time.

DERVISH   Moslem mystic, ascetic holy man, religious fanatic.

DHARMA   Sanskrit word meaning "law." Also used to denote the universal law of nature, a spiritual code of behavior.

DOWSING   Searching for water or metals by psychic means, usually with an instrument called a dowsing rod.

DRUID   Priest or medicine man of the ancient Celts.

ECTOPLASM   A white substance pouring from a medium's body openings, allegedly denoting the presence of a spirit.

ELECTROENCEPHALOGRAPH   Apparatus for recording brain waves (EEG).

ENGRAM   A trauma caused by shock, usually prenatal.

ESP   Extrasensory perception; a term embracing such paranormal abilities as clairvoyance, telepathy and precognition.

EXORCISM   Driving out an evil spirit by means of religious ritual.

FAKIR   or Faquir, a Moslem or Hindu holy man who mortifies his flesh in order to control it. Frequently attributed with phenomenal psychic or physical powers.

FOURTH DIMENSION   That which lies beyond the three physical dimensions: height, length, width. Can mean time, but in the occult sense it refers to a realm of mystery.

GRAPHOLOGY   Character analysis based on handwriting.

GURU   Spiritual teacher or leader.

HOLY GRAIL   A vessel invested with sacred powers, figures in both Anglo-Saxon and German mythology.

I CHING   Also Yi King The Chinese Book of Changes, contains methods and explanations of prophecy.

INCUBUS   (See also Succubus.) Demon in male form, given to sexual intercourse with human women.

KABALA   Hebrew mystery lore based on occult interpretation of the Bible.

KARMA   In Hinduism the law of cause and effect which rules man's life and the conditions of his next reincarnation.
KISMET   Arabic for fate.

LAMA   Tibetan priest or monk.
LUCIFER   Satan.

MAGUS   A seer, divine, magician or philosopher.
MAGIC CIRCLE   Ring drawn by magicians to protect them from the spirits and demons they invoke.
MEDIUM   A sensitive or psychically gifted person.
MESMERISM   Archaic term for hypnotism, after its most famous practitioner, Dr. Anton Mesmer.
METAPHYSICS   The science of ultimate causes, of the supernatural.
MONOTHEISM   The belief in one universal God.
MU   Lemuria.

NUMEROLOGY   The analysis of the hidden—supposedly prophetic —meaning of numbers.

OCCULTISM   Belief in supernatural, paranormal forces and beings.

PANTHEISM   Doctrine that identifies God with the entire universe, every particle being part of Him.
PARAPSYCHOLOGY   Study of psychic phenomena through scientific research.
PENTAGRAM   Five-pointed star used in magic rituals.
POLTERGEIST   German for noisy, racketing, destructive spirit.
PRECOGNITION   Advance knowledge of coming events.
PSI   The mysterious unstable factor behind ESP, the root cause of the ability to perform extrasensory actions.

REINCARNATION   The belief that souls return to earth in other— sometimes animal—bodies.

SÉANCE   A gathering for the purpose of contacting spirits, usually headed by a medium.

SHAMAN A medicine man, witch doctor.
SHAMBALAH Mystical city in Oriental folklore. A kind of occult Shangri-la.
SHINTO Japanese religion of ancestor worship.
SIBYL Prophetess, a female divine.
SOMNAMBULISM State of trance.
SUCCUBUS (See Incubus.) Female demon specializing in sex relations with human males.
SUFISM Persian mystical creed, based on Mohammedanism.

TAROT Deck of 78 cards which can supposedly reveal the secrets of man and the universe. Contrary to the claims of some occultists, its origins are unknown.
TETRAGRAM A magic diagram in shape of a four-pointed star.
TELEKINESIS Also called psychokinesis. The ability to move objects by force of will alone.
TELEPATHY Communication between minds by extrasensory means.
THOUGHTOGRAPHY The ability to photograph mental images.
TRUMPET MEDIUM A psychic who produces "spirit voices" through a trumpet at séances.

VALHALLAH The paradise of Nordic mythology.
VEDA The sacred literature of Hinduism.
VOODOO West Indian witchcraft of African origin.

WARLOCK Sorcerer, wizard.

YOGA A frequently misused term meaning the development of physical, moral and spiritual powers in order to achieve God-nearness.

ZEN Japanese form of Buddhism.
ZOMBI Haitian word for a corpse reanimated by sorcery and subject to the sorcerer's will.
ZOROASTRIANISM Persian religion of fire worship, founded by Zoroaster (or Zarathustra). Its modern derivation is the Parsee faith.

INDEX